LETTERS TO ANOTHER ROOM

Ravil Bukharaev, 1951–2012

CONTENTS

ॐ

'Some details relating to my ancestry and to myself – for my Lydia, written sometime after she acquired a curiosity and a more sympathetic inclination to learn about them.'

Memoirs for my Daughter Laurence Sterne
October 1767

'You are perfectly right,' said Goethe; 'and the only matter of importance in such compositions is, that the single masses should be clear and significant, while the whole always remains incommensurable – and even on that account, like an unsolved problem, constantly lures mankind to study it again and again.'

Conversations with Goethe Johann Peter Eckermann
Sunday, February 13, 1831

1

TEN MINUTES OF SOLITUDE

80

'IN ENGLAND, SPRING is rising: should it be ever rising thus, and coming alive within the human soul?' So, impeccably attired as a gentleman, might I scribble with a golden Parker pen upon my snow-white cuff on a melancholy March evening at the Athenaeum Club…

Or rather, I might if I were one of those dusty relics whose entire existence devolves into ritually serving out their allotted time in deep, green leather chairs, sipping weak, sepia tea dutifully delivered by albine waiters, or wafting desultorily through the newspapers.

It is, of course, extremely flattering to be admitted to the Athenaeum's hallowed inner sanctum. Yet I confess I am a poor connoisseur of its ancient and time-honoured privileges, being rather better acquainted with much more modest old curiosity shops. I rarely wear bow-ties, and my sole pair of golden cufflinks bears only the singular coat of arms of the Tatars – not exactly buoyant currency in today's bonfire of the vanities!

To be honest, I was never destined for such a serene and regulated life, and I have not yet quite reached that pinched age when I do actually need to scrawl liverish notes upon my sleeves.

Indeed, I still retain some fleeting memories, amid a host of which sits that delicious riposte of Oscar Wilde, the supreme Irish arbiter of fashionable wit: 'We are all in the gutter, but some of us are looking at the stars.'

I also maintain that to thoroughly inhabit a gentleman's being, rather than simply resemble a gentleman, one must actually be born wearing a Saville Row suit and bow-tie, and then take up residence in them in infancy. Otherwise, the entire thing is an utter masquerade. And despite the natural obligation to dissemble, I know I don't look at my best in masks, which are apt to slip – even though I also know the hardest thing in life is to be what you are, regardless of the consequences.

Just between us – beneath this sneaking yen to not merely appear like a true gentleman but actually be one – I admit an even deeper longing to be a man of noble qualities, in contradiction to the advice of Confucius, who observed that, 'the genuinely noble man is not worried when his merits go unnoticed; he is far more concerned with his own imperfections'.

Ironic, then, that this narrative, the invisible creation of which has brought its author so many pangs of conscience, should unconsciously and uncharacteristically commence with starched cuffs and vague sartorial musings!

What then took me on this diversion, and almost led me astray? Perhaps it was that absurd and theatrical procession along the Staroluzhski embankment in Karlovy Vary, when, past the common folk watching from the pavement cafés, there paraded grandly towards the Mill Colonnade such a gaudy, peacock array of young and not so young aristocrats – the elite of the Old World.

Observers marvelled at them and instantly diagnosed their blue blood from their haute-couture garments – those green velvet tail-coats and black tuxedos, those ballgowns in all shades of red from Bermudan dawn to Sinai sundown; the flowing silk mantles and luxurious capes; the ladies' shimmering elbow gloves and lustrous beaded purses; all polished off by extravagantly costly shoes and exquisite canes.

That evening, I tell you truly, the Fifth Congress of the European nobility was holding a Vampire Festival! And it all culminated spectacularly, late that night, with fireworks brilliantly streaking the darkness above the Castle Tower – followed by a drunken braying in the streets beneath our wrought-iron curlicued fourth-floor balcony – that very balcony from which everyday I gazed out across the way on that old-fashioned but charmingly refurbished house Zum Pomeranzenbaum, its eaves intriguingly adorned with a colourful oval emblem depicting a green orange tree hung with plump sunset fruits.

The following day, the host gathered once more to celebrate: those barons and baronesses, counts and countesses, marquises and crown princes, and a plethora of other pinnacles of the peerage – all those Waldsteins and Thuns, Likhovskys and Esterhazys, from whose resplendent ancestors Mozart and Beethoven had to beg their daily bread.

This time, however, they went the other way, upstream against the Tepla River towards the grand and newly renovated empire-style spa. Yet the sheer perfection of their garments, which demanded such an exacting performance from them, and such undivided attention, especially from the ladies, awoke in those who witnessed the procession a train of thought that led ineluctably to an appraisal of their own earthly fortunes.

Indeed, it was a tableaux of a life unknown to most people, a startling invasion courtesy of the lacquered pages of the spa's

photo-chronicles, an effusion that projected itself like a rainbow upon the curious vision of those ordinary leisure-seekers
enjoying coffee with cream at the gold and marble tables of
the Elephant, those holidaymakers who everyday pass, without special thoughtfulness, without the inquisitiveness that
entices a child, the houses of the erstwhile Carlsbad where
Beethoven and Batyushkov, Gogol and Goethe (yes, the great
Goethe) domiciled as they took the waters – houses like the
elegant pastel green and gold Mozart Hotel once called The
Three Scarlet Roses and now slightly rundown; the mud-
hued house dubbed The White Rabbit pedimentally and
suitably adorned with twin rabbits in relief; and the pearly-
yellow mansion known as The Three Moors which squats
upon the old Market Place not far from the Plague Column
and is decked out with bizarre bas-reliefs of three thick-lipped
negros, not to mention the Daliesque plastic mouldings of
orange trees, vines and bushes that should be utterly taste-
less, and yet are beguilingly entertaining and beautiful in that
authentic way that excites the fancy of a child.

If you give this inner desire for authenticity even the
slightest freedom, then even here, amongst all the paying
trippers from Minusinsk and from Liechtenstein and from
Monaco, amongst all the gaudy mirages of life that command the attention of the promenading crowds just as from
the heights the lofty Imperial Hotel reigns over the lower
hotels of this spa, you may suddenly see – for a moment, for
a second – reality, fresh and green as spring upon the mountain; the original, as if touched by Allah's answer to the heart's
most fervent prayer; and the actual, like a genuine memory.
The truth of life the enlightened soul longs to experience.

Maybe there will come a vision – and not just a vision, but
sounds and smells and even tangible sensations – in which

time and its conventionalities have no meaning: a vision in which Johann Wolfgang von Goethe, perhaps in 1812, perhaps in 1820 (it is not yet clear), is walking before you, attired in a long grey frock-coat and snow-white linen shirt and neck scarf, taking his usual path by the darkly transparent Tepla, as gentle airs whisper and waft the scents of the blossoming bird-cherry trees from high in the mountains above.

He walks, then takes a draught of Carlsbad's restorative waters and strides away on a constitutional stroll amidst the ashes, beeches, limes and sycamores beyond the town where they cleave to the mountain slopes near the Post Yard. Every now and then, he meets on the way himself a little younger and even youthful, from 1786 and 1791, and believes this is an ordinary and matter-of-fact occurrence – as it should be, and entirely typical for an elevated spirit thinking about something deeply and intimately personal...

...And here I am, I can see, still holding on to his proletarian youth, not to say his vulgar haste, provoked by a greed for things that seem most important in the moment, running far ahead of the field lines of the limited time and space of my narrative in divergent spirals – and for this I should whip myself on the hand with a cane, like a grey-haired teacher (which no doubt is how I look to some people) – whip myself, a smug student who hasn't even got the basic grammar, yet is already presuming to subvert the rules of the game and overturn the true canons of composition.

In reality, it wasn't a time for starched cuffs and cufflinks, but a very ordinary London morning, when I indulged myself in passing judgement on spring and the human soul, as if this judgement was not to be disputed – and just as a truly impartial blast of storms and snow beat down from the English north for the next few weeks to expose my all-too-human error. Only in May did spring bless the islands – and even then somewhat reluctantly.

Yet though of course I soon discovered my error, I would not admit it straightaway. I simply amused myself with this illusion. And no wonder, after such an endlessly long and dark winter.

So, coming down that morning after the Muslim prayer that had become mandatory for working with a calm heart, I entered the kitchen and boiled filtered water for my coffee – two lumps of brown sugar and two teaspoons of instant – and as usual, ambled through those mundane solitary ten minutes preparing to go to work. I opened the door to our haphazard garden, sat down on the step with my red delft mug, sipped the still scalding coffee and, striking a match, lit my rough cherrywood pipe from Karlovy Vary. And after this simple personal ritual developed over the years, I finally opened my sleepy eyes and, through my ancient spectacles, looked and saw: it has happened.

Yet, the bold simplicity of my assessment again turned out to be an error; in reality, it was only just starting to happen, and the conception was far from certain. In my haste, I had once more shot far ahead, rashly outpacing the proper time. Meanwhile, the sky turned pellucid blue before I truly woke; and the aromatic, incense smoke of Mac Baren tobacco (an offering to the idol of defective pleasures) hung in the moist, clear and slightly dim air and diffused gradually. The morning was fresh, but not too chilly, and I was warm enough in that green, quilted and rather stiff dressing gown given to me in wintry Tashkent – so comfortable and convenient for the morning, yet also very traditional in its lack of pockets and buttons, which means you can quickly wrap it around you and belt it with a twisted scarf – now where is that scarf? So again, I was sitting on the kitchen step and doing what had become usual for me – seeing what I wanted to see.

Collecting my thoughts and dragging myself back to reality, of course I sought authentic perceptions, but each day of life for just a single soul has already proved that although the authenticity of prayer is an absolutely necessary condition, it's not always enough. Action is needed – not just any action, but one formed and matured from lessons of previous existence and which slowly flows from the soul with the clear light of labour and compassion to the world – an action that begins without my frail, capricious will, and once begun has no mortal end but joins the Unity of immortalities.

This soul action, which was meant to happen and, maybe, has long been imprinted with a moving script, must foster all other efforts in life and ensure they are not futile; so everything must happen constantly, rather than stagnate, and it is starting even now, and secretly, in the inner life of the first primroses, birds and trees...

And so the puffs of vanilla incense that hovered and floated in the morning air, conjoining and dispersing, were like awakening imagination that without your conscious will conjures seeming facts in your passage through the world – that imagination which the moment it arises brings ideas to the soul, Sufi-like in its moving script, the same Fancy that Laurence Sterne admonishes: 'Thou art a seduced, and a seducing slut; and albeit thou cheatest us seven times a day with thy pictures and images, yet with so many charms dost thou do it, and thou deckest out thy pictures in the shapes of so many angels of light, 't is a shame to break with thee.'

7

That is how spring entered my imagination, as on the verdant lawn amidst the plain grass a tiny wild crocus shone its soft lilac light, while above on the strong boughs of the spreading maple tree two stock-doves perched saucily, along with a fickle magpie that occasionally picked a fight with the squirrel family that long ago took a liking to this mysteriously hollow and exotic tree in the corner of the garden.

Then the birds took flight, but the maple remained, as it probably will long after me and my philosophizing are gone. Climbing into the sky like some giant branched fountain, the tree was still completely bare, yet so dense and ample with branches that even the unadorned candour of its naked form still hid its pure, natural essence – and isn't this like the legendary Lady Godiva who covered her marvellous nakedness beneath the golden veil of her down-fallen dale of hair? So she rode past the greedy gaze of the people on her black, or was it white, horse? In the same way, the ambient reality of life slipped undiscovered through my morning, overfilled as it was with the fancies common to all mankind, while reality in its complete authenticity was lived out within the bushes and crocuses. There awoke in my heart a wrenching and insatiable jealousy of how completely they fulfilled their purpose in their brief existence.

Everything I saw through the small circle of my glasses made me ache with its unreachable authenticity, its absolute compliance with intention. Everything was explicit, and without any sly concealment. If there is one all-embracing word to describe this super-real sense of the garden, it would be 'honesty'. Isn't it true, though, that frankness in men is not always honest?

Frankness may be disingenuous when it breeds narcissism, and derives from that deliberate invention of conventions from chance human meetings, in which a clever script conjures hidden meanings and associations, establishes links with petitions and entreaties and the explanatory notes with which it is sometimes possible to justify oneself – but it is impossible to reckon and exhaust the guilt of life, the guilt which years not only fail to diminish but ceaselessly multiply.

Honesty, on the other hand, draws on silence – not because of any dark secrecy, but because it is impossible with even the best writing and speaking to be completely honest in a way that is understandable – yet still I keep trying. Can words ever be as honest as true music, which is ever replete with unspoken nobility, love and loyalty to one's spiritual and earthly home; honest as music that directly and unequivocally connects soul to soul and expresses for solitary humans conjugations of authentically present realities, rather than just the visible, the manifest, the apparent?

I cannot compose or even record music, yet I cannot be honestly quiet, and just like a beloved woman, I am always demanding words.

In the meanwhile, in the world of plants and birds, and the world of cats, foxes and squirrels, two different aspects of reality – the visible and the true – were merging into one, their corporeal union free of human disorder; a conjoined existence which feels all the unseen, unheard sadness and pain of living things, yet does not sow the bitter seeds of distemper and doubt that flourish in human hearts and souls.

By now, dawn had fully broken. Yet the sun still hid behind low, trailing clouds, and you could only wonder at the innate colour of the sky. This saddened me greatly and it seemed that if day's dawn begins only with the sun, then the soul's dawn can come only when its light marries the visible and the true.

Oh Allah, if I did not know, and could not imagine, what heights exist! And how steep the vertex of human destiny! If the truth of the Unity didn't at times shine into the soul with such unbearable brilliance and burn into it forever an unquenchable thirst for everything to be accomplished as intended! If I was not so profoundly aware of that summit – sublime, poised, fitting – which might be achieved once and forever...then if only I might know how and what to sacrifice for it.

That human and artistic imperfection, unspoken but felt from afar like the music of the spheres, was troubling me again this morning, and again I could neither express nor capture the truth of the moment, mundanely realizing that all things captured in haste stagnate in the mire of monosemantic meaning. The visible made me forlorn, and the true was so far, so infinitely far, away, and ever receding – leaving me in my dull bondage to a world which, like an idle woman, is drawn to light chatter and superficial folly – a world loosed from the mutual obligations which, in her opinion, no-one follows anyway.

And so there I was, wearing the Tashkent robe and smoking my Czech cherrywood chibout, sitting on the kitchen doorstep, poised between house and garden as if on the threshold between the two realities – one of which held me in its eclectic image of the present, and the other which drew me, without ever letting me in – provoking and perplexing me with tenebrous hints, tips and reminders of the Unity.

I knew nothing thoroughly, yet after five minutes silence, I imagined a new call – a call to a path that seemed mine at once and for certain. It seemed so easy for me to rise from the threshold entirely as I was and go wherever my eyes led me – for on this path, one by one, would be torn all super-fluous trappings and bonds, and the soul (for the soul does exist) would exult from the return flow of sensation from the universe's imperceptible movement and unfading growth – yet I remembered how this happens.

Why did I have to confuse frankness and honesty – integrity and self, too? Do eyes always follow where the heart yearns? The truth is that there exist mutual bonds of existence, and tearing them will not spread light – only the utter darkness of despair.

Didn't I know that my longest path led always to you, and that for so many years, any road, wherever it took me, always began and ended with you?

After losing yourself in work or reading until after midnight as so often, you slept on serenely upstairs, rather closer to the sky, and these penetrating questions melted in the moist calm of the morning – unseemly in your dreams, the guardian and shepherd of which I was long ago destined to be.

Unfathomable and far off, you slept, slept as always, like the first time, and through the window in our mansard bedroom gazed bushy cedars, their dark purply green needles and dozy pillars entwined in curling ivy, and beside them a ghostly willow and an oriental poplar. Through the gaps in the branches the great expanse of London climbed to the horizon of its northern hills, draped by low skies, and beyond intriguing but not unlimited distances.

And now like the blue tit, perfectly Russian, darting from the aspiring branches of the one apple tree not planted by us, a thought flashes up into these deep silences – that from long ago, and for a long time, we have been wandering, together.

This morning, you slept while I awoke alone – a morning of separation and farewell for the day. In the evening, past midnight, it was you awake alone, while I slept, embracing my illusions, illusions which any other woman might dismiss as pure balderdash and baloney. But you know, so well, that someone else's present world is untangible and unimaginable, like a foreign country filled with great happiness and great sorrow. In our mutual love, we have caused each other so much anguish and unacknowledged misery, but it has finally become clear that in the unique love for either a woman, or a homeland, one learns the meaning and idea of the world – love for the One and Only Authentic Existence, which created us from one soul alone, the same for men and for women:

> O mankind! Be careful of your duty to your Lord, who created you from a single soul and from it created its mate and from them has spread abroad a multitude of men and women, and fear Allah in whose name you appear to one another, and fear Him particularly respecting ties of relationship.
>
> Al-Nisa 4–1

How little life we are given, Oh God, for learning and understanding!

The house, on the threshold of which these minutes were trifled away, our stone house on the hill, was girded on the northern side by the dormant buds of the woods scaling the slope, and on the south by a brick wall festooned with curls of ubiquitous ivy and by the small garden, a-brim with daffodils, crocuses and hyacinths, created by your own hard work.

For all its sturdiness, it was not our last home, but an enduring shelter on the way to another shimmering place. Bestowed on us as a challenge at the crossroads of our wanderings, it grew on us, with its simple objects, which also bore memories of previous homes. Every object is an accumulator of memories and feelings, memories and feelings that can sometimes surge back with the odd glance or touch to remind us that we have shared experiences – that our two lives, though so different, are intimately entangled and, for some purpose, lastingly conjugated.

This house, so different from those other time-worn homes, does not bring our lives together by force, but is sympathetic to the natural separateness of human existence, with its two studies, its two disparate worlds where each can shelter to read and write, with a shared wall but opening to opposite points of the wind rose – my windows looking out south and east, yours to the north and west.

Our beliefs and ambitions are so different in many ways, but this makes the mutual connections that much clearer as they lodge within our home, bringing together both worlds. All their variegated differences mingle here in unity, allowing the grace of occasional mutual silences to penetrate commonplace reality, as the point of a young leaf penetrates the maple bud, or a tear disturbs an impassive countenance.

Now it's happened, and there's no time – and I didn't even notice where the time went. In my heart, you see, there gathered so clear, so earnest a wish to explain, to explain myself with all the guilty prolixity and diversions of words – those words I never have enough of from day to day for your more substantial grievances. But even words are given to me in unmindful silence, like the radiance of familiar objects that brings back emotions from the past.

And the traces of the past are slipping ever further away – the start of our mutual destiny is receding – the time when we, two people, two differences, two lonelinesses, had neither a common home nor even common memories. When did those memories begin?

No, it wasn't that secluded summer at Butharovo, under the roof of the rented cottage with the carved terrace, deep amidst the forest in a landscape alien to both of us. It wasn't then that began our life of love, a love which then and for long after seemed a simple story of dark temptation and glorious but brief passion, a seduction by fate – a perishable romance that is born and dies in the pride of either man or woman.

'She didn't understand him.'... 'He didn't understand her.'

However one begins such a humdrum tale, its humdrum end will loom all too plainly. Was this meant for us? Who knows? If it weren't for the irresistible gravitational attraction of fate, and not another conjugation whose heavenly justice will only later be revealed, would we have been able to resist the centrifugal force of unrestrained egoism that at the time seemed for me and you the self-preservation of talent? We will only discover the answer in the many-layered joys and sorrows of life; the pain of mutual existence is the need for us to sacrifice even those things sweetest to our hearts, the strident ghosts of our unmutual past.

I think we chose to meet under the roof only rarely, but as the rains kept falling, so we were brought together – for where else could we go in that dull village? We walked together, yes, but somehow singly. We adapted to each other, but the arguments were terrible and the silences filled with tension, leading to new arguments. But in everything around us – in the ripening leaves of the alien forests, in the distant murmur of a brook, in the drizzle drops on burdock and nettles, in the unexpected birds of our foreign garden, in the maple reflections on the country ponds where I fished to be alone and waken to the real world – everything was filled with the inevitability of life, and shone with the possibility of unity.

In your words:

Here's a soul's garden neglected and dank
without love without care a desolate blank
dense jasmine and lilac grow over the bank
raspberries and blackberries thorny and rank

if some bold stranger ventures inside
in the green shadows where lost truths now hide
crunching like ice underfoot with each stride
on leaves and blooms fallen in piles deep and wide

the anguish is neither implied nor intended
but it's magnified greatly by fear and doubt
so I'm unsure what's broken can ever be mended:
if one entered here – would they ever get out?[1]

Why were we staying in Butharovo if not for your wish to test our feelings again? I have only understood at last – it takes a long time for plain but unpalatable truths to reach the liver. All the human bonds in your life were snapping then, and every attempt at unity left only blank emptiness, and despite that hard-won stubbornness which shone through the loss of your parent, your dreams of what your life should be were lost in a mist of uncertainty. The highest power endowed you with immense vitality. Yet the death of your young

---

[1] Poem by Lydia Grigorieva.

father in an aircraft fire deep in the Arctic circle then deprived you yet again of any strong shelter, and left you with the sense that even the ground could give way beneath your feet.

Could I then be your solid earth? Could I be not a charming prince, a Prince Yelisei[2] whose fairy tale inevitably ends, but the one you needed all your life – your comforter, father and brother, your wall and shield from the evils of the world, the strong and disinterested patron of your golden talent?

No, I could not. I did not know how to. People learn to do it, giving their whole life to learning. Your striving to be brave in the face of despair drew me but I was terrified by it, because it was so overwhelmingly demanding – not only for me then, but for the future me, of which I had no inkling then.

So Butharovo, where my best poems were written, failed to become our joint shelter, and has sunk into your past like a painful coincidence, lacking the happy memories that might bind it into your life. We were not aware then that we should not stay in one place, locking ourselves for years into meaningless restrictions. For you and me, it turned out, it was ever better to be on the road.

The minutes of silence were running out. You slept on upstairs. And the light that augured spring cascaded into the mansard through the twin windows, beyond which the clouds and trees were flooding with dreams anticipating new shapes – shapes that will be formed once and never again.

---

[2] The hero of *The Tale of The Dead Princess*, Pushkin's telling of the Snow White fairy story. The princess, who is protected by seven knights, is tricked into eating a poisoned apple and falls into a deathlike trance, only to be awakened, finally, by the brave young Prince Yelisei.

Sometimes I allow myself to wake at dawn, like a little boy for whom, odd as it sounds, everything is yet to happen. But I see through my drowsiness how the streams and flows and flickers of light happened without me this morning, and I remember the light-lured pink of budding apple-blossoms, uncertain and moist, in those lost secluded gardens at Kuskovo[3] where the light of our first mutual feelings budded and shone towards the foreign lands destined for both of us.

If I could write this life like a novel, I could make up the beginnings of the story as if it was a prophesied meeting of two existences after years of separation, in such surroundings and scenery, a classic unity of time, place and action: amid the generously blooming apple and cherry trees of an orchard on the outskirts of Kuskovo, in the rented room of a shabby wooden house near the station, not far from the palace parks with their lakes and waterways, humpback bridges and well-proportioned marble statues, an ancient and steady harmony far from the mental strife, and far from the inevitable restless and rootless rage and remorse bought on by life's desires.

I loved – you didn't believe and wanted to believe and didn't believe again, just as you're not believing now, when it can be sweet not to believe. But to all the shocks, dreams and true torments of the heart, there was a Witness, who was creating balance and proportionality; all that was needed was to look deeply, not with the eyes but with the heart.

Why with such a lack of faith, and a woman's eternal need for words, were both of us, once our wanders

---

[3] With its sumptuous palace and magnificent formal gardens, Kuskovo is sometimes called the Russian Versailles, created in the eighteenth century by Pyotr Sheremetyev, the wealthy son of one of Peter the Great's key generals, as a luxurious summer retreat on the fringes of Moscow.

had begun, always drawn to the same places: to Kuskovo with its shiny sprinkles of leaves and silvery waters, its Dutch house dedicated to Peter the Great, its museum of Shuvalov porcelain, and the time-defying oak near the Orangery fenced off by a cast-iron chain from Kasli; to Archangelskoe, on our last few kopeks, with its palatial cascades of terraces, amid the russet and gold autumn forests to the west of Moscow; to Pavlovsk on the fringes of Saint Petersburg and its natural looking English park; and of course that first prophetic journey which precipitated our nomadic life.

It was a quarter of a century ago when, golden-headed and warmed by the September sun, we stepped down from the train in Leningrad and I, remember, said to you – as a joke or consolation: 'Welcome to Paris!'

Then after many years, we did go to Paris for real, and although I didn't repeat the phrase on the Gare du Nord, you joked about it. But perhaps how it appeared to me then rebelled against my many images of Paris before it became an effective memory of the heart.

If you ask me, even now, what single memory of love I would choose, it may be that coloured vividly in red and gold on green, of leaf fall on grass on the Pavlov Hills near the arbour of the dowager empress, from where with a gasp of happiness and unguarded faith – yellowy shimmering birch, scarlet Russian maples, deep azure of mountain air, silvery shafts of sunlight, shining golden curls in your warm-wind-caressed hair – you ran into my open arms, and for the very first time we came together in that devout impulse to human unity which, Oh Lord My God, happens truly only once, to leave ever after its inescapable presence and a yearning for it to come back.

I confess: my entire life I have been waiting for a return of that glorious moment of fulfilment and alignment, of that irresistible triumph of unselfish happiness. It is part of our shared past, and it beckons and teases me with its constant presence and its foretold uniqueness amid the normal strains of life. But of course you can never retrieve true unity; it has to be accomplished anew each time. It must happen afresh and not become a memory. It must appear to the soul as another new dawn, in which I must understand you and myself entirely, from the beginning.

Yes, you were sleeping in the heavens above the garden in which things were happening and being achieved. My ten minutes have already departed, like the unified wholeness, and the silence has lifted, to return only as scattered moments in the happenstances of an ordinary day. Once more, I was leaving you for a day, to come back in the evening with a heart exhausted by the pressing vanity and powerlessness of the necessities of life, in the silence of tiredness which I can never share.

Time has not stretched, and the urgency of our unmatched dreams, and our perceptions of visible realities, separates us far more often now. So forgive my manly silence, if you can – authenticity cannot be explained in spoken words, but may sometimes be written down.

What was formed in the silence of the morning was a message to your inner life and your separate existence. What had concerned me for so long was to be written down like a letter to another room of our shared house, and it turned out to be a reflection on silence – a simple composition in four extended parts with a brief additional story that in my flush of honesty emulated a moral parable...

For us humans even honesty is impulsive, but the open authenticity of the garden is mantled with marvellous nobility, and possesses, as if leading on perfectly from the past, a wonderful classic unity and balance of shapes, where every detail is distinguished and transformed to a centre of gravity.

Whatever we verily love about the world, a lover or a homeland, we love about God – about the ancient Unity, partially reflected in the mirror of a troubled soul and in the muted secrecies of a mortal heart.

Si tu n'existais pas, dis-moi, pourquoi j'existerai?
(And if you didn't exist...)

Devoted people are the first to be betrayed. You can rely on people like this. They will always be there for you. But I can vouch that just over twenty years ago, one summer's day, around Moscow's Sokol metro station not a living soul had this sort of idle thought in their head. In one green quadrangle stood substantial apartment blocks which had only one, but I must say significant, drawback, which was the constant traffic on the nearby circular railway. Every night, heavy-goods trains without any apparent end seemed to slow down then pull away again right next to the apartments with a fearful fusillade of metallic clangs from the truck couplings. The residents, though, long ceased to pay any attention – can people get used to anything? In fact, this place wasn't especially quiet even during the day.

On one side, the eight-story apartment block overlooked the Volokokamsky Highway, and on the other, the side on which Elizaveta Osipovna lived, the 23 tram regularly clattered by. For three kopeks you could ride the tram to Koptevsky market, where moustached Azerbaijanis royally traded scarlet persimmons, richly coloured apples and grapes as pale as teardrops – where did they get such ripe fruits in June? Piled high on their stalls, too, were lush bunches of coriander and sweet brown Georgian churchkhela[4] – jumbled, for some reason with wonderful pickles, huge, waxy marinated garlic, and delicious crimson-stained Gurian cabbage bound in sheaf-like bundles with salty green ramson.

Of course, there were also many other Moscow treats, especially rich, butterlike soured cream, the purest most trickling cottage cheese, village butter in golden millstones, freshly drawn meat ruddy and steaming, juicy vigourous radish, giant dense onions, plump washed carrots and lush green celery and parsley.

Yet Elizaveta Osipovna had long ceased going to the market. A butchers, a dairy, a baker and a fish shop were conveniently at hand, next to the tram stop. The greengrocer's was a disappointment with last year's spongey potatoes and straggly damp carrots covered with the soil that was smeared all over the floor. The soil was often dry and the smell of the dust filled the shop. Not far away, though, near the beer dispensers and a recently opened *rumochnaya*,[5] there were almost always old women selling herbs such as dill and parsley much cheaper than in the market.

True, the bunches the old women sold were sparse, but, lonely as a finger, Elizaveta Osipovna didn't need much. She was terrified of anything not fresh, so every single day she went to the local shops to top up. She'd buy 50 g of

---

[4] Sausage-shaped sweets from the Caucasus made by threading almonds, walnuts, hazel nuts and raisins on to a string, dipping them in grape juice and drying them in the shape of a sausage.

[5] A soviet variation on a pub, where people went simply to drink. The word *rumochnaya* comes from the Russian word for 'wine glass'.

butter, a couple of slices of *doktorskaya* smoked sausage or, on pension day, a few slices of ham, a morsel of soured grain, and a sliver of cheese – just a smattering of each. Strangely, her fear of stale food harmonized perfectly with her pension of 56 soviet roubles. She learned how to eke out that sum over the entire month, yet at the same time, out of the kindness of her heart and the natural diplomacy essential in communal flats, she managed to give a rouble to the local wino to tide him through to the next pay day. Well, one couldn't dare refuse.

All her neighbours were, as a rule, drinkers. Some drank more. Some drank less. Some drank because they were young and foolish. Some of the older ones were so fossilized into the habit that they drank like fish. Her nearest neighbour was, in this sense, just reaching maturity. Through the working days, he imbibed moderately, but on Saturday he got roaring drunk, fighting with the girl he'd just picked up; and Elizaveta Osipovna, consumed by a black and viperous fit of anger, locked herself in her room and convulsed at each clatter as furniture was thrown over in the flat next door. It was lucky, then, that she had no children with her, as she did much of the time, since the neighbours would often hand their offspring to her to look after while they had a break from boozing at home, and a break from playing the songs of the highly fashionable (in those long-gone times) Joe Dassin.[6]

That summer, it was especially hard to get away from Joe Dassin. Sweet and catchy tunes spilled out into the warm summer air, if not from one window then another. 'Si tu

---

[6] Joe Dassin was an American singer-songwriter famous in the 1960s and 1970s for his French songs.

n'existais pas, dis-moi, pourquoi j'existerai?' the handsome foreign singer was convincing some girl, and if only Elizaveta knew French she'd have recognized the haunting lyrics: 'If you didn't exist, then why should I?'

But Elizaveta Osipovna didn't understand French. She knew a little Azerbaijani, because she was from Baku. But all her family lived in that faraway place by the Caspian Sea. In Moscow she had no-one, no-one at all, apart from her neighbours, who were entirely convinced she was a native of Moscow because of her incorrigible love of theatre and her stubborn intelligence. They were truly astounded when her sister and nephew arrived from Baku to arrange her funeral.

In the past, before her retirement, she went to the theatre regularly, and never missed a key premiere, although she always bought the cheapest seats. Her pension wouldn't stretch even to the cheap seats, so whenever she could she got a free season ticket to the lectures in Bakhrushin theatre museum, and was always up on the latest theatre news. In the past, too, Elizaveta Osipovna had visited Baku almost every year. This summer, though, it was getting hard for her to even walk to the shops.

So she relied on her TV, small and black and white. She'd saved her pension for quite a few years to get it. Then finally she had enough. With the help of another neighbour, a giddy young father from across the stairwell who, thanks to her child-minding, had plenty of time on his hands, she went to the shop, selected the very cheapest set and brought it home in a cab, worrying all the way that it might get broken and stop working. But the TV did work, and Elizaveta Osipovna, who suffered senile insomnia, watched and listened to every programme right up to the anthem of the Soviet Union that closed broadcasting for the day. In the past, before the TV, she had read a lot, but now her eyes were letting her down. 'I'm so afraid I'll go blind,' Elizaveta Osipovna would say, weeping bitterly. But that was when she was in hospital.

Before she was taken into hospital, on a quiet night when the lips of the ever-present Joe Dassin were momentarily stilled on the insistence of Soviet regulations, then a single nightingale, or even a pair, that swooped into the yard between the blocks from the Streshnevsky ponds might just be heard. In between the clanging and rumbling of the goods trains, Elizaveta Osipovna, holding her breath, listened intently to their leaping song. Sometimes, when it was hard to stay lying down, she went to the window and tried to guess in which of the yard's trees the nightingales were hidden.

One might imagine that hearing the silvery warbling of the nightingale, singing out through the sudden silence of the dark yard and ascending to the stars, might bring to Elizaveta Osipovna some sweet, or even sad, memories, but did not – and even if it did, we, her ex-neighbours, will never know. If you do let free the dreamy capriciousness of the imagination, then much more plausible in this ordinary world would be her sudden wish to have the strength to walk in the morning across the railway and along the white, beaten path to the Streshnekovsky ponds and sit on a bench to watch the flashing ripples in the water, the soft to and fro of the reeds, the ever-shifting reflections of the pines. And maybe she'd catch the watery scent of overblown bird-cherry blossom, strewn across the pond in blankets of white stars.

After all, do any of us, here and now, realize what a joy it is simply to be conscious of our own existence and, while there is still time, feel alive – realize not what life was, but what it is, before, ahead of time and carelessly, we bid it goodbye?

To really feel, experience, see, hear and comprehend — without some exaggerated sixth sense and redundant imagination — how the living branch of the tree near to you shades the grass; how gently and sympathetically the warm summer breeze touches your hair, while at the same time rippling the sparkling water and waving the reeds; how the pine trees on the far bank stand straight and while they are alive, stretch up through the air towards the heavens, up to the clouds that are tenderly spun by the same soft wind of life. All that is in the world is perceived together in such a moment, like the summer's warmth, and appears as it truly is — a miraculously bright, gratefully received yet undeserved blessing.

How warm, how fresh and light, how easy to forget debts and guilt and all the confusing details in the vision — which, thank God, the eyes can still see — and see with all the simple clarity of the children playing in the sandpit and on the grass who will remember all their lives some chance view of an ant busily climbing a straw of grass, or a crimson and black fire beetle, or a gleaming, brassy water-beetle flashing amber on the pond — where, the adults say, also live the scary tritons with those bright red spots on their white bellies. Ah!

Elizaveta Osipovna died that summer in the regional hospital. So now there was no-one to leave the children with. The young neighbour who helped her buy the TV visited her in the hospital only once, and found her sitting on the bed, wearing a grey hospital robe, which slipped off her yellow shoulder to reveal a pitifully thin clavicle. When she saw him, she started to cry, and said she was so scared of going blind. There was a phone call later, informing him that she'd died.

Elizaveta Osipovna's relatives from Baku arrived for the funeral, and the young neighbour went with them to the crematorium, and as the coffin glided slowly between the open furnace doors, a taped voice solemnly sang Massenet's 'Elegy' 'O-o-o, where are they, the light days, the tender nights of spring?...' And on the way home, the neighbour couldn't help humming that haunting melody, again and again out loud and in his head, until the moment he walked into the yard and it was overwhelmed by Joe Dassin:

Si tu n'existais pas, dis-moi, pourquoi j'existerai...

Yet, extraordinarily, as he walks through the yard, enters the porch and goes up in the lift back to normality, he has no idea that for all his life he will remember that music, and every time he moves on, or changes his life in any way, that music will awaken in him an inevitable, unquenchable longing, a perpetual reminder of the involuntary betrayals that lodge guiltily in his core. He might have forgotten it entirely – for was there really any fault – but what is anyone left with if you take away their last treasure, their secret and very personal guilt?

Only shame is then left, but with shame it is completely impossible to live, dear neighbours.

2

THE GOUT FLOWER

ॐ

MEMORIES ARE CRUCIAL when you're craving to be reunited with life – when you long to be aware simultaneously of the present, past and future. The future, which is in any case filled with the past, is seen only dimly and slips away in vague guesses, while the present is by definition uneventful. But the past is with us always – without permission, pacing through any scene as unconditional reality.

And so like this, memories came striding towards me that spring in the early 80s. With it came dejection as I, with pointless humility, punished myself for misdemeanours in some past setting where, for absence of proper achievement, I was brought by life and fate...

That setting was a concrete and asphalt and grey-brick world where the Gorky Railway is crossed by the Enthusiasts' Highway, which long ago was called the Vladimirka[7] and stretched away from the might of Moscow into the gloaming

---

[7] A diminutive name for the road running east from Moscow to Vladimir, made famous in a great painting by Isaac Levitan from 1892 (now hanging in Moscow's Tretyakovsky Gallery), which shows the lonely, open road stretching into the distance.

of a memory that once palely hurt me in the remote and beautiful woods and fields of the Vladimir region.

Here, in Vladimir, is the small white and blue Church of the Intercession on the Nerl.[8] The square and ancient church with its central tower stands on a low mound above an oxbow lake formed by the snow melt. It looks entirely self-sufficient, and without need of anyone − or so it seemed to me, confused and empty at heart.

Even this scene failed to wake any particular tender emotions in my soul, and yet it was deeply beautiful and even disturbing in its unique harmony, with its miniature white walls and the vast sky around in such perfect balance that in my imagination it became weightless, and seemed to float and shimmer like its reflection in the lake, the two images separated only by the band of limp reeds that grew between the floodlines. In those vague days of non-existence, there was nothing I wanted more than such freedom from gravity, but my earthweight dragged me down, and even in my dreams I had forgotten how to fly.

At the time, thanks to my foolish extravagance, I had neither home nor wife, nor any significant money. I was spending every kopek I had on necessities and could not save at all. Lacking even a proper home, I was staying with a kind friend in a room from the tall windows of which could be seen, mirrored in glass on the opposite side of Enthusiasts' Highway, the whole of the grey, apartment block with its ground-floor foodstore, its shelves entirely empty but for ranks of

---

[8] The Church of the Intercession on the Nerl is one of Russia's most treasured architectural monuments, a perfectly square twelfth-century church in white stone built on a man-made mound above the Nerl river.

then ubiquitous 'Siberian' vodka. The room stuck in my memory because it was so hard to sleep in, even when very drunk, yet waking up in it was harder still and I never, never wanted to get up. I was in that foolish frame of mind where I was just existing, with nothing happening around me, and this fake existence, like everything devoid of a beginning and end, charged itself into the general guilt of life, meaningless and useless.

Yet even this dark winter, long as it was, did pass, and I started to peer gingerly outside, each time looking further and further from my shelter — until once I managed to walk to Izmailovsky Park, where above the last vestiges of blackened snow the restorative pussy-willows were starting to bloom, and the muddy ditches were awash with the clear snow melt of Moscow's foreign to me spring.

It was there in Izmailovsky that my eye was taken by a golden-yellow mother-and-stepmother flower,[9] emerging from a bank of poor clay soil washed out by the spring rains. A zealous bee buzzed around this early source of nectar. I took the plant with me, dislodging its roots so easily from its native clay that it seemed almost accidental — the reddish-brown, tomentose roots led up the reedy stem to the heart of the floral corolla, shining like a miniature sun.

When I reached my room again, I stowed the flower in a delft tea cup and soon forgot about it — because the reality of non-existence is actually rather self-obsessed. You suddenly want to do something, ignite your remaining powers, only for them to be snuffed straight out, since nothing in

---

[9] The flower known in English as coltsfoot, once widely used in herbal medicine in the treatment of gout, but which has been found to contain alkaloids that cause liver damage.

non-existence retains any meaning for long, even the express delight of a new spring. In this dimmed life, apart from such occasional flashes, there's no engagement or connection because everything is dictated by only dismal ambition or boredom. No talent is ever engaged or else it is abused by the agony of self-love which artfully pretends to be a life.

Even that first spring flower, captured in the white-inside brown cup sitting on the broad, paint-peeled sill between the piles of worn-out books, prompted no revelations to the soul about the future. It was merely a reminder of the past, implying that the past, and so all our life, is a matter of chance – in other words, even the living spring bloom was turning the unchanging recurrence of separate particles of time into yet another sweet lie, another seduction, turning everything towards the paltry self-deception of non-existence.

Mother-and-stepmother, *Tussilago farfara,* the Gout Flower: if it weren't for the reductive power of non-existence, each word of this composite botanic name could and would encourage some kind of true fulfilment or action, or maybe even some true words. Yet these names awoke nothing in my soul, apart from dull sensations that became manifest only as a dying echo or wisps of dust from the ashes of burned out love. I somehow imagined these ashes being whisked away from my homeland to the rest of the world, because the pain of love for a woman, in all its inexplicability, is a kind of homeland, a soil of life – and the loss of this scarce soil leaves only a dreadful foreign land. All natural connections were torn from inside of me – apart from the single root that thrived without sunshine but still could not bring me joy – merely reverberating in the great void of shame and pain of loss, which I took simply as proof of my own worthlessness.

Putting down yet another worn-out book in which I was trying to escape reality, my vacant gaze fell by chance upon the mother-and-stepmother flower and through the fog of my non-existence an image came to me from my recent past of the River Lopasnya on Moscow's hem, a ribbon of blue and light-blue surrounded by spring forests in which snow was quickly melting, dripping down the pine trunks and liquefying in the glades – those bare places amid the trees where amber shafts of sun can needle in to bring life to the rare ant herbs of Russia's middle band.

I was staying in a sanatorium there for almost nothing on a family pass card I got by chance through a friend. But I wasn't there for nervous exhaustion from work – rather because the continuation of our love, then an undiagnosable illness, had reached a crisis which must end in the death of my 'I', or a final cure, and this week-long stay was the last test, a natural break from the addictive pain of emotions, a respite imposed before the decisive and irretraceable step into a new homeland that still looked to me like, and actually was, a cloudy foreign land.

For that whole week, languishing from unresolved love, I walked among these unfamiliar surroundings, wandering as far as I could into the still forests along muddy tracks. At dawn, the mud was hard from the tenacious frost, and the spongy, shallow spring snow was covered with a sparkling crust. There in the early morning calm, my ears filled with the soft chatter of woodpeckers and the light trill of blue tits, I saw a huge forest deer. It slowly observed me with its large, moist eyes and then retired with graceful dignity, and the image struck into my memory as if I was born to it – with the greedy force of one who can steal from another life, when their own is not enough.

The Lopasnya here swept out a broad, deep bend, and the spring breeze that flowed in the clear air followed its curve – fresh and free-spirited, it followed the water. I too was drawn there, but the sticky, ribbed clay banks were not overgrown yet as they are in summer with waxy-topped, velvet under-sided leaves of mother-and-stepmother, with lush burdock and with strong-stemmed horsetails, and it was impossible to get down to the river, especially as the spring melt was flooding ever more of the shallow banks.

But there was the small blue wooden bridge, which I crossed to meet you from the local bus that came out from Moscow once a day. It was a hard meeting. It was clear you wanted to break with me, yet didn't know how to, which is why you were so sharp – rough and desperate because you knew nothing would work out, this way or that, because life, despite its dreams and vague desires, was already plunging into the chill flow of obscurity, swept away in deep, strong currents that surged under the blue, blue bridge.

What we didn't know then was that bridge bound us together forever, eye-to-eye as we toiled with bitter jealousy of our separate pasts – I jealous of the things I didn't know and would never discover, and you of the constant Sene-zhes and Intercession on the Nerls of my flights to going-nowhere isolation.

The sky was blue. The wind flapped and spread the droop-ing branches of the birches, their trunks full of sun near the top but pink from sap near the bole. Stunted, pale-green pines were candling together up to the sky, while in the damp soil on the river slope yellow and shining mother-and-stepmother blooms spilled almost to the inaccessible water's edge. Muddying my boots, I snatched a flower for you – but it was no use, and soon it flew from the bridge into the churning, unstoppable currents of the Lopasnya.

Even after a few years our emotions were still disturbed, and their continuation was so acutely painful that they culminated in what was to me an appalling separation that seemed so belated that it could have neither success nor justification. Only unconscious non-existence and desperate reading saved me from the dark abyss. Day and night, traffic streamed along the Enthusiasts' Highway, and trains clattered under the bridge, slowed down through Novaya station and rumbled punctually on. The tall window glowed with the morning light or the bright stripes shining up at night from the streetlights below, and on I read and re-read, reading someone else's words and mistaking them for my own. Then one day I looked at the little flower from Izmailovsky Park again and found to my surprise that it not only had not withered, but was growing so stubbornly it had spilled right over the edge and crept across the edge of the window sill, extending its ringed, scaly indestructible stem.

This will for life so struck me that I started to observe the mother-and-stepmother flower daily – and maybe because of my bookishness I began to think there was something symbolic about it, some sign for me – but of course there was nothing, and where would it come from anyway? Yet the flower kept on stretching and growing and sprouting in front of my eyes, and simultaneously I sensed life beginning outside, and what had seemed irretrievable flowing back – until finally I woke up and realized I had no burden and I closed my eyes, opened my heart and took flight into the new space in which there was everything but the fear of darkness.

The darkness, of course, was there, but there were stars too – each one, if you looked closely, resembling that radiant flower, that in authentic reality is a giant, dazzling sun,compared to which the sun that shines from the sky is just a weak spring sun, surrounded by the busy bees of our attention.

KARAOKE

By the time Nina got back from Klayz'ma, it was already nearly dark in Moscow. Snow, yellow under the streetlights, was flying down for the second time this year. The first fall had come in November and soon melted, leaving a ghastly slush. It was uncertain if this new snow would settle itself lastingly on the ground – if it would tame the sticky slime of puddles and stir, even for a while, an indifferent gaze with its infant purity, or if it would quickly and futilely melt away according to the newly established, indifferent mechanics of natural processes, in which a misty winter delivers rain that can bring neither joy nor disappointment to now wing-less souls – and where every unconscious impulse becomes enfeebled and dwindles to nothing like the Sunday snow uselessly scattering its flakes under the streetlamps in Moscow's damp dusk.

The descending darkness nearly caught Nina on the road. But it didn't. The car, a new Lada, had run like clockwork. In the lobby, Nina, relaxed by the journey, smiled at the unsleeping concierge. The lobby light was working, and the lift didn't let her down either. As she entered her single flat, Nina was wrapped by its reliable warmth and felt the small irritations of life drop away. Not only was there hot water, but the tap in the bathroom omitted to bark back with its habitual ferocity. And the other day the plumber, surprisingly sober, had fixed the shower by changing the ancient and leaking chrome hose for a shiny new Italian one.

Now, after throwing off her purple sheepskin coat with its furry cowl, she filled the bath with scented herbal foam, just as she used to. She could sink into it, close her eyes and ignore the little icy drops that fell occasionally on her face. She could put some gentle music on, and leave the bathroom door slightly ajar, too – so that the air from the entrance hall kept the big, oval mirror from clouding as it did if she shut the door completely, leaving Nina to wipe it crossly with the end of her thick towel in order to reveal her flushed face, her refreshed chestnut curls rumpled with drying, and her still strong body in its pure and uncomplicated nakedness.

Anyway, even without the music, there was no reason to shut the door. Nobody could see her in the secure seclusion of her little flat, that was like a handy cosmetic box in which all things, both useful and useless, can find their own special place. In Nina's wardrobe, for instance, hung a forgotten fur coat that once seemed so alive and animated that it begged to be stroked and spoken to. In the living room, that was at the same time a bedroom and a studio, there was her computer, her books and paintings. And on the kitchen wall dangled the shiny gold circle of a frying pan, with a long polished handle, in which she'd had such fun in former times making gooseberry jam.

To a casual visitor, Nina's apartment block might look like a grim fortress tower where someone might hide from the inevitable grievances of being. But Nina didn't encourage visitors. On her salary from the advertising agency, she could actually have afforded a bigger place, but in her personal retreat nothing annoyed or disturbed her. The flat suited Nina because it was a perfect fit, like the bathroom, for her new routine of life. She could draw the drapes on her eighth floor windows, leave just the kitchen light on and a candle burning in front of the tiny icon of the Mother of God brought from Cyprus, undress entirely, wrap herself in a dressing gown, take the few steps to the bathroom and slide into the piping hot water.

As she lay in the bath, the sensation of the water suddenly took her back to some long forgotten time when she was a child. Clear blue sky. Vest, knickers, a panama hat. A host of evocative smells. And the dark, smooth path to the bathhouse, over nettles and star-shaped night blindness[10] with its soft hairs, past dense thickets of raspberry-red fireweeds, past yellow tansies and lacy snow-white lungwort. Young pines exuding a rich aroma of sun. Lacewings and pop-eyed dragonflies flitting and hovering in the shimmering air. Behind was the carved wooden verandah of the kindergarten's dacha, from which they were led in small groups to bathe nearby in the spacious borrowed bathhouse on the fringes of the village. Beyond the bathhouse spread a vast field, green with ears of wheat but splashed blue with cornflowers, wheat waving in the breeze – going on, on, on, right to the far blue sky, never ending, like the life within the ripening seeds. And finally that pure sensation of the skin stepping into the water – so sharp, bright, wonderful. As she lay in the bath, Nina, held by the imperishable spirit in her, waited for it all to flood back to her. But not this time.

Now the shock of the water reminded her of something completely different – the foggy, pre-winter lane from the dacha where that afternoon she had parted from her husband for the week again. It was three years now they had been living apart, without thinking about divorce – he, a physicist working in the defence industry in some institutional settlement in the Moscow suburbs, while she,

---

[10] The Russian common name for meadow buttercup.

who remembered Moscow's dissipation, moved into the centre. 'I am a bad physicist and a bad wife ...' she joked with that old phrase, culled from a sixties movie. Even now, they understood each other better than anyone else, but life was turning out in such a way that they saw each other only at weekends. It was always Nina who visited him, either at the settlement, or at the dacha if the weather was ok.

Today, an old friend they hadn't seen for some time dropped in at the dacha. Yet as the conversation gained momentum, Nina had suddenly got up to rush back to Moscow. Aleksei walked her to the car, and then stood for some time watching the car rumble off down the lane. Finally, he vanished from her sight in the rear-view mirror – along with the little cluster of houses; along with the neat rows of American maples, their branches hung with propeller seeds that looked like dragonflies' wings; along with the bridge across the black, icy still flowing river. And after that came the slipway on to the main road.

There was a time when Nina had really loved that road. On each side spread vast, open fields, and the river was sporadically visible on the right, its banks picked out by pale bundles of ginger grass, by the thin, drooping black branches of weeping birches, and by stunted willows from which withies protruded like scribbles smeared in pencil in a child's sketchbook. Alongside the road marched groves of purplish, glaucous-leaved trees, mixed with the odd cloud of dark green spruce.

Nina was driving fast, mechanically sliding past the naked winter trees in the raking rays of the equally unconscious setting sun, as the groves darkened and thickened, merging with the damp, descending dusk. The twilight spaces flooded with a dank silence and the first flurries of snow slanted across the fields. Good, Nina thought, wanting precisely the soft,

longed for calm whiteness of nature at rest, a natural refuge for the pain of her unseen mental torpor. The aching
depths of that autumn soil, she hoped, would soon be buried — sweetly, thoughtlessly, benumbed — and there would
be no more need to live, to labour, to give birth throughout
the long, fierce, icy winter, while above in the pure, white
snow-swept fields, shivering spikes of wormwood[11] would
turn dark-gold in the setting sun.

How sad it is, how thick the mist...

Wrapping her head with a towel, Nina suddenly caught
herself humming an old romance — the one her husband
had started today on the guitar. It was at that moment
she'd suddenly remembered she had to get to Moscow.
He, bless him, didn't get offended or act surprised, but put
aside the battered instrument, a veteran of many hiking
trips, and went with her to the car. Now the words from
that romance appeared on her lips by themselves and she,
just as suddenly as she'd wanted to escape from the chatter in the dacha, wanted to banish the now oppressive
silence by singing aloud, with the backing of the karaoke
machine she had bought on impulse. Nina switched on
the electronic orchestra, picked up the microphone and,
sensing the beat, started to sing.

And the past seems a dream...

---

[11] In Russia, wormwood is often used in herbal medicine and its bitter
taste is a symbol of a bitter truth that must be acknowledged. In contemporary Russian poetry, it is often a symbol of the loss of illusory
beliefs.

Nina sang, and the snow flew outside the window, and the orchestra boom-boomed on and on with its relentless rhythm. The mechanical pop tempo was a little too fast for Nina, so she couldn't sing with the proper expression. It is the accompanist who must listen to the singer sympathetically. But sadly a karaoke machine has no sympathy. Still, you don't have to talk to it. You don't have to share the unconscious impulses of the all-enduring heart. You can, without offending anyone, simply fling the microphone on the armchair and walk to the window to gaze at the snow again from behind the curtain.

That snow was tirelessly covering Moscow, and in the suburbs everything was maybe already white, whitening the darknesses and the endless nooks and open spaces in which no soul could find an earthly answer to their prayers or relief for that unbearable, for Nina, poignancy; nor was there any consolation in the candle guttering weakly in front of the Cypriot icon of she who, as Nina was told, in the very death of her son found comfort and example, and her own immortality.

Snow flew, flew and fell – in big fluffy flakes now. The pavements began to turn white and even the ugliest trees near the block were transformed by slipping on snow-white furs for a while. Snow clung to their branches, lodged in their forks in moist threads, and sat like white dough on their gleaming, naked twigs. But whenever too much snow piled up, it collapsed with a thump to the pavement beneath, and it was becoming clear that the snow wouldn't stay until morning, that it would melt in the never-ending repetition of wet weather, as if it was trying with all its being not to remember how icy, how invigorating, how ringing and crisp it once knew how to be.

There was a place on the way back from Klyaz'ma, a mixed grove where one November we picked mushrooms in the first snows. That day, remember, was also foggy, but the sky was still bright above. The road was smeared with such terrible sludge that the old car with its bald summer tyres shot into the ditch. Fortunately, we were driving slowly – so got away with just a little fright. Aleksei set off back to the dachas on foot to get help, while we, not wanting to hang around on the road, walked deep into the winter grove with Lenechka.

Soft, clinging snow was lying on the pine needles and yellow leaf-fall, thickening the arms of the spruces and forming fringes along the branches of birches and aspens. It was Lenechka who spotted a cluster of small snowy mounds in a shallow dip, and scattering away the snow revealed huge, creamy milk mushrooms[12] – real milk mushrooms, freshly fringed, beaded on their silvery undersides with white dew drops of their secret juices.

Lenechka skipped back to the car for a penknife and they, lost in awe, cut half a dozen mature mushrooms, and were struck by the rich aroma which brought the soul alive with its sense of warm summer rain and dew-soaked forests plants. It emanated not only from the exposed milky caps, but rolled in waves from their leafy nests that were laced with the whitish threads of their hidden mycelium. Life itself, continuing against the odds, smiled on them in that white grove, where it seemed, every living thing was held forever in suspense.

---

[12] Milk mushrooms or milk-caps, known as gruzd in Russia, are mushrooms of the genus Lactarius, and get their name from the milky liquid they secrete when you cut them. They are little thought of in the West, but Russians love them. There is a Russian proverb, 'If you think yourself gruzd, get into the basket' – that is, if you're as good as you say you are, get on with the job.

Lenechka would have already been twenty-two. He died four years back, appallingly and stupidly – not in Chechnya, but during a student winter hike in Kolsky.[13] He broke his leg and froze to death in the tent, while the rest went vainly to get help.

After that, Nina couldn't look at snow for a long time. She'd even had to find a job in Cyprus to escape it. But she couldn't settle in the Mediterranean and had eventually returned to Russia and learned to face the snow again. Now it flew and beat the window and smothered, smothered everything, and her heart, Nina felt, was humbled in waiting for the coming white, pure, infinite spaces of eternal winter, so light and perfect that her soul would feel neither warmth nor cold but reflect only the light of the skies that still glows even in the total Russian darkness.

The electronic orchestra, mechanical and predictable as the duties of existence, went on boom-boom, boom-boom, officiously leading Nina back to the banalities of life, but she wouldn't turn it off. She suddenly regretted that she'd let the idea fill her head that she must come home so early, because nothing now seemed to save her from mortal vanity, not even calling her husband's name, nor screaming, nor howling aloud to the God of the Just for Justice – and all that was left to her was to swallow her usual strong sleeping pills and slump at once into a deep sleep.

But before that she must still dry her hair – and kill another two hours, or else she would wake before it was light. And she'd have to while away the hours in silence, because those snooty neighbours wouldn't tolerate music late.

---

[13] A district in the extreme north of Russia, on the Kola peninsular deep within the Arctic circle.

3

THE GHOST OF THE
BIRD-CHERRY TREE

&

COMING BACK TO the present day from the past, from Karlovy Vary where the freedom from schedules gave me those
mountain walks so good for the heart, spring has arrived at
last – and it has arrived on the heights of London, too.

I once thought of London as flat, like a tourist's map. But,
no, to the south and to the north of the Thames, first gently,
then more dramatically, this great city rises to various hills,
some completely built over, others sweetening the view with
the dark green of mature trees rising above the lighter green
of grassy parks and open spaces.

Hampstead Heath to the north is famous, known for
its absurdly expensive mansions and conserved woods and
heathland, but I dwell in the south, amongst lesser known
hills, with less appeal to tourists. Indeed, so little is their
appeal that even the whimsical drivers of London's black
cabs cannot always be persuaded to venture 'south of the
river'. But if you take the bus from Waterloo, as we often
do, you find the ups and downs begin even in Camber-
well, reminding us continually that to reach the next crest,

you must always first descend – so there is no need to be upset when your life takes a downturn …

All the hills around Sydenham, on top of one of which nestled our house, have their own names: Honor Oak, Gypsy Hill, Denmark Hill, Forest Hill, Norwood. When you're approaching this domain, already from the crest of Denmark Hill you can see that, alone among the southern hills, our hill, a deep overturned bowl, is entirely mantled in green, and from the taxi home after the night shift at the BBC, you can't see a single light twinkling on it – as if it was left entirely untouched from those ancient times when all of London's southern hills were the province of thick forests inhabited by deer and bears.

But it's neither down to the English love of nature or divine disinterest that this wooded hill survives barely fifteen minutes drive from Buckingham Palace, and that the village of Dulwich at its foothills looks so historic. The reason, I discovered, is bears – or rather baiting bears for the pleasure of Londoners, arranging which considerably enrichened Shakespeare's chum, the famous Elizabethan actor Edward Alleyn. It was Alleyn that bought the village of Dulwich and then bequeathed his estate to a special trust that has managed all the local land for four centuries, and prevents any unfortunate changes. Alleyn's name is preserved in the names of roads. At the foot of the hill there is an old mill dam, and on the site of the ancient mill now stands the famous Dulwich College, founded, like the local public art gallery (the oldest in England) by the same Alleyn.

Despite the continual recession of reality, history keeps its grip in Dulwich in the old names of places. A road skirts the hill near Dulwich College and the upmarket sports and riding clubs (one of which is even named the Old Club of

Alleyn) and runs into Lordship Lane next to the Harvester pub. It used to be the only road to London. Even this road recalls in its name Dulwich Common, the time when around Dulwich spread only fields of oats and barley and pastures for cows and sheep.

Cereals once sent up their fruitful stems in fields all over south London. Take, for instance, Peckham, not far from Dulwich, where before the railway era people grew rye, which is why the green expanse of the local park is still called Peckham Rye, and once stretched all the way up the hill to Honor Oak. That oak, in turn, gained its fame because in Shakespearean times, the Virgin Queen Bess, Elizabeth I, honoured it with a picnic;[14] so even a lone tree, growing on just another hill amongst the fields, has etched its way into the life story of these London suburbs.

And in Dulwich College, set up by Alleyn in 1619 as a school for twelve poor children, are kept ancient court archives from Dulwich's history, including some documents that seem rather funny today, like the one describing how, in 1334, one William Hayward ran off with the wife of com-moner Richard Rolfe, taking not just all her jewellery but a cow worth ten shillings. And it's not only family dramas that are recorded here. It should not be forgotten that in 1333, poor William Collin was obliged to fork out three pence because his pig had the unheard of audacity to wander into the oat fields of his local feudal lord.

---

[14] Legend has it that on Mayday 1602, Queen Elizabeth sat down for an alfresco lunch by the oak tree on top of the hill with Sir Rich-ard Bulkeley of Beaumaris. The tree, thereafter known as the Oak of Honor, is in turn honoured by an oak planted in 1905 to replace the historic tree.

So, I think, what is history, when even a damned pig is not forgotten, and nor is Julian Farrow who was dragged to court by the scruff of the neck in the year 1440 for missing a day's work on his lord's fields? What is history, if not a mirage or a fantasy, in which you have to imagine there really once existed Edward Alleyn, Shakespeare's chum, and that other about who we'd never know – and so wouldn't have existed at all – if his pig hadn't strayed into someone else's field.

But let's get back to reality, where the time was certainly the present, and the English spring really was happening.

At night, from beyond our windows in the wooded ravine overgrown with elderberry and brambles came the hoarse, hysterical squealing of foxes, while in the garden that morning I saw baby squirrels in the tall tree. In the fresh green leaf buds, in the singing birds and blue-pink primroses spring was indeed rising and coming to life in the tangled woods of Dulwich that climbed, as I said before, the stepped slope of Sydenham Hill right up to our house.

So as not to forget spring in the mountain forests of Karlovy Vary, I had adopted the habit of walking through the restorative green of the woods both on my way out in the morning and on my way back in the evening. I could get a bus to work right by the house and that was the logical, conventional way to go, but that's what made me sick of it. There are always other ways, unnecessary ways it would seem – but it's these needless deviations that lead you to that longed for balance in the soul. As long as I stayed on damp and muddy paths, it seemed to me that our home, with its surrounding woods already preserved for five centuries from financial pressures, existed beyond the starkly painted vicissitudes of fate.

Despite the obvious benefits, the decision to abandon the bus stop three minutes from home to hike through the woods wasn't made easily. It meant I had to leave half an hour earlier, which entailed not just tearing myself from my sleep but from writing – I didn't have, and still don't have, any other time apart from that early time in which to follow this obligation of the heart, and I was greedy.

Yet there is a silver lining to every cloud, and the extra half hour's walk gave me time to reflect, and to develop a sense of the wood – which, as it turned out, I had for five years lost in the fevered dash for the red double-decker bus on which, ensconced on the upper deck, I could for 45 minutes hungrily read sources for another historical book about Islam in Russia. But I realized that for these letters to another room there is only one dependable source – that is me, myself – and so there was no need to scrape and cram: what will happen will happen.

There are many paths through the Dulwich woods to the more distant bus stop, but by taking three little tracks down from the crossroads, I could find my way along the sparsely grassed gravel bed of a disused narrow-gauge railway. Whenever I set foot on that long-abandoned track, I had a sense of my own long-forgotten narrow tracks from the past.

One of these once led me and my father to the August hunt in Tatarstan – in the chilly white predawn mist on a high crest that rose, silvered with dew, above our Tatar meadows, with their knolls of knotted willows entwined with brambles, stubbornly blooming wild roses and hops with their clusters of pale-honey coloured cones. But all of this, you will see later, when the sun rises....

You know how it happens: unbearably beautiful, it pours into the world fresh and newborn, pale gold and soft brilliance, and then, becoming hotter and shining with devout, intense clarity, it melts away the haze and greyness of the dawn smoking above the meadow glades and illuminates the dew on grasses and branches, and its joyful brightness washes all the intermingled colours of the invisible rainbow of life, knowing no boundaries in breadth or height, earthwards and skywards, and goes on forever, inextinguishable.

But I recall that morning, just before dawn, on to the open meadow there darted the daftest rabbit, loopily sitting upright for a moment, staring straight at us, before bounding away into the pale mist.

Another narrow track from the past, this one carpeted with wilting grass and yellowing pine needles, with my brother Almaz, in our first youth, when with limitless enthusiasm we vanished into the virgin forests of our homeland. Once we walked all day through the November taiga with heavy rucksacks to reach the sacred lake. At night, the frost was bitter, and in the tent, pitched on the shores, it was so utterly freezing that we spent the whole night huddled next to the fire. It was the first time I was ever awake to experience the gelification of the lake waters as it happened. The chill, exposed thickets by the lake basked palely in the light of a vast moon, which cast shifting, glittering spars on the surface of the lake as the water froze, later accompanied by a startling, starry crunch and crackle, like distant gunshot, as the ice formed out beyond the shallows. Long, lightning bolts and zigzags of moonlit crystals spread, like the brilliant cross-cuts on fine Moser crystal, yet continually changing direction. Enchanted flames of icefire sprang from the twigs of pine and birch and found their echo in the glowing embers flying vivid orange into the dark sky from our fire, with the resounding crack of the present.

The Dulwich narrow-gauge track comes to an abrupt halt nowadays in front of the welded iron gates and thick rusty cage that bars the entrance to the old tunnel, from which padlocked and mysterious darkness always blows a scent of fungal dampness and desolation. The mighty arch which thus forbids entry rises in the wood's twilight as a citadel, fortified like a Czech castle or the Pope's Palace in Avignon. Up the steep brick slopes, creep and swarm besieging strands of dark and ancient ivy, marking the end of the line and the beginning of oblivion.

In Victorian times, the ornate red-carriaged, copper-handled trains of the Express Electronic Service company whisked smartly dressed people from Victoria station in central London to the modern wonder of the world – the glass pavilion of the Crystal Palace, which dazzled the grey-bearded Camille Pissarro as he wandered among these trees with his easel. But the smoking chimneys of trains have long since diffused into the past and the carriages no longer jangle through the dark tunnel, even as ghosts. And the great transparent palace, constructed entirely of glass and cast-iron tracery by Joseph Paxton in Hyde Park to house the Great Exhibition of 1851, then dismantled and rebuilt near Sydenham, burned down entirely in a single night in 1936, and photos of those infamous flames decorate the walls of the local pub, the Dulwich Wood House, designed, like the palace, by Paxton.

Besides the photos, the pub's walls are hung with newspaper reports of the great fire, and a yellowed, framed bill, announcing, in letters of different sizes that after the royal family's visit to the Festival of Empire in the glass colossus in June 1911, the Crystal Palace, together with the Concert Hall and central portal, and also the pavilions of the Chinese, Ancient Egypt and Rome, the Byzantine, the French Farmstead, the Chambers of the Moorish Alhambra and the Renaissance era, besides a Medieval English Court, and also the adjacent park with man-made lakes, with their humpback bridges and small islands – will be put at once up for auction. But even then, no-one was actually willing to stump up any cash for this onetime pride of the empire.

It's a short walk from the pub to the park, where you can still see amongst the weeds the wide flights of ruined stone staircases, imperial lions and statues that survived the flames. But the Palace itself has merged with history and become not merely transparent but invisible. And it comes to mind that those everyday worries that force us into alien schedules burn and crackle away to nought, and so do those imaginary palaces of the heart and chambers of the soul – those Chinese pagodas on Formosa lakes, those ancient stone-pines of Cyprus, those Byzantine churches and Roman temples, those luminous lagoons of Renaissance Venice, our own personal Alhambra, our Sinai deserts, our English Middle Ages – are all blown through the gaps of consciousness, through any imposed reality, like the Mistral sweeping down through the French valleys from the Alps, verifying that the past is not completed...that everything is being accomplished and everything happens outside time, outside the here and now, as in the human soul.

And that's quite enough justifications for these apparent confusions of thought before those who won't welcome them anyway, just as they won't welcome in spring the insane winds of autumn – like that furious mistral in ever-sunny Provence that recently and yet so infinitely long blew in our presence with such energy that it almost blew us and our love off the famous Avignon bridge into the chill font of the deep, plethoric Rhone...

Oh Allah, what was I meant to realize at that moment, when it was so freshly and so terribly imprinted into my memory and consciousness, that moment which could so easily inspire, but even more easily bring grief:

> Sur le Pont d'Avignon,
> L'on y danse, l'on y danse
> Sur le Pont d'Avignon,
> L'on y danse tous en rond[15]

Out on the remains of the medieval bridge stranded in the river: around us the penetrating, maddening mistral that knocked you off your feet, below the icy azure waters flowing as they had for tens of thousands of years, and behind, on a hill, the vast and imposing Palais des Papes – its thick walls faceted with cubes and rhomboids and corresponding spaces: a labyrinth, a charade, an enigma, a conundrum of history that stimulates the imagination perhaps more than it should.

And so we wandered through the deserted stone halls, quietly pleased that the mistral had already blown away most of the idle-eyed tourists, leaving only a handful to shuffle around that palace where, like a repository in time, the papacy was exiled for a century when the light in Rome was dimmed. Through the empty palace, through its connecting

---

[15] On the bridge of Avignon
We all dance there, we all dance there
On the bridge of Avignon
We all dance there in a ring

(Old French song)

echoing halls and galleries and through the wide open doors, gusted the mistral, the one visitor which had a right to visit freely, earned by long service.

And who were we with our lonely earth love in this stone shell, this ancient masonry undefeated by time which we naively touched to sense immortality? The chill of the stone shot through the fingers and penetrated the heart, which so rarely obeys the mind. And again there was the question — what is in the world beyond the illusion of our historic existence? After all, if history itself is a mirage, an illusion of the mind, a delirium of the calendar, an unembraceable dream, then you cannot touch it, and you cannot just feel the truth. We can only reckon when we want to feel and be present, because only when we are present does this seem an action. But there was only the mistral, the sun-stirred wind and the Rhone, rolling its full, blue, icy waters past the Avignon bridge, which you can't cross.

Everyone has their own tongue. Everyone has their own truth. Everyone has their own history. And these variations of people's sufferings interact only on dates, in the numbers that rule the world of people. The age of the Avignon retreat, the age of Babylon's captivity, the age of purgatory before the brief deceptive paradise of the Renaissance — you can call them what you will, and all will be true and nothing will be true. Yes, these ages that overload us with knowledge and lure the mistral in the mind to murmur to the heart. The age of the Hundred Years War, the age of Dante, of Giotto, of Bocaccio, the time of Petrarch, of the Great Plague, the years of darkness and foreboding, the times of plots and brutal dictatorships, the ages of grumbling by the illiterate rabble forever seeking bread and circuses... And in the mirror of ages, this present age of quiescent changes that are neither visible nor yet have brought

anything but lost illusions and everyday suffering. The trap of ages.

Who else but us will remember our presence in the Pope's palace, when, chance visitors, we strolled from hall to hall, from one floor to another, witnessed only by the secret eyes of the ancient stone walls newly uncovered by restorers? Yes, stones can see, but it takes them long to learn how.

In the streets of Avignon – a poor village compared to Rome even though stubbornly electing its own pontiffs – cattle both large and small loiter in the day, while at night lurk restless gangs of medieval lads. In the echoing halls of the palace, its bedrooms and corridors, trail vile intrigues and the smell of death, mingling with smells of cooking as smoky aromas fill the lofty refectory from the spit-roasting of a lamb the size of a small bull. Aromas of death still linger secretly in the palace chambers where the mistral can't reach, where lived and died the first Avignon pope, Clement V – who tried to unite Europe with a new crusade against the Saracens and met his demise after treating indigestion with crushed emeralds; who outlawed the Knights Templar and blessed their brutal execution; who smiles at us from a dark corner with his public smile, since he went down in history as a pious, placid and pleasant priest, and there must be some truth in the reports.

Accompanied by that unsettling smile, we escaped the Pope's chamber, recognizing that it was locked up in time – a time not ours.

And outside, the mistral was blowing, the wind that drives people mad, that confuses the mind of even the toughest husband, by blowing out from the soul and from the heart the dusk of self-possessed pride.

The mistral blew, filling up the sunny spaces of autumn with the ghosts and memories of things unhappened,

unhappened because everything that truly was, was different from how we imagined.

The mistral blew, turning the heads of northerners and driving Van Gogh crazy in canvases of scarlet vineyards and twisted cypresses near Arles, yet invigorating the mind of Cézanne who, as it turns out, did not invent, but precisely impressed with his brush the motley, smoky scene around Mont St Victoire. That is what Provence is, with its Aix, its Arles, its Avignon and Marseilles, and its vivid blue calanques that gnaw the rocky coast, overgrown by the stone-pines of the infinite imagination.

A human being – seeks to justify his being and his wanderings through life. A human being – understands that his brief stay within nature and geography is like the existence of a leaf that once quivers on a plane-tree branch then is carried off by the wind in an unknown direction, and there's no human being whose existence is fixed like a stone.

Everything that happens, happens inside the soul. Only the soul can sense invisible connections that slip away unnoticed from so much knowledge. But the soul can slumber, or shiver in fear, and only earthly love and God's mistral can help it see and comprehend how everything in the world is interconnected – even those things that seem utterly disparate.

Yet do they really understand this, these chance observers, these frequent trippers, these earnest tourists in Avignon and Turin, the Holy Land and Sinai, where a wily Bedouin, wrapped in a *keffiyeh*, gives them a ride on his asthmatic camel to the monastery of St Catherine which holds behind its stone walls Moses's 'burning bush', the first images of Christ and an original handprint of the Holy Prophet of Islam. The only thing they'll really remember is the camel ride, because they paid for the ride. Only very rarely will one of this mixed crew look up and feel with the trembling heart that they all, so different, are inextricably connected to each other by the common air of the world, our one atmosphere, that looks from space like a soft blue haze above this planet of people in which each of who, you must remember, Mozart is killed...

People, people, nameless as the wandering clouds that shine so brightly in the heights of love above other spaces where live the northern, the sick, the grieving, the Russian – spaces for long uninhabited and careless in their vacancy, spaces where now and forever reverberates the chaos of shrieking hatred and its strident echo: the unctuous teaching of lies.

And in these spaces, vanquished people, tired of passive flesh and of the heart that alone can vanquish the fear of death in life – this is what it comes to.

Sur le Pont d'Avignon,
L'on y danse, l'on y danse
Sur le Pont d'Avignon,
L'on y danse tous en rond

Any river has two banks and the wind blows above each. And what can we do if we do not dance on the bridge that leads to nowhere but to and fro – dance like the dessicated plane-tree leaves whisked through Avignon's cobbled strets, dance like the mistral – and smile to your beloved, and try not to think but to live ....

I could walk straight down from my house to the abandoned tunnel, but I chose other paths. If you go right, say, after just five minutes, you find yourself on a meandering track, curling through the twittering of goldfinches and the fluting of red-breasted robins, between young hornbeams and ash trees entwined with mistletoe and honeysuckle, past early spring flowers – pale bluebells, anemones white as ivory, anemones like tiny stars peeping from the tangled grass, violas and foxgloves – *digitales* with their fleshy, geranium-like leaves and crimson bell-shaped blooms.

You can then climb up to a Cedar of Lebanon, so ancient and tall, that spreads a tent so broad and dense that nothing grows beneath, not even the most tenacious bramble. In this bare space, exposed sandstone is blanketed in fallen needles.

In the thick base of this great cedar, nestling deeply into its tough bole and knotted sinews, is set a bench for contemplating the dark pond below, a pond which even in spring is short of water. So this place is not a happy place, but filled with melancholy, like any place that does not fulfil its purpose. At first, I came here often to sit on the bench and think, but the sight of the exposed mudslime and seeps of the pond bed brought only dreary thoughts, so I gave up draining my imagination and heart here, along with the duckweed and water fern – and followed other paths through the wood and found other benches, some set up in memory of English people who had loved these places when they were alive. On the copper plates screwed to the bench, I read Gus Berger, Phillip Heath, Brian Seymour...

Then the path winds further on, under the shady canopy with its flashes of sunlight, past constellations of snowdrops and wild garlic with their lanced leaves, past blackberry and raspberry bushes, and ferns with fronds still curled in yellow spirals like a bishop's mitre, and then after a while emerging past what seems like a ruined chapel where rocks fused into a gothic arch.

And everywhere in the gloom of the trail beneath the trees, it seemed to me there beckoned the deceptive scent of bird-cherry blossom. I looked for it with my eyes, but it wasn't there − only the faint scent, bitter, brusque but beloved, drifting past − but where from?

Maybe it was the mingling of moist morning air and whiff of muddy puddles with the fragrant bouquet of flower scents − the pinky froth of hawthorn, fluffy rosettes of rowan blossom, golden showers of meadowsweet, subtle jasmine, wild garlic and lily-of-the-valley invisible amid the grass. Maybe they all conspired to compose for me that longed for breath of pure happiness.

Gus Berger, Phillip Heath, Brian Seymour (vanished descendants of the Victorian imperial era), Cedar of Lebanon and artificial ponds with small oak islands, wide, grassy banks with bluebells and angelica, dandelions and fireweed and thistles, and English birch trees and may alders with their sticky seedpods primed to fluff up and fly over the glades where are bedded lungworts (pink but turning purple), glades which, after the moist gloom under trees...all of these suddenly stir a marvellous thought in the passerby's mind: this isn't just for me to wonder at snow-plumed and pink starry flowers, nor even to foster my contact with the Unity, but for those working hard on the Earth − for Gus Berger, Phillip Heath and Brian Seymour, the walkers of the many paths, the black-wet paths with the staccato signature of dog-runs leading into thickets and the dry sandy paths in spots of sun, the paths on which I could as easily go astray as I do in these letters, yet, glory to Allah, always find my way out. Let peace be with you in the truths of the Father's spring, where the memory of you so carefully ministers today to the regular visitors and chance passers-by to this ancient English wood, who, sadly however, have no idea that in the world there exist entirely different kinds of wood...

...where also in the beginning there was silence, undisturbed by a single memorable sound, and only later did the sun pierce the deep blue and gold gaps in the clouds to break the chill – drip-drop, splash, little by little – and suddenly a stiff breeze stirs the uncaring leaves, and sunlight flushes glittering gold from birch and aspen in clearings still spread with white, and sparkles the pearly frosted webs that in autumn glimmer through the tall grass – in autumn, filled with taiga briar, gangly pink honeysuckle, dizzy elder, as well as copper-rusty angelica, yellow-eyed tansy and marvellous magenta fireweed...

...in autumn, when helpful fatigue forces you to find moments of midday repose – the blissfully stretched out body with no sense of its final shape, lying supine on the grass and merging into one with the season happening around, and just barely, out of the corner of your eye, you glimpse moments of your life flowing by – a gun and backpack; fresh animal trail winding through birch glade and past pine windbreak; flash of sunlight on dragonfly wings; sun-baked mushroom umbrella – but even those visit only vaguely before again comes, drip-drop, honest, sensitive, wonderful silence, and you soon can't tell what was, what is and what will be, and events swap over and over in the undelineated reality of memory, happening before and after, after and before, flowing in and out, joining, transposing, stretching and shrinking...

...just as this onflowing sentence which, like a dream, can only be broken by waking...

...and will slip again, slithering through brown shadows under pines over the mesh of crimson cranberry and emerald taiga mosses to the capercaillie lek, where amid hog-hued shadows, a trio of capercaillie cocks flurry from boughs to view the brace of hens that squat on silvery needles strewn on the close-compacted sandy forest floor – and the old grey cock perches on palings, sprinkled beak to tail with beads of icy, autumn dew.

It's so good to doze in the last heat of the autumn, so good to feel the whole day open before you, open to impressions, amongst which will be the forest river Ilet, with its confined channel, sandbanks and deep pools, running smoothly past trees that plunge in their roots and trunks, and bifurcating into three limpid streams that quietly murmur in sympathy with the whispering wind and the soft rustle of glowing-in-the-sun leaves.

If you gaze from the bank or, mayhap, the knotty bole of a pine where it drops to rapids: shoals of dark-backed, double-edged ide, riding the current on scarlet fins, head upriver: the flicker and glitter of silvery roach; a deep hole where the novice might be seduced into angling for red-scaled perch, unaware that the first catch will scare off the rest, leaving you to fish in vain all day. Taiga rivers demand movement, not just when hunting with a gun, but even fishing will knock your legs out, walking from catch to catch up the stream in search of the perfect bowl of *ukha*.[16]

Will you come back to this extraordinary, fleeting experience at least once again? Or of all that truly *was*, will the lasting memory be waking in the dusk – awakening from sleep before night falls, before the coming of mortal loneliness,

---

[16] *Ukha* is a rich Russian broth made with fish caught in rivers such as perch and tench, along with carrots and potatoes and herbs such as tarragon and dill.

with the sudden, distressing realization that reality endures more memorably than any dream.

These twilight moments are so familiar – these moments when all around becomes imperceptibly more vague and melancholy; when each joyful tree, its boisterous rustling briefly stilled and suspended from the innocent festival of life, and the purling river, too, slipping into quiet abstraction, accentuate the coming silence with their remoteness. These moments of detachment when barely lingering day yields to the clarity of night, and you seem to sense directly each tree and flower and bird – birds especially seem to sense this time of withdrawal, becoming quieter.

You see, there were a few of us at the time. I joined the group by chance, before sunrise at the rest in the Mari[17] – I think we were en route to some tourist spot where I hoped to meet my friends, or something – and we all, I don't remember why, dropped off to sleep by the river. We'd just sat down after a long hike with heavy rucksacks – but the sun shone warmly, the river burbled softly and the breeze with gentle persistence was inclined to weave the fresh withies on the banks and diffuse the scent of bird-cherry. In short, the casual chatter dwindled into drowsiness then slipped into slumber. And then I woke suddenly.

I'll never forget that melancholy twilight longing. I'd happily banish it from my memory, but from that time on, a sad longing returns at the most unexpected times – comes back and touches my heart with its chill hand. And then I remember straightaway the infinite emptiness of that withdrawal that so abruptly caught me by the murmuring stream – such

---

[17] The Mari Depression, a vast area of swamp and taiga in the west of the Mari El republic, a small Russian federal republic next to the Volga.

an emptiness that while I was lightly sleeping in the fresh air it seemed as if some genie or other supernatural creature had stolen my sleeping soul, and would not return it until they'd done with their games.

My companions slept on, but even their human presence failed to comfort this aggrieved orphan, lost in the empty font of the soul. I was suddenly aware of how little our fellowship meant in the face of the stark and inexpressible reality of life happening now, and continuing to happen in the future, without us.

I sat for some time gazing at the river's rapids, it being my habit at the time to indulge any longing, but everything ends. Then there was time to; now there is not.

And the water flowed full; flooding and muscling aside with its youthful vigour the bankside bushes and bent grasses, the ever-shifting streams of its gushing snow melt impossible to track. It was a long time until autumn, when the river would finally run blue and clear, opening to the world in its last sincerity the secret light painting of its bed – but I could already imagine it then, the autumn river and her bravery and sorrow.

See – I've barely managed a few paces without these punctuations of memory. It's my greediness; my insatiable wish to have my fill of these fragmentary hypostases of existence. But now I see a face – your face, framed by flowing to the shoulders fair hair, your face clouded by long non-understanding as the shadows of alienation descend between us. That alienation was already happening in the Altai, where I once dragged you, reluctant to spoil my fun that you could not share.

After a long and arduous journey – by plane, by suffocating bus and by helicopter – everything upset you and nothing could console you – not the wild scenery, nor the green folds in the hills, nor the jagged cliffs above the azure Chulyshman river, nor the orange blooms of zharka[18] or mauve Lenten roses.[19] You were terrified of a rock dislodging from the ledges above to start a landslide; terrified that the icy blue, bottomless waters of Teletskoye[20] want to suck us in.

Now, looking at the pink-flowered, wide-leaved Altai bergenia,[21] which here in English gardens are purely ornamental, I understand that then in the Altai, I had forced you yet again to another strange land.

No, not catching grayling together in the tumbling Chulyshman, overlapping on the fly and remembering how you angled in the Lelvyrgyrgyn in your tundra childhood; not that mad whitewater descent in a motorboat from Teletskoye to the Biya through boulders and gullies; not the mountain larches in dazzling sun, and the clouded slopes from which soared clear the icy wastes and snow-capped pinnacles of Korbu and Altyn-Tuu; not Teletskoye itself, golden and blue, the icy fount of my early memory and easily distressed heart – no, none of these, to my huge disappointment, gave you any pleasure or solace.

Yet now, remembering the sunset of alienation that so confused me after that sleep by the river, I think, isn't that how you felt in Altai, how you could do nothing by yourself and knew nothing? Everything then seemed to threaten

---

[18] The local name for globe flowers.

[19] Oriental hellebore.

[20] Teletskoye is the largest and deepest lake in the Altai. Its name means Golden Lake in the Altai language.

[21] The pink flowering saxifrage from the Altai region often known in England by the name 'elephant's ears' because of its broad, leathery leaves.

you with distress. The big heifers that blocked our path in the sunlit spray in the glade, the slippery boulders blanketed in emerald moss and rust-red lichen, the growling dog, the tangled thickets of purple ledum and poisonous clusters of white berries, and even the huge cedars – none of these, which meant so much to me, were yours, nor echoed with emotional memory, and so could only bite, bruise or sting.

The de-invention of these vast Altai tracts... And isn't it true that a woman's existence, lovelier though so much smaller, is enough to complete the picture and the pattern of any true life?

And so Karlovy Vary, Carlsbad – your gift, your unselfish gift, surrounded by mountains which at once resonated for me with the alpine cool, gushing rivers and greenery of the Altai. There, at dawn, when this enchanted town still sleeps by the hushed murmur of the Tepla, and life lies motionless high up on the Diana Tower and other woody heights, like the nearby hill of Eternal Life, just as Artybash, grey and shrouded in damp mist, lies by Teletskoye... Then, as it has to, the sun rises, the clouds melt, and the skies, if you're lucky with the weather, turn dazzlingly blue above the fresh green of the mountains, poised and frozen in high in the air waves that stretch to the horizon.

You and I were walking on the slopes of the English park of Richmond Sanatorium, perched right on the mountain's foot by a bend in the Tepla. Only this name, and the then closed Anglican church of Saint Like with its stained glassed windows, recall the time when Carlsbad was visited by the English aristocracy.

And the park: sloping meadows dotted with pines, silver birches and blossoming lindens; a track snaking up, covered

in yellow-flowered oaks which stand undaunted by the
hustle of foreign azaleas and rhododendrons which under
their scarlet and white inflorescences hide flute-playing fauns
with bronze navels; cast-iron statues of deer with spreading
antlers; and a pool, filled steadily with water cascading down
from an unseen stream above – a hand-made pool in which
a stony round-bellied young faun grasps the graceful neck of
a stony crane.

And their flight, echoed in the fluttering of newly budded
leaves, spread out through the classical symmetry and balance
of the English park created, like Pavlovsk Park, in imitation
of nature, so that just as in the Dulwich woods, it was hard to
see where natural vegetation ends and man's additions begin.

So the stream, taken briefly captive by the artificial pool,
escaped from its limbo to tumble down to the river below,
while above, beyond the footbridge, this eternal life flowed
untouched. It went on singing softly amid the mossy stones
and beech twigs, rolling and falling from one natural step to
another with that pure chushing burble...

...chushing like the 'ch' in Richmond, like the ch-chir-
ruping of birds...

...and incidentally resonating in the soul with the name
of another brook of the heart's memory, the Chiri,[22] above
the boiling stream of which I sat on my first visit to Teletskoye, distinctly feeling that I might never again see the great
perfection in the life around.

This strongly flowing taiga stream of living water, raged,
rumbled and churned to Teletskoye down the steep, birch-clad
ravine, once a precipice in its path but now bedded with a con-
cave channel, worn diligently smooth and strewn with mossy

---

[22] Chiri is also the name of a bird common in Russia.

boulders veined in fiery turquoise. The sun laced through curling branches to fill the stream with a golden glow and create a rainbow in the spray where it jetted into the lake – scintillating like crystal the drops of water that clung to blades of grass emerging between mossy stones in the perfect proportion of a Japanese garden. Above, a golden oriole called. Perfect proportions, too, appeared in the harmonies of rocks in the grove and the fans of ferns that sprung from the ancient trees.

> The river; a mighty stream – the Chiri as wild birds warble
> (in a gorge down rocky steps where perfect light is playing)
> below like clear blown glass, the current's silvery bubbles,
> (in a gorge of thundering stones, the rain's forever pouring).
>
> Over the river's bed (you remember, dearest) –
> the soft and tender stream (my love, where did you go?) –
> between the mossy boulders, hid like a woman's breast,
> in a cool and pale pool, the limpid waters flow.
>
> The warbling of the birds confirms the day is clement;
> shadows are sharply cast and branches nicely warm too;
> the splashes on wet stones, the moss is like green velvet,
> (where?) – the rocky steps – (oh my love, where are you?).[23]

There too grew wild peonies – taiga peonies with firm red buds – and fragile pink mountain aquilegia and, modestly bedded by the stones, fragrant creeping thyme that with its delicate scent so characteristic of the steppes unsettled my solitude and called, no, demanded me to bring you to Teletskoye, because to have beauty and truth to yourself is simply unfair.

---

[23] Poem by Ravil Bukharaev.

Why after taking your gifts and others, though not straightaway, do I go so long through life with my own — who reclaims them?

After all these moments pass, Dulwich wood is coming to an end; the hornbeams give way to oak, the wood is lighter and more open and fills with the chirruping of birds, and at the huge feet of ancient oaks protrude blades of emerald herbs covered in white, living stars; after undulating erratically, the path suddenly becomes sandy and flat and, on the left, behind a silvery aluminium fence, the well-watered, well-tended and well-swept clearings of a golf club appear; the sand becomes white gravel and, beyond the wind-stirred willows, a pole topped by a red and black flag, a bunker, an oval puddle on the green and neat clusters of azaleas, along with other golf course paraphernalia; and I reflect that due to lack of time I cannot indulge in this eminently useful form of idleness like that gentlemen in the red pullover, yellow trousers and white sun-cap, who rolls up behind him a black caddy stuffed with silver clubs as he tries to catch up with his companions — while I'm only catching up with time, which doesn't exist, and the scent of bird-cherry that is certainly present but still elusive...

And the heart, in spite of all, keeps aching, and the eyes see less well than they did. Before I emerge in the alley to the bus, I embrace an oak, chosen by chance: that's what you recommend to relieve the heaviness of the heart.

Then faster, down the alley between the oaks, through nettles and buttercups and burdock, with just a few minutes of authentic life left, before the exit through the green wicket gate on to the road, where knots of ancient hawthorn bushes wreathed in white blooms unexpectedly appear — and I suddenly understand from where, wafting through a little

English wood, came that watery, ghostly, obsessive odour of bird-cherry, with all the pungence of home – my spiritual homeland, irrecoverable, like childhood. Then as I step on between the buttercups and burdock, the thorny mistletoe and azalea, there hovers unprohibited in the fresh morning air, the tormenting, giddy scent of another hemisphere: snow-traced rosettes of hemlock from my homeland, too – hemlock with its carroty leaves, poisonous cowbane,[24] everlasting *tsikuta*, bringing home to me that there is no choice in love, nor in running away, nor in the final homecoming...

At last, as the double-decker bus slows down for the corner by the Harvester pub and the timetable of life so shamefully hurries me on, I see, behind the pub's low fence, in a garden filled with rows of wooden tables and benches, two great chestnut trees rising – linking their branches and creating a conjugal mixing of their starry, white and pink blooms.

And I, getting on to the bus, take with me into nowhere this last valuable thought that, spring or autumn, there stands this neighbourly pair of chestnut trees, each remaining itself like us, yet mingling their branches in unity and merging their roots in an unmutual past...

THE MONTH OF LITTLE HEAT

Arzhana only just managed to keep calm and humble herself; only just – for the sake of the three children or the restless hopes of a woman's heart – took back her tipsy husband. But

---

[24] The author here conflates two kinds of hemlock – *Conium maculatum* (known in Russian as *boligolov* and cowbane (*Cicuta virosa*, or, in Russian, *tsikuta*). Both are poisonous and historians dispute over which was used by the Greeks to poison Socrates.

in the morning, she found him absent from the bed again. She also found missing two buckets of sour milk *chegen*[25] that she'd fermented for cheese in the deep *hadka*.[26]

He had run away and taken the *chegen* with him. And there, out of the smoke hole of some neighbouring *ail* (an eight-sided cedar yurt where Altai people live in the summer) grey puffs of smoke were already spiralling, and out of her *chegen*, in the age-old process, the whey was already being driven[27] to make milk *arachka*,[28] so that the first drive is supped as soon as its ready, while it's still warm from the battered pan, turning men into animals with slobbery, uncontrolled mouths and swollen eyes – cloudy, like the damn drink itself.

She'd hoped he'd stay dry at least until the mowing, but her hopes were clearly vain. June, the month of little heat, was the mowing time. In the woods on the mountain slopes, extending from their *delyanka*[29] right to the thundering brink of a turbulent, boulder-strewn stream, the grasses stood high, flashing in the sun – but, *oi-li*, they'd been left standing too long; early birds were already clearing their nebs and twittering in the branches. It was such a fine place to mow, to move through the fragrant grass, swinging the sharp scythe to and fro, shirk, shirk, slicing through the stems, taking care around the stumps and stones that might be hidden by new growth, until hot and perspiring you washed your face in the clear, shooting water. She so loved the foamy bank and the icy jets, as she had since she was child – the golden, life-giving flow

---

[25] A cultured milk product common in the Altai.
[26] An Altaisky wooden tub.
[27] In Russia, the process of home distillation is called 'driving'.
[28] A strong local drink made by distillation.
[29] The family plot.

of water, and no wonder that her name in Altaisky meant 'sacred source'. Or rather, just 'source', but is there any true source that is not sacred?

Arzhana milked the ginger-coloured cow and led it from the yard, though like all her neighbours' cows it was free to wander wherever it pleased, up to the cedar fence on the outskirts of the village. Like a mother eagle, she looked out over the village that in recent years had fallen into decay. It was a substantial place, about a hundred houses, stretching far as the eye could see, and that was a long way – right to the clear, turquoise river which, beyond a spur cloaked in boulders and trees, ran over a sandbar and into the azure fount of the fathomless lake, as long and twisting as a woman's lot. This valley, Arzhana always told the children in their lessons on local history, could easily contain the whole of Liechtenstein, not to mention Monaco – but this didn't mean much either to the children or their parents.

Beyond the cold, shooting stream, the steeply ascending stone ridges soon reached the taiga where marals[30] roamed; higher still, among the pines and cedars, full, red buds of wild peony glowed, while across the stream, there were succulent, dew-sparkled pastures that had tempted the cows since time immemorial, and the cows, not bothering to look for a ford, huddled together and lifted their muzzles to plunge into a reach of the stream where the waters looked smooth but were actually strong and fast-flowing. Calves couldn't manage it at first; sometimes, they'd get swept right down to the first *izluka*.[31] But then the local cows were famous for their remarkable cleanliness, and no wonder, since they bathed

---

[30] Red mountain deer.
[31] Sharp bend.

every day in the crystal waters so well that there was no need to even wipe their udders for milking.

Further upstream, through a deep ravine of birches and flower-splashed green meadows, was a bridge over waters bubbling on yellow stones to a place where the view opened wide, wide as the world, on a valley filled with thickets of blooming buckthorn and ancient barrows, and in the middle distance, a lone mountain shaped like a saddle, or a two-humped camel lying prone. Under that mountain, named after the epic of *Batyr*,[32] was in the past a common site for archaeologists to dig, throwing out mounds of unwanted skulls and bones, and there used to be more tourists here, but regulations, which a while ago wouldn't let you breathe, now tightened around your neck like a garrotte. Shuttle helicopters no longer flew to the village; the motorship *Altai Pioneer* stopped ploughing the lake in '92 and was now lying beached on the far side of the lake; there were no pioneers in school; there was no petrol for the motorboats; the broken windows of the abandoned shops sold only wind and rain; and the villagers were reduced to bartering, as they did long ago, exchanging bulls for mirrors with the Russian merchants, collecting pine cones, milking their cows and basic hand-to-hand trading, as well as foraging in the taiga, and poaching – not to mention blatant theft and drunken robbery.

The *sovkhoz*,[33] or whatever they call it now, was still sowing barley in the valley for its own use, and made a bit of cash by

---

[32] The tale of Ural-batyr is the great ancient epic poem of the Bashkirs, about a legendary hero and his brave battles and encounters with magical creatures. It was first translated into English only in 1999 by Sagit Shafikov.

[33] State farm.

selling goat's wool and untreated sheep skins to dealers from Barnaul at just five roubles a time. Those dealers, by the way, after curing the skins, sold them for 150 roubles for making luxury sheepskin coats, which, of course, sold for over ten times as much. But how could you start your own leather goods business when the electricity supply was intermittent even to the school – the school that was falling down, and lodged in an ancient building of smoke-blackened logs, the only remnant of the long abandoned Orthodox monastery?

And anyway, what kind of 'bizniz' is it when meat is sold for seven roubles a kilo and goat wool for even less? Salaries aren't paid – out of what profits? So how come some people in the village have satellite dishes? But why the surprise. No, the truth is, there's no money, and people are forced to slaughter the remaining cattle for food...it's easy to die of starvation, these days... And you have to get the children ready for school, don't you? And how do you pay for that? That's why the villagers give away meat, wool and skins for a pittance; there's no other way.

Arzhana's sons, both teenagers, got lucky that summer, though. One was a shepherd up at the *coshara*;[34] the other one, the younger one, was an apprentice wood carver, away at the far end of the lake, carving ladles and souvenir bears from cedar blanks – ah, let them burn in the flames of the new age – the taiga will always feed the Altaisky, it will always feed them, their dear taiga will.

Arzhana was no ordinary *Altayka*. She was descended from the ancient Turkuts. She was a striking woman, with a thick, dark-blond plait draped down her back, high cheekbones, an eagle's nose and blue, blue eyes like the Altai skies.

---

[34] The high-altitude sheep pastures.

A warrior-woman, one of those Amazons from Hyperborea, utterly convinced they descended from the stars and will leave this life fully armed for the heavenly meads of their ancestors.

But the people had fallen a long way. They were bogged down in gossip, and with no work they lost their pride, and they gave themselves up entirely to Erlik, lord of the underworld, no longer even dreaming of celestial pastures. Kudai, the god of the mountain meadows, who had already long been angrily hurling space launch vehicles and fuel tanks back to earth, had given up pledging the zaisans[35] golden grace – and was instead inflicting yellow rain, psychosis and deformities never seen here before, even among the heaviest drinking families. Heptyl rain,[36] scattered from rocket fuel, left behind puddles skinned in wrinkled yellow, and scorched vegetable patches; it left infants bald and greying; it led adolescents to go mad and try to strangle themselves; and adults began to die of cancer.

Those who could, those sober enough, escaped this bleak wilderness to earn a poor wage in Gorno-Altaysk, in Biysk, or even Barnaul. The rest, or so it seemed in her grieving heart, secretly blamed each other for their shared miseries, and instead of helping out, they only undermined each other; and they were digging a hole for her, maybe because

---

[35] Tribal leaders.

[36] People of the Altai are regularly bombarded with both rocket debris and rain polluted by toxic heptyl rocket fuel from space launches from the nearby Baikonur Cosmodrome in Kazakhstan, since the Altai lies along their flight path. Unlike rockets launched from the Kennedy Space Center in Florida, which shed stages into the Atlantic, sections from rockets launched from Baikonur drop on land, usually in the Altai.

she once wrote poems, or maybe because she doesn't submit to the burdens of life and always looks far away and high up, and rarely under her feet.

Arzhana, though, really did see further than some people. Her home, the farm and the house and the indispensable ail, was set high on a ledge on the mountain slope, beneath a steep rock wall, up which wound, invisible from below, a goat-track to the under-sky cliffs, still wet in places with slushy snow clinging to dwarf birches and cedars – but on the high shelf above, between the scree, squealing pikas and susliks scurried, and in the mountain grass beside the rills there, with yellow blooms, was slowly ripening the golden, healing root, *Rhodiola Rosea*.[37] If she only had company, Arzhana would climb to the celestial meadows to get the root, and also *shilajit*,[38] and if she were desperate, maybe she could sell it to tourists for real money. But only penniless cranks floated this way, and with a tiny three year-old daughter, a gift of the last reconciliation with her husband, who was here tugging at her skirt and twittering, 'Mama, why are you crying? Here, take my doll…' – well, alone with an infant… and it won't be easy doing the mowing…

Not easy, but necessary. 'The weather won't wait; I can cry when it rains,' Arzhana decided. She saddled the horse,

---

[37] Also known as Aaron's Rod or Golden Root, and known to have psycho-active properties that may help improve the mood and alleviate depression.

[38] Shilajit or momijo is a sticky, tarlike substance found in the Altai and Tibet, and long used in Ayurvedic medicine. Once processed it is a dark brown paste. Scientific research on its health benefits have so far been inconclusive.

strapped on a leather *archimak*,[39] tied on the ready-sharpened scythe in its canvas case, and sat her daughter in front with her favourite doll, dressed in a little coat with a tightening hood just like mama's to protect against acari bites – and after ambling by the huts of her indifferent neighbours, she rode out into the silky meadows and the sun-pierced groves beyond the cedar fence.

A light breeze was blowing, stirring the fresh leaves and playing with spots of light on the grasses and the great stones rolled down from the ridge in ancient times. On the left, shushing like heavy rain, flowed the river, and above it, hovering then suddenly stopping, were large mica-winged dragonflies, while in the honey meadows bumblebees buzzed and the grass was dotted with blazing orange and red blooms of zharka: the most loved flowers of any young Altaisky. The whole wide ravine was blooming and fragrant, as on the day the world was created: with temple hellebore rising like a Chinese pagoda; shining bergenia with vivid pink cluster cups and dark-green glossed leaves; violet ledum flickering in the shade; giant angelica, already tall as a person, holding sunwards its fragile, snow-laced rosettes – and a cuckoo calling...

The little daughter purred a tune to herself; the reinless horse stepped steadily, knowing every hoof-fall of the way; and breathing in deeply, Arzhana marvelled at the Earth's power of renewal and the female persistence of Mother Nature. After all, no matter how you assault her with acid and poison, no matter how you tear her to shreds with greed, or bombard her with litter from the sky, she will embrace

---

[39] A pair of saddle bags linked by two leather straps so that you can simply flip them over the horse.

you and comfort you, the eternal child of the most beautiful mother, who will never age, and never die, forever on.

And is the will to live stronger in a flower than in a human, who plucks or tramples the flower? Each taiga peony, each bush of bergenia confidently asserts its purpose: to sow beauty and make it flourish. Each cedar tree reaches for the sky and dies standing, mingling silence with the rustle of leaves. Each birch tree leaf affirms itself as it chatters in the wind with other leaves. All in confidence that God permits it, and would rather replace humans than nature, which despite suffering offers love and gratitude.

'Where, where,' Arzhana asks, 'where did our people lose their natural wish to help one another? What's happened to our pride – the pride of the Altaisky who are ancient like the Altai ridges and tough as the mountain juniper;[40] the Altaisky who survived the darkest times and always stood up to their enemies? Even the bleakest moments in the past left us with stories and songs of heroism. But what will be left from this mockery of the soul? Oh we've been mocked in the past, but to be wiped out by the cheery grin of a commercial...

The voiceless fish – the silver grayling lured by the artificial fly, and the copper trout that swallow spoon-bait with a red feather – they fight until the end, and may even break the hook in the fight; bees die as they sting to protect the hive; grey lizards leave their tails in the hands of a fool and run away to the scree; a bear, mortally wounded by a bullet, walks towards the barrel; an eagle dies in flight; a dying red deer retains its nobility – and people? People who only live

---

[40] The mountain juniper or archa has special significance for the people of the Altai.

in expectation of looser laws and handouts from the authorities and feeble pity for themselves?'

Suddenly, the breeze swayed the grasses and leaves, and the shuffling of branches broke its harmony with the buzzing bees and the chirruping birds to bring to Arzhana's ears the vague at first then more distinct sounds of orchestral music. 'It's probably a radio,' she decided. But she was wrong; on a bend in the track, next to two bicycles with spokes glittering in the sun, two young men were lying on their backs on a bank listening to a portable CD player through two mini-speakers. They lay and they lay, and so what: there'd been no casual chat with tourists for a long time – people from the outside world had been well-warned about the thieving wildness of the Altaisky. But these two in their carelessness didn't notice her coming, and nor did she pay much attention to them.

But the music! The music that rose in great waves up to the sky and lifted the oppressed soul with its celebration of life, immortal but simple. Music that leads to a sigh of gratitude, to the hope of understanding human greatness and generosity. Forgotten music. Where did she know it from? Maybe she remembered it from her childhood, when the radio still transmitted classical music amid the rubbish? Or had she heard it in the town when she was studying at the pedagogic institute? But no, these soaring violins and cellos were churning up yet another memory. Yes, of course...

It is the Czech composer Smetana, *Vltava*.[41]

She recalled the quiet words from the not so distant yet still irrecoverable past – on the planed table strewn with blossom

---

[41] One of the six symphonic poems from Smetana's Má Vlast, portraying Bohemia's great rivers in music, known in German as the Moldau.

from wizened apple trees, with her deceased father-in-law Ivanov, a venerable Russian already eighty years-old then. Ivanov had settled by the lake in the 30s, a warden on the reserve, and selected for himself a *zaimka*[42] by the mouth of a strong-flowing river – the Birds' River, that ran down from the cedar wood to the lake through a leafy ravine cascading over mossy rocks and stones. He'd married a local Altai woman, and through years of tough work he'd cultivated – in the remotest taiga, on bare ground – a real orchard, paying no attention to those know-alls who ridiculed him, but later carried apples by the boatload across the lake.

And he always did everything alone. Alone, he dug out stumps, roots and boulders. Alone, he cultivated the land and crushed each handful of soil in his palms. Alone, he built up his farm, bought cattle, and built hives, and even a greenhouse for tomatoes, cucumbers and starry asters and dahlias to remind him of times past, though this was later, when you could get glass at the lake. During the autumn hunts, he'd drive bears from his house. During the winter, wolves. He was fed by the taiga, fishing with wicker nets. He even delivered his wife's babies, though they had no luck with their children. Two boys died young, drowned in the spring melt as they came home from school; three daughters got married and were spread all over Siberia; and the last boy – damn him, to think about him again, that *alkash!*[43] He didn't take after his father, that was for sure. He drank away his mind, and his soul, and without it, a man goes wild at once.

---

[42] A newly settled piece of land in uninhabited areas, mostly Siberia, occupied on a first come basis – normally just one house and some farmland.

[43] Altai word for an alcoholic.

Grandpa Ivanov, as they called him on the lake, would never let himself be lazy, and even when old would never sit idly, but read books and newspapers, and listened to music on the radio. There was no-one else on the lake better informed or more cultured than he. How did he manage this, despite the blows of fate? And he had suffered. Under dekulakization,[44] he lost everything – his cows, his sheep, his goats, and even his bees – and he lamented the injustice but started all over again, and built everything up until the next time the authorities paid him attention.

Arzhana, fascinated by the fate and life of this man, visited him enough for all his children. Sometimes she rode around through the taiga. Sometimes she took the straight track. Sometimes she took the motorboat over the aquamarine *ples,*[45] watching the lakeside ridges rise to the sky – covered in autumn by yellow larches and swirling cedars, in summer with vivid green and the silent jets of cascading water – and even higher still, the sparkling ice steeples of the *golcy,*[46] shining white above the clouds.

She was always trying to help the old man and her mother-in-law, whenever she could – in the house, or with the hives, mowing the grass in the orchard with the old scythe, placing the net in the lake for the old man when it got too hard for him to bend. And as always she was given tea under the apple trees, and it was rarely packet tea, since Grandpa made his own, with bergenia, wild currants, or willowherb... all

---

[44] The repression of kulaks, the better-off farmers and peasants, under Stalin between 1929 and 1932, during which millions of kulaks were deprived of their farms, arrested, deported and executed.

[45] The deepest part of the river.

[46] The local word for the highest peaks.

sipped with clear, dark, gooey golden honey from his bees.
They were talking.

Pavel Ivanovich was getting worked up about how stupid
the authorities were, how he'd honestly tried to understand
what he read in the newspapers delivered to him once a week
on the *Altai Pioneer*. At the time, everyone was talking and
writing about the All-Union Food Programme, and experts
descended by helicopter to lecture the villagers. 'But what is
the point in making people work, if their souls are not taught
too?' Grandpa was saying, 'Why don't they understand – if
you don't work with your heart, yet keep working, your heart
will seize you, and your soul will torment you?' Grandpa
turned the knob on the Spidola to look for news, and suddenly came upon this music, and stood silent, spellbound, to
listen. Then he rose from the table – he was tall, even as a bent
old man, and his grey hair wasn't yellowy ash like other people but shone – and he took off his round spectacles, mended
with copper wire, and spoke slowly and clearly:

'It is the Czech composer Smetana, *Vltava*,' he declared, 'I
have lived a long time, as long as Methelusah,[47] yet I still don't
understand how such a tiny country can inspire such majestic
music, with such bright and clear love that even far away at
the ends of the earth, it can bring a foreigner to tears with
an innocent and childish love for his own homeland. Everything in the world seems to fall away before such love, everything else seems petty and unimportant – and it is so obvious
that the soul is indeed meant to have wings like a bird, and
the purpose of its existence is not mundane sufferings but

---

[47] In Russia, they use the phrase *aredovy veki* (meaning one will live a
long life) rather than Methelusah, after Jared, the Biblical figure who
lived 962 years.

constant flight, in the intensity of such love... God! And the saddest thing – most people, it seems, can't be helped...'

Arzhana was rather surprised by this unexpected, other-worldly speech – but then she'd already got used to Pavel Ivanovich's oddities, and wouldn't let anyone make fun of him behind his back. Coming back to the village around the lake late one evening (while her mama was alive and helped look after her boys), she was thinking about things and saw how the lake creates the clouds – how over the clear surface of the lake there appeared here and there ghostly palaces and castles of smoke, drifting off from the *ples* and ascending into a sky already dotted with twinkling constellations.

Pavel Ivanovic was dead now, dying before the new age and buried right here on his *zaimka* by the lake, on the stony terrace, where the roses bloomed large and a sound like never-ending rain filled the air from the forceful mountain stream with a name that sounds like birdsong. From here, all the southern shore of the lake was visible and in clear weather you could see on the far side of the lake the reflection of snow-capped Golden Mountain, rising to a plateau forever shrouded in cloud, a reminder to those who don't wish for and don't expect immortality. There were stories that, in ancient times, in years of great hunger and troubles, one Altai man had discovered a nugget of gold the size of a horse's head. But no matter how hard he tried, he couldn't use his gold; not for all the gold in the world will a hungry man give up his food. So the hunter climbed a cliff on the mountain and flung his great nugget into the depths of the lake, after which both the mountain and the lake are called Golden.[48]

---

[48] The legend may have been inspired by the gold found in placer deposits in the Altai, which is sometimes washed into streams.

The mother-in-law lived out the rest of her life in summer on the gradually disintegrating *zaimka* and in winter in Biysk with her older daughter, who grew cold towards Arzhana after she broke up with her husband. Arzhana no longer had any reason to visit, and little time anyway. Yet she, probably, was the only one who'd understood the old man; the only one who bothered to, and so inherited his spirit of sweat-and-blood idealism and zealous integrity. And she suddenly had a thought as she emerged on to the broad expanses of the upper valley, where, above the sacred source, on the side of the valley down which rushed two torrents, there stood a pagan tree, dressed in colourful ribbons. Maybe any selfless devotion is such a rare thing that at all times it is worthy of legends and stories. And the epic hero Batyr, who gave his name to the saddle mountain, may have seemed a crank, or something worse, to his sharp and niggardly-souled fellow tribesmen. And only the unknown folk narrator, who was perhaps ridiculed and persecuted as well, kept his memory alive and gave him the only true immortality there is on earth.

'Mama, let's tie a ribbon to the tree, too!' begged her infant daughter, and so Arzhana dismounted, lamenting to herself that she probably doesn't have any sacred wishes left. The little girl stuck her tongue out with zealous effort as she tried to tie a torn-off strip of white handkerchief to a lower branch, while Arzhana, with a sudden sad longing, gazed out as if surveying her past over the broad vernal valley, above which, level with the peaks around, young kites circled. The road to the mowing meadows ran on into the distance, past the camel-backed mountain, across the col and beyond to further life-giving ridges, where, from a hundred sources,

THE GHOST OF THE BIRD–CHERRY TREE

streams and torrents were being born, gaining strength as they surged over stony riffles, whooshed down mountain slopes and thundered over rapids. On that mountain, beneath stocky cedars and overgrown by pink stems of rabbits' cabbage[49] and blooming *solodka,*[50] the silver cladding of a rocket had already lain for years, looking from a distance as if someone was trying to set fire to the mountain with the rays of the sun focused through a giant magnifying glass.

'It's so mesmerizing,' Arzhana thought, then, hearing voices behind her, turned slowly around. Petr Semenych, her neighbour from three doors down, and his son, who'd been completely unnoticeable in school as a teenager, were looking at her from their unsaddled horses, as if they'd only just finished mowing...

'Why didn't you ask for help? Ah, but you're proud, aren't you? Well, we see – your husband is off to the ail again to wet his neck, and you're alone again... So my son said – let's help the teacher. Our meadow is not fully mowed yet, but I thought, well let's go, there's no time to waste – we can dream as much as we want later...'

And so – does someone need much to be happy? Look at her: she is happy, the little girl is laughing, and the golden oriole is whistling in the branches as the scythes sweep in smooth semicircles, laying down between the trees and boulders the ineffable life of the grasses – and what is most wonderful, the God of Unity (to Who no-one pays much attention except to complain) is present and at the same time smiling at these small movements of the human heart as if the world truly does live by His Justice, and any darkness is

---

[49] Wood sorrel.
[50] Chinese liquorice, *Glycyrrhiza.*

fleeting, a temporary sad place not yet reached by its dazzling light – and its healing, comforting warmth.

And people, well, you don't often see this. So now all there is left is the blue sky, the mountains rising around the great bowl of the valley, the streams foaming over rocks, the whirling kites and the cedars on the heights. And that lonely tree, dressed up in ribbons above the sacred source, didn't it deserve attention in the end, because, besides the false hopes, it is a witness? Each spring that quenches thirst is sacred, and the earth doesn't create unsacred springs.

4

THE ESCAPE, AND TWENTY YEARS
OF NON-EXISTENCE

෯

'Now, TELL US what's going on when nothing is happening...'

That's what Vladimir Nikolaevich Sokolov asked once,
and I took this odd question too much to heart – as if one
moment of extraordinary insight from our ever-present poet
should really become a programme for action. It seems to
me that among other things, this is really all about getting
tired of being noble; and noticing how and when a moment
of nobility becomes such a heroic, rare thing that it seems
like a great enough deed to stretch throughout your life.

Of course, a noble person can fall in and out of love – there
is no direction, beyond that granted from above. But there are
things of the soul that he cannot choose – honour, justice and
loyalty. He cannot neglect them even briefly to become selfish through self-pity; the weak place in the soul cannot stay
empty, but will be visited at once by betrayal and injustice.

Be visited – no that's utterly wrong. Open just a tiny loop-
hole and they will *burst* in, gushing into the hard-working
river of the soul like a flood of sewage, turning its smooth

and clean-running waters into a foul and churning mass of self-torment.

So I wonder if our entire life after childhood is just the redemption of betrayals, little and large, and any channel is just a return there, to the first shining, all-forgiving waters — shining like the young leaves in which even I sometimes see the instantaneous and eternal flicker of Allah's smile ...

'It's time to gather the stones,' I mutter under my breath into my greying moustache, remembering how, moustacheless, I had once sat with a friend now lost on the high Jurassic cliffs above the Kama river,[51] from where we could see through the autumn mists both the smooth flowing deeps sparkling with ripples and becalmed backwaters and, beyond, meanders cut-off long ago to become oxbow lakes.

That unforgettable spot on the Kama cliffs, richly coloured and cut with gullies, which was visible before the rains suddenly swept in, hasn't disturbed my sleepy imagination until now, and I imagine it is still there and still called Krasny Bor.[52] But the pine and spruce forests that gave its name, and still exist further downstream near Shiskin's Yelabuga,[53] were long ago brought to nothing, leaving only the autumn blaze of fiery maples and burnished scarlet elms with silvery

---

[51] The Kama river is one of Tatarstan's major rivers, the largest tributary of the Volga — a vast river with a huge discharge.

[52] Krasny Bor, which means 'red pine forest,' although an old village is actually now a community of smart dachas, which hit the headlines in 2008 when a lion belonging to one of the dacha owners escaped and swam across the river.

[53] An ancient town on the Kama where one of Russia's greatest landscape painters, Ivan Shiskin (1832–98), was born — and famously painted a view of the Kama in 1888 similar to that the author describes.

gold and yellow birches, poplars, aspens, wild cherries and currants, along with rose hips and hazels. The large, old village is below us, under the Kama heights, with the wharf at a distance, and only a few straggling houses climbing up the bank, from the brink of which begin the already-reaped croplands and rain-sodden potato fields, dotted with *kolki*[54] and villages and hamlets connected either by the old high-road, or rough country tracks.

I have many memories from here, but I'll mention only that, sitting on the scarp near a neglected graveyard – above the leaning crosses and crumbling tombstones where elms shook their last russet leaves in the damp wind – I was ardently explaining something to my friend, and he, much more down-to-earth and realistic than me, answered calmly: 'Do you really want everyone to think the same? Just imagine a world inhabited only by Ravilkas[55] Bukharaevs – wouldn't that be awful?'

Awful, I agreed, though I persisted with my explanation. We were, I have to say, bright boys, and on the whole had a good picture of the life we were yet to live. Anyway, we were both living the way we imagined, and my only authentic discovery since, and it wasn't even a glimmer in my soul then, has been the revelation that there's no need to make up and invent things in life; any commonplace event, without needing to be invented, can turn into a brief miracle – just give it enough time.

'Time to gather the stones,' I muttered in my present time, but even the most obliging thoughts are, from time to time, overshadowed by conscience.

---

[54] Copses in the middle of fields.
[55] A familiar form of the author's name.

Because although the endless loneliness of childhood is in time replaced by chance friendships, in old age it comes back, that great loneliness. It seems as if in that first immeasurable sadness, any friendship is unexpected and gives us wings, and I was secretly trying to understand – how did I deserve this joy of forgiveness and understanding? And will lost friends still understand our complaints? Do we even speak the same language now? Or did that language die at the time of separation when mutual stories were lost? No wonder, if so. Because we were trying so hard to forget and push away what we should have selflessly and unfoolishly pressed to the heart...

And yet what are we looking for when we go searching for old friends years after? Perhaps we're looking for ourselves, lost in the independent struggles of life? Or perhaps the innermost, unhealed, incurable loneliness has become so unbearable that we just want to begin anew and throw ourselves into the illusions and mirages of the past – to escape, like the clear water cut-off in an oxbow lake, into that first innocence of existence? That luminous innocence that seems so surpassingly more attractive than the wisdom of later moments of clarity, even though this calm wisdom of age is unafraid of disappointments and of the inexorable passing of time – and the only thing it laments is the lack of time left.

And so I peer warily into the future – how much more time is meted out for the fulfilment of my task? And hence this morning moaning about irrelevant, purposeless actions that persistently distract me from my plans in the many lonely silences. And where are they coming from, these pressing troubles that don't leave hours, nor sometimes even minutes for human concerns, not to mention simple friendly conversation, from which, by the way, I once so thought-lessly ran away in my student youth, obsessed by the arguable idea that true work requires undivided attention and can't endure the jealous rivalry of other activities, not even love and friendship.

I got it into my head back then that only these rivalries – mathematics and its continual exams, friends' parties and the ferocious torment of unrequited love – only they prevented me from achieving that full authenticity that I already sus-pected in me. The loneliness of the task enticed the vanity of my soul, encouraging me to leave everything behind and withdraw from people in the name of God, to leave all that business that you can only deplore, but never change.

You know – I entirely remember my first escape.

There near Kazan, close to where the pine forests are thinned by birch and aspen groves as they near the sandy banks of the Volga, were two places – Zeleny Bor[56] and Boro-voe Matushkino – that bore happy memories from my ado-lescence because they were not, as Krasny Bor already was, overrun with dachas, and remained pleasingly unpopulated.

There were at most twenty legal houses on the margins of the forest in Zeleny Bor, if, of course, you don't count those of the fishing village unceremoniously encamped by the giant willows of the Volga's bank and its creeks, which were hammered together from driftwood and so entitled Shanghai. In the creek with its still, clear water, where shoals of silver fry flashed amid the underwater weeds, motor-boats were chained, and between them skated large water strider spiders, sliding over the water without disturbing it. Behind the low garden gates of the shanty village houses,

---

[56] 'Green pine forest'.

fine-meshed nets hung to dry and illegal plots of cucumbers and tomatoes flourished, but the other seasonal visitors to Zeleny Bor were only interested in hunting for mushrooms and dreamily dangling fishing rods, not thinking about the time when the grassy, knapweed-bright meadows between the Volga and the forest would be divided into *sotkas*,[57] and it would become impossible to walk along the river because of all the fences. Even without looking closely at just what was lost, I feel sharply now the hour of farewell to the primary purity of these blessed places. And isn't any loss more memorable if it's been possessed for a long time?

It was late in autumn, already very cold and wet, when they finished the annual burning of the yellow and red leaf fall in Kazan. In my parents' flat, where from the glass fifth floor balcony you could almost touch the wide branches of the oak tree in the yard, the student party had been going on since morning after my parents left. Someone was reading poetry. A guitar was twanging. And intense philosophical debates and profound chit-chat rumbled on. The drowsiness of drink was already obvious by the time my brother Almaz dropped in to say goodbye because, still in training,[58] he had to leave for service in East Germany. It would be usual to have a drink on such an occasion, but he couldn't this time because he was driving Dad's car – the already un-new Lada, which he later drove right through to the third millennium to keep Dad's memory alive.

Then – put it down maybe to idle boldness or just intense depression – I decided on an outing to Zeleny Bor – and

---

[57] 100 square-metre plots.

[58] The phrase the author uses is 'not-fired yet' – that is, he hadn't yet fired a gun in battle.

good that I did, since it turned out to be the last time in our mutual life that we did together something we both wanted. Taking a flat brandy flask filled with pink and aromatic peach Georgian *chacha*,[59] I left the party to walk down from the flat with Almaz, and we were soon racing along the empty suburban highway, between the pre-sunset quiet and slowly dusking autumn forests.

And so, God, how could I forget turning right off the highway to Borovoe Matushkino, and roaring along the narrow, asphalted lane through joint-pines wreathed with juniper and delicate Tatar honeysuckle? We stopped when we found the way blocked by the chain entrance to the already built-up Zeleny Bor and got out to look for some time for a way down to the Volga past all the fences and barriers. Finally, we found a path pressed right to the edge of the creek to the ineradicable Shanghai and made our way up the steep bank to sit down at the wooden trestle table and benches we'd discovered there, dug into the sand amid the fir-grove planted in our childhood and long since grown to full height.

We two brothers, we barely spoke a word, settling into easy silence and gazing out over the Volga of autumn, absorbing the sunset that glowed on the river between the dark islands by the shore and the smooth *ples*. Oh God, how unspeakably sad, and intensely beautiful that infinite autumn was!

The cool crimson sun rolled down the cliff; the solitary river gull slid over the surface swell, its singular swirls showing drafts of air; the dearest sadnesses of home and their

---

[59] A strong, clear liqueur that used to be made in illegal home stills in Georgia from, typically, grape juice, and also known as vine vodka. Now it's made and sold commercially. It can be coloured and flavoured with peaches, apples and other fruits.

unembraceable vastness spread far under the gloomy sky; and a flock of crows, after crowing as they should, made an end to this prewinter day by flying noiselessly over the Volga as if behind the forested hills was another life — a life without partings and the pain that goes with joy.

It wash, of course, not the first parting at Zeleny Bor. There were memorable farewells here before, especially one — in the time of low water, when close to the bank, a bare, grey sand islet was exposed, on which the iron-gleaming waves left all kinds of flotsam and jetsam. We crossed to it with just two strokes in the skiff, carelessly caught some silver bream — and then it all seemed to end, like autumn. Darkness fell as we brought the yellow-scarlet flames of a fire to this ephemeral island; the wind got up and dispersed the flames; and the fire crackled and spat and tried to overcome the coming night. Back then, the river ran just as cold and the air above had the same chill freshness, and I felt a pit in my stomach open with a presentiment of alienation, and with that eternal beautiful longing, which did not yet know how to mercilessly squeeze the sinless heart.

Yet now something different settled in the chill air; if it weren't for the rosy, aromatic *chacha*, the soul might have seen this leavetaking with the same clarity as the fishing, the skies and the glowing skies of old. But we were sitting on the bench in silence looking at the Volga, and I was smoking — the will was blowing lightly with the Volgan breeze and sparkling with the last freedom of autumn, but the barely adult heart was unaware of the meaning of farewells and the soul could not taste the calm of remorse, lit only by the lingering oblique, glow of youthful fatigue and trying, like the unruly fire, to break the non-existence between light and night.

After that autumn outing, there was no more Zeleny Bor in our lives. Why visit the ashes of a burned out fire? Especially since the area was soon built up, with every patch sequestered and shared between each incomer, and the grass and pine-strewn lane buried under asphalt and straightened, where once it wandered along the forest edge, echoing the shape of pine, birch and oak.

But let me come back instead to my planned, and accomplished, escape to Borovoe Matushkino, which was luckier than Zeleny Bor, because it was situated near the ancient Russian village of Bolgary,[60] and there were no land seizures then. Everything was as it should be: the river *trams-omiks*[61] were running on time from Kazan and the dachas were appanages[62] distributed between factories in Kazan. It was in one of these appanages, situated in a bay on the forest edge, that I was going to take refuge from the irritations of life. Taking with me a portable typewriter loaded with black-red ribbon and a week-long voucher for the dacha secured by friends, I took the river tram, and leapt off eagerly as it bumped into the tyres of the quay for the village and was soon settling into a dacha with a glazed veranda.

It seemed to me as if I must have got there between holidays; all the other wooden dachas were empty. At first, I was very happy about this – nobody to distract me from listen-

---

[60] Near the village lie the ruins of the medieval capital of Bolgariya Volga-Kama which was destroyed by the Golden Horde of Timur in 1361, but dates back to at least the sixth century. Archaeological excavations on the site of the city began in 1870.
[61] A regular passenger boat service running on the Volga and its tributaries.
[62] Grants of land.

ing to the wind in the ship pines and nobody bothering me with questions, and so I could give myself up entirely to the blissful dream of creativity. Yet I dallied, even though the first thing I did was unpack the typewriter – taking it like a child's accordion from its case and placing it on the aluminium table where tomatoes, vobla[63] and a bottle of Zhigu-levskoye beer would have looked more picturesque. The first chill of apprehension at how out of place I was here seemed to touch my heart; it struck me that I wouldn't be able to live in this dacha to work, and that's how it turned out. But I still swanned about and even slotted a clean, cream sheet of paper into my tiny typewriter, in case of sudden inspiration.

I'll remind you – who I was then in that self-seeking escape, in that vacuum beyond obligations. That vacuum so *full* of personal time it was as limitless as the shining skies above, limitless as the Volga deeps, limitless as the noisome trees stretching to the horizon. And from the three wooden porch steps, I could see again the other, opposite bank of the Volga, high, cloaked in hazel, garlanded in rowan, hemmed in bird-cherry and embroidered with all the other elements of a life discarded.

There seemed to be, and really was, so much time that it frightened me and I went round in circles, lost in idle thoughts, overwhelmed by the abundance of hours and min-utes – with no idea that this preparation will bear fruit not in a few hours but after twenty years, when I finally learn to take my stubborn soul by the throat if it obstinately refuses to be appeased by honestly witnessing the unity and gentleness of God's world.

---

[63] Caspian roach fish.

I persisted with my ambitious dreams and desires then, yet had no idea that the simple secrets of the craft lie in continuous self-discovery, and in rejecting any experience except that endured until it vanishes from memory – until it is sunk so deeply into the flesh and blood, the mind and hands, that it rules you without your will, directing you to create one way and not another – because you cannot do anything else. Only then do we dare speak as we wish once more with the natural simplicity of a child, so that each sign of repentance at parting seems honest, like the two final verbs before the honest silence of united immortalities, so final no more can be said:

Forgive, and show mercy…
…for everything that I've left in the past with no memory, for everything that has come back to me, almost from oblivion, barely held by the shining threads of torn connections… for anything that has come back to the present me from the past me, from the sleep on the grass to some forgotten yet ever-fluttering daisy in a field.
For there is no greater happiness than remorse when it suddenly discovers its lost purpose…

Yet I thought then that the experience of existence corrupts the soul and brings ample disappointments, and so I believed my childish illusions and my feeble sins worldly wisdom. And what could I unfalsely witness with such a deluded soul but my own foolishness? Yet the existing God, about Whom, in my presumptious new non-existence I wasn't even thinking, was merciful – and kept my lips sealed for all but a few moments when, out of fatherly sympathy, he'd send, suddenly and surprisingly, the semblance of true inspiration, enough for a few poems amid the business of life. Not understand-ing the source, I didn't yet deserve freedom from work, as I struggled to invent life, to invent myself, as I laboured to write, unaware that any such writing is a sad lie.

That is how the first day of futile escape went. Then evening came, followed by a humid summer night. Exhausted by pure idleness, I went to bed early, but as I dozed off I was rudely woken by a deafening roll of thunder – a July thunderstorm, brewed in secret above river with the sorrows of the day, then unleashed in crackling, fiery forks of lightning and a torrential downpour on the hushed forests of Borovoe Matushkino.

I quickly rose and opened the rattling veranda door and stared out on the storm as sporadic flashes vividly lit the wide grass space between the unoccupied government dachas. From the hipped, asphalt roofs, water gushed and gurgled in unstoppable streams into churning puddles all over the grass. Pine trees shrieked as their tops swung like the black masts of ships at sea. Each flash of lightning was quickly followed by deep thunder that cracked the dark air already filled with the sudden gusts of sodden storm wind. And that wind swooped down on the clearing, flinging the downpour sideways, and desperately whipping the branch of a rowan against the tear-drenched glass of the veranda. Beyond, in the thick night, leaves rattled and spun in God's natural forests. Yet in this divine storm, my soul, instead of filling with joy at being part of this great action of the elements, was sharply struck with that unsatisfiable sense of worldly misery and alienation – so sharply that even now, remembering the stormy streams of that matushkin night, I feel that painful sense of transience, that once felt settled in me forever.

The rain died down and the storm drifted off beyond the Volga hills that grew lighter in the distance beneath the billowing, dark-blue clouds intermittently glowing with each soundless flash. I couldn't sleep, and kept feeling all over again the acuteness of mortal sorrow – the beckoning void of infinite loneliness. I was twenty then, a young, strong animal driven to act only by the appearance of life, but if it weren't for that longing for Authentic Existence that settled so suddenly in my orphaned soul, I would never have responded in my forties to that inner call of the Unity, already predestined – after twenty years of non-existence, twenty years of heart-rending dreams, empty struggles and countless betrayals, each measured out for me from that beautiful but unanswering night of storm.

...Barefoot as I was, I stepped out on to the grass aflood with heaven's waters, and my feet felt the chill of the soaked ground. I stood a long while, looking motionless at the river where in the diffuse darkness a single lonely beacon twinkled back at the stormlit haze of the hills. Behind me the branches sighed and unhurriedly shed their water until the matushinsk forests fell into the blissful stillness that had once soothed my adolescence. In these forests were spent the crucial years of my first contact with the world, ever enlightened by the healingly silent brotherhood of Almaz,[64] my constant companion and constant mirror of my actions – who was imbued, just like his name, with natural, inexhaustible and luminous nobility.

You know that whenever and wherever in the world I felt suddenly lonely, I saw the very fact of his existence justified continuing with life. But did I really remember him?

Did I remember that not so long ago summer of wonderful mushrooms, when early in the morning we went deep into Zeleny Bor between the canopy of branches and wound

---

[64] *Almaz* means 'diamond' in Russian.

up to Borovoe Matushkino by trails known only to us — through rowan and elderberry undergrowth beneath pines, pale birches and thick green-stemmed aspens into those hidden thickets where, in amber blankets of pine needles under green fir branches, every one of God's days new ceps pushed up into the light with their tough, cherry caps and dew-besprinkled spores beneath.

Did I remember that time half a kilo or more of dazzlingly-white-when-sliced mushrooms appeared on our route to our daily harvest of firgrove born ceps and filled the bottom of the basket straightaway — those mushrooms with yellowy caps bent so intricately above stout stems and stacked around a birch tree with leaves thinned by age. And maybe the translucent sunlit groves that distracted us from our mushroom hunt with ripe clusters of red bramble berries that peeked through the leaves — and then at dusk the bilberry thickets or patches of wild strawberry amid blizzard-white umbrellate inflorescences of cowbane, aromatic *tsikuta*. And then the loopy rabbit that popped out from a squat bush, pulled itself to its haunches then lolloped away…

Sometimes, we would wander out into the sparser forest edges between ancient oaks and sit down on the grass to gaze out over that sparkling and so familiar creek — its waters opening into the *pleses* of the Volga. Closer to the banks, the river was braided with islands covered in kingcups and strawberries, with withies and dog roses scrambling over the solid sand banks interlaced with channels lined with rushes and water lilies that emerged from lagoons of red-streaked perch.

Suspended in tightly drawn floamy clusters above the still waters and forest wreathed huge, slowly shifting clouds in which the sun created great mountain ridges and deep ravines, strange faces and physiognomies, giant monsters and odd shapes… And the tall-stemmed ox-eye daisy swaying near us in the breeze – did I remember her?

But no, I didn't.

The inextinguishable, generous light-fall of early childhood that once poured so freely was already then barely dripping through the non-existence of my residency in the world – one of those residencies that is concerned only for itself – with rain and leafy dripping whispering in the damp darkness. And the soul was disconsolately quiet in those initial times of oblivion.

But to forget – does mean to betray.

And now, after twenty years of sham escapes, I'm still trying to break free from these betrayals in work and the persistent hope that any tale of suffering has a happy end – and it truly does because everything that comes from that fleeting patch of first light is not in vain. And so, I give what I have, and willingly – let those accept who will that any non-existence is transient, and only existence has no end.

And what do we need time for if not for the joy of returned forgiveness? What has happened, has happened, but the conscience continues, coming back to the beginning again and again, as if it can be no other way.

ON TO THE OTHER SIDE

The river was just like any other; there are dozens of rivers like this in Povolzhe, meandering rivers, straying beyond their bounds, eroding new channels according to their strength, spilling out on to meadows or wandering out of sight behind spurs.

Sometimes, you'd climb to the high bank and it seemed as if the river surrounded you – this leisured unhurried, smooth river, with an almost perfect loop embracing the truncated sand or clay, the outer slopes full of swifts' burrows and, at their feet, pussy willow, bag willow and silver willow, while on top, in ore and gruss grassy plants of the middle band – blue rimes of wormwood, silvery orach, golden tansy, bushy thistle and layers of ground burrs with notched leaves and countless other honest, unknown grasses that you never bother to discover the name of.

The far, inner bank is always low, and covered, necessarily, in willows and basket willows, in alders, in brooms and white willows that are first to bud in spring, when they display above the snow their fluffy grey *verbeshkas*[65] dusted in golden pollen. In the distance, beyond the fields, there is normally forest, both replanted pine and deciduous, or mixed – though only in mature man-made pine forest wander God-given oaks, birches, viburnum, elder and, of course, rowan – without which the autumn joy-sadness cannot be the same, the riverine autumn when the river falls subdued, the sun shines clear and candid and without fear into the river depths to reveal the bottom grasses with their locks swirling in the current.

No matter how small the Kubnya river is compared to the Sviyaga that gratefully accepts its tributary waters and is itself gratefully accepted by the Volga not far away, the Kubnya is so deep that it cannot be forded by cows or people. If you have to get to the far side, you have to know where to cross, otherwise you'll get exhausted just looking for a way across. Even when you do know where the crossing is, it's not so easy. And what kind of a life is that, when you find the crossing you need is the wrong way from where you want to be, especially if you have to carry a box full of tiny live chicks?

---

[65] Willow tree buds.

It's a philosophical question, and a woman likes to think practically, and Zulfiya, although a programmer at the city's computer centre, came to the conclusion, without any philosophy, that it's all the chicks' fault. If it wasn't for the chicks, she decided, she wouldn't now be looking at the collapsed weir across the Kubnya, carried away by the early April flood as if to spite its usual mildness with brimful rages.

The tractor-rammed earth dam, from which last year local fisherman were catching small carp from the dark flower and grass overgrown sides, was completely washed away. The black spillway pipe, with its gaping muzzle reminiscent of the great Tsar Cannon in the Moscow Kremlin,[66] was covered at the top by the wide, unstoppable coffee coloured waters. The Kubnya, so usually a half asleep willowy river, was evidently reminding people not to take it for granted – with self-willed, innocent delight it was rolling its waters anyway it wanted, paying no attention to the wishes of those same people.

The small newly built (and constantly shut) mosque in the Tatar village, which Zufiya absolutely had to get to, was in plain sight, a stone's throw away – just down to the Kubnya through the chernozemed fruit and vegetable gardens where the last blackened snow was concealed in the shadows. To cross the road bridge, she'd have to walk at least ten kilometres to the *fazenda*[67] in the spring slush, so Zulfiya could with a clear conscience easily have just walked back to the railway station, and even walked home to her dull husband, if it wasn't for those chicks bought in the morning market.

---

[66] The world's largest cannon, almost 6 m long and cast by the master caster Andrey Chokhov in 1586 but never fired in war.

[67] Country house.

The question is, what was to become of these tiny living creatures in the hands of two fairly intelligent people, qualified mathematicians who had taken it into their heads to buy an *izba*[68] in a remote village so that they might get some fresh air and start a vegetable garden to provide them with potatoes and other vegetables to tide them over between the constantly late salary payments? They'd bought the *izba* with funny soviet money at the dawn of democracy, when there were no post-reform delays in salary. (The shops were entirely empty then, but that is another story.) Because of the troubles, they'd put off having children in the hope of more prosperous times. The husband Shamil had some time ago joined a firm assembling and fixing computers and kept going with that kulak's steadiness, but Zulfiya was already bored sick. Still they were living no worse than anyone they knew, especially since no-one they knew was exactly catching stars in the sky.

But the chicks – it was all a bit much! It was obvious that these small, yellow balls of fluff would tie them to everyday chores – feeding them, watering them, keeping them warm, sheltering them from crows and kites, until eventually they start to cluck and crow! You have to tend to them whether you want to or not. Their tender-hearted neighbour Nasima might be persuaded to look after the little brood, but it's not good offloading your burden on to someone else! Shamil – well, he wasn't noted for his perception, but Zulfiya sometimes sensed, even without getting someone else to look after the chicks, the dirty looks the true villagers gave to the

---

[68] A traditional Russian log-house.

dacha folk,[69] and tried hard to be seen bending her back in her vegetable garden as often as possible. She could foresee all the shrill arguments if she left the chicks with her neighbour, which is actually what did happen in the end, but right now she just needed to get to the other side – the rest could wait.

But that's what's interesting. With luxuries, maybe it's not true, but if someone really needs something badly, they'll usually find a way. Especially if that person is a woman in her middle, but certainly not excessive, years, with the maturing of that beauty, proud and refined, which had made such a huge impression in her first year at university, but left all who laid siege empty-handed. Especially one, the famous university poet, who could have been thoroughly attractive, but for the fact that he terrified Zulfiya with his regular reveries, by his far too earnest love, and by the fact that he took her every word and action so seriously, as if he was trying to find in them some sacral meaning.

'You are probably *thinking* all the time?' he once asked Zulfiya. She didn't listen then, just as she didn't that other time when they were one-to-one, when the circumstances conspired and all he had to was just show at least a spark, just a vague semblance of manly resolution. Like a fool, he missed that moment, and it serves him right that there was another who didn't think too much and better understood how she would like to live.

After setting down the box with the chicks on grass caught by the late frosts but already thawing in the sunshine, Zulfiya walked along the river, first one way then the other until,

---

[69] The dacha folk are the wealthy weekenders and ephemeral summer visitors from town.

just beyond the first bend, she saw a boat, slightly hidden in the thick of blossoming willows. The boat was wooden, tied to the bushes with a simple knot – and both oars were lying in its dry hull. It was a huge stroke of luck, and she was actually very lucky most of her life. Fetching the box of chicks, Zulfiya clumsily inserted one oar into the rowlock, and with the second pushed the boat away from the bank to start her short voyage.

But who'd have guessed that the second rowlock, that simple mechanism, was missing in this stupid tub? Resting the second oar in the wooden groove, Zulfiya tried hard to hold the boat straight, but the oar kept slipping out of the groove. The boat refused to obey, and the Kubnya's unruly spring strength soon swept Zulfiya on past where she wanted to go – further, further and further on. She soon gave up with the oars, and the boat began to revolve slowly in the currents, round and round. The chickens squealed pitifully in the stern. The village fell far behind, then disappeared altogether behind a wall of willows and alders along the bank. And the farms fell behind, too, and the cow pastures, and the iron roadbridge that just missed her head, and then completely unfamiliar places, still so deserted it would have been pointless to call for help, even if Zulfiya had wanted to announce to the world her absurd situation.

Whenever the boat came close to the bank, no matter which one, Zulfiya stretched out to grab blossoming willow branches. Twice she almost caught one, but her frozen hands slipped to leave her clasping only handfuls of yellow buds. Finally she succeeded, as the boat became wedged in a jam of branches near the hoped-for bank. She managed to yank herself into the bushes with the box of chicks under her arm, then after alternately sinking her green welling-

tons into the squelching mud and fighting her way through
tangles of willow, Zulfiya reached solid ground at last. Only
then, as she recovered her breath and sorted herself out, did
she realize what a scrape she'd emerged from safe and sound,
thank God!

The ground was too wet to sit on, and anyway Zulfiya
realized she had a long trek back to the village – and it'd be
good to get there before sunset. She set off briskly to warm
herself up and save the chicks getting completely chilled. But
by the time the village finally appeared and she reached that
desired point B of the morning, the crimson sun had dipped
below the birch groves with their rooks' nests. The clear air
was already thickening with the spring cool, and somewhere
across the damp silence of the ploughed field, a brook purled.
The sky above the fields and groves was growing dark and
the first stars were beginning to shine. The chicks were silent
and Zulfiya looked at the box in concern.

But the nestlings, fluffy and defenceless, were clustered
together trembling on top of the tatty old thrownout shami-
levsky jumper. And Zulfiya sighed with relief that, after all,
she will get them alive through this starry chill, and only
began to hurry again, when for no rhyme nor reason, she
remembered that quite forgotten poem written just for her:

Do you hear it? Sad and low,
Water dripping from the trees…
Do you hear it? Strange and slow
Departs the long and bitter freeze.

It's not clear what has roused her, or maybe even awoken
something in her soul, but Zulfiya, who had already reached
the empty *fazenda*, felt as if she had suddenly fallen out of

her own time. It was probably all the fault of the stars and their constellations which had somehow imperceptibly spilled into the overarching sky and so completed the picture of existence. And the dark wet ploughed fields, the dim birch groves and the silent village where no-one was waiting, suddenly seemed accidental, random, yet at the same time, amazingly, inexpressibly beautiful, as if in the plain ordinariness of evening they were somehow revived and brought into the life of the world again – and with them came twinkling in the damp spring air the possibility, no the practicality, of compassionate and generous love. And this isn't to say that this woman realized her life could have turned out differently. Of course, it could have done, easily. It could have done, but it didn't turn out that way because Zulfiya didn't include it in her calculations. And it's nothing to do with the poet, even though she triumphantly thought that nowhere – not in Moscow, nor abroad – will he be able to find true peace; in every woman he will look for her and not find her, because for some reason he is not there and she is here, where despite all her calculations life has brought her – to fields of infinite loneliness above which persuasively, and invitingly, flicker the same ever-burning spring stars, for all those who can to see – and for all those who have learned to see again.

And what remained, as the starry world easily, hopefully, wounded the heart with its eternal and beautiful independence from life's details, was the return to one woman's soul of the tempting and dangerous possibility of recklessness – and Zulfiya recognized in that moment that such chances, so clearly and rationally avoided in the past, are not simply present as she prepared to carry on her life amid the ploughed fields, the birches and the tireless constellations, but remain a crucial possibility – so crucial that nothing else really matters:

Leaves' snowy down shines softly on
To reassure me like before;
Love lingers briefly, then is gone –
And winter's coat comes down once more.

'What have you done, then?' said Zulfiya, looking at the chicks. 'Were you really so sensible? Just a hand, a hand you couldn't reach out and touch. That's all. And everything could've been different.'

5

'NOT ALWAYS FLYING…'

ℰℐ

JUST THINK OF this: the more honest a person is with himself, the less he's understood by others. And I would give away a dozen lessons of experience for just one youthful illusion – because in the unity of those unearned hopes there is more sense and truth than in all the minute insights gained in life as it flows away.

So no matter how much I'd like to say, I sometimes stay silent – despite the fact that my silence is even less eloquent than that of the fantastical frog from Taiwan that squats by the mirror in our hallway near the Tunisian camel – that enigmatic stone Bactrian with its three legs and blue all-knowing eyes. That frog, of course, is supposed to stay silent, its mouth filled with an opal-centred silver coin to draw prosperity under our roof – but you know that's not the reason we brought it home.

It doesn't befit me as a Muslim, who of course completely avoids superstition, to call on amulets and talismans, even though the estimable Dahl informs us in his cherished dictionary that both these words are of Arab origin. But then, I'm not Arab either, and this frog is just another relic of our travels – who merely flashed her azure pupils from the white silk upholstery of her box and pleaded with us to take her away from the tourist shop on the mountain lake of the Moon and Sun...

...that lake which glimmered so calmly the morning after our journey from the typhoon through the steamy, *banya*-like mists, past landslides up the winding and precipitous roads...

...through Taiwan mountains drowned in ever-shifting, slowly thinning haze; to upper slopes where – langouring in cloudy veils and rich with camphor laurels, spruces, firs and tree-ferns – deciduous and mixed woods rose to cliffs clad only in tenacious rhododendrons and alpine herbs, while below, the cloud-forest gleamed with evergreening palms and other trees fringed with liana tangles and dressed in stilt-stemmed pandans dangling their aerial roots from high branches to reach the soil below.

In the distance, we could see grey clouds writhing over dark emerald green, and, near to, pale and feathery bamboo, waving in the gusting wind and rattling in the lashing rain. But as night came, the rain ceased, the thick clouds cleared away, and under the newly shining stars, we went out to look at that white orchid whose strange aroma filled the darkness. Tall and glamourous and with a neck bedecked in fragrant golden stamens, this Beauty of the Night came out but once every few years, to shine alone in the pitch-dark of the flowingly fresh night with its tropical sky embroidered in stars and its moon quivering in the lake where, according to Chinese legend, two dragons once played with the balls of the Moon and Sun they stole from the people.

Wide-eyed we gaze at the shimmering Moon,
And think of Citizen Xiao who pays

For this brief time so opportune
On Formosa – these September days.

This is the kind of rather odd verse we were writing then, and
yet that invitation to the World Congress of Poets and a trip
around Taiwan wasn't a matter of chance, nor had the Taipei
officials tracked us down themselves. No, our noble friend,
Turkish Cypriot Osman Türkai,[70] ex-president of the World
Congress of Poets, laureate of fifty international prizes, widely
translated around the world yet barely known in Russia – it
was Osman Türkai who wrote to the congress leaders and
persuaded them to invite us to this beautiful place.

Not that we could have forgotten that night in our old flat
in south London's Croydon (the so evocative name of which
means 'crocus valley'[71]) when the late-night phone startled
us awake. Yet instead of disturbing news, there came the soft
and courteous tones of a Taiwanese man inviting us to this
congress, offering to pay for our travel and asking us to bring
a small compilation of modern Russian poetry.

Nor could I forget that long flight from Amsterdam to
Bangkok in the chance company of three low-lifes, one of
whom, a shallow womanizer, talked with gleeful anticipation
of a sex-tour around Thai brothels – but I have no wish to
drag this into the same frame of memory as the conscientious and chaste heart of Osman Türkai.

---

[70] Osman Türkai (1927-2001) was a Turkish Cypriot poet born in Kyrenia but living in London, who was nominated for the Nobel Prize in
1988.

[71] It is thought Croydon was a centre of crocus growing in Roman
times, supplying saffron to London.

The last time I saw Osman, we were in that blank room of the Alexander House hospice on the edge of London's West End. After he had become ill and forgetful, his landlady forced him out of the flat in Finchley where he had lived and worked twenty years – and as his life neared its end he was exiled to a small corner room in a state nursing home with all his worldly goods – just a suitcase containing a few suits and a couple of copies of his own books. In this small cell with its white walls and washbasin, there was neither desk nor bookshelves – just a window from which you could see tall sycamores in a yard enclosed by a cast iron fence with curly ornaments. Here, suddenly aged, grey and vacant, he sat on the edge of the bed in pyjamas and boots with no socks, detachedly flipping through a collection of his space age dramas and tragedies published in Turkey...

'They ask me why I never married,' he said suddenly, 'But I was married to Poetry and had no feelings left for anything else.'

His loneliness did not prevent him from remaining elegantly British until the last days of his life. No matter where he was, he'd wear only well-tailored suits – whether in the foyer of the five-star Asia Plaza hotel in Taiwan or in the corridors of the hospice with its wizened old men and fidgety women.

He was so out of place in this transitory accommodation that I was immensely relieved when once, coming back from a trip to Moscow, I found his Cypriot relatives had taken him on a trip to Kyrenia, his childhood home. And that's where he died shortly after, living just long enough to see in the third millennium, and was buried as humbly as he'd lived on the mountain with the stone pines from which you could see in the distance the glittering, ever-changing azure sea.

He always knew he'd return to his homeland at some time but London's anonymity suited him, because London is a remarkable refuge for those who are not afraid of the silences of loneliness and not afraid to talk to themselves.

'I was born to be a poet and nothing else,' he said to us once as we sat in that nice Turkish restaurant named Efes. But such self-sufficiency has an obvious outcome; Osman Türkai remained lonely in the soul, lonely in the flesh, and you can look in vain in his poetic symphonies for love limited to a particular Lady Beautiful. He was twice almost caught by rather banal would-be brides, but never married. Yet love, that fills his poems, became neither a despair nor yet a disappointment – but simply turned to the entire visible and non-visible world. That love, directed with the searing intensity of the soul and heart to a tree or a bird or a star, might have frightened lovers of more wayward and homely feelings away from his poems, but it could create whole worlds because it was so unselfish.

In this present-day world of multiple mysteries, the simple integrity of his life and poetry could easily seem like the most unfathomable mystery of all. It would be possible to invent Osman Türkai if you wanted to write a novel about a pure poet adrift in an increasingly meaningless and prosaic world, suffering the mechanical routines of life. This fabricated literary hero would be condemned to utter loneliness, would not yield for anything to the glorious temptations of television and would only be able to write at night in touch only with the starry skies and his own myths, so alive and so authentic. Amazingly, though, this strange creation is simply a true description of how Osman Türkai did live – and the worlds that live in his writing can be read about by anyone who dares to look at themselves.

In this perfect storyline of an existence, Osman Türkai, in his youthful commitment to the call of poetry, is the equal of the legendary poets of yore – all the more so because his muse from the early days thrilled to images of antiquity and sported in the dazzling Mediterranean sun of his native Cyprus – the beloved isle of Aphrodite, goddess of love, an isle with a history steeped like the immortal soul of Türkai in the intermingling of Islam's Sufi mysteries and the Byzantine luxury of Christianity, of the refined paganism of the Greeks and the Romans and the majestic priesthood of Phoenicians, of the gloomy gothic of Crusaders and baroque intrigues and cunning of Venice – not to mention the later history of British imperial dominion which ended with the isle of love exploding in strife that drove Osman Türkai from his native land, turned alien.

The cosmogeny of stellar nebulae shimmers brightly in Türkai's poetry, its cultural layers devoid of calculated restraint: a poem, like a word and deed of love appearing afresh before our eyes, capturing in the all-encompassing process of creation not just the reader's imagination but the poetic impulse of the poet himself. Everything in Türkai's poems is ever on the move, like a pre-autumn flock of birds on the universal wind that swoops towards the horizon then suddenly comes back as if nostalgic for the past and separates in rising vortices of air before reuniting as a single flock:

God is a vortex

Ticky-tak-tak
Track-trik-tak...

So the map is drawn in your mind.

It is either God or Human!

And
The Sun
Is in its very own
natural system. Saikal
smiled, pointing to this enlargement
of the inner structure of the atom. One of
the inner particles scorches the world... Then
in came Isikan. And the mystery is mirrored in
another indicator. Life is constant, he was told,
in every organ of man: in the planets and stars.
He pictured his new nature. Flooded by the light
Shining forth, as it opened like a mother's womb.
Unbalanced now. It meant: time to search for God.
The oculus flickers. And words roll on waves of sound.
One corpuscle flutters to another, as if she
Obeys the law of attraction on his command.
Colour-coded chromosomes outside the body.
Acid, that essential device, turns like a sphere.
Oh look how the universe spins to my whistle!
Sound-signs and movement: symbols of the search.
The proof of a connection. The beginning in the Inner
Order; the essence in the Outer Structure. Purple Planet. Her
Distant indicators flashing out. It is the true verification of
God's elasticity and infinity. Blu–blu–luu! Numbers.
Date. In vision, a body, brought by Cosmos,
And eagerly a voice goes chop–chop!
A robot now waiting your orders on the Red Planet.
What was that tongue of fire the giants speak? They press

A button. They see their voices. They find their hair is wet.
They press another, hoping to tell us where they came from
Somewhere? Time, Mind, Space – everything has flown from there!

I looked at the Dawn. I saw my mind, burgeoning in
its blood. Let its Time and Cosmos halt. Let its oculi
see-read the secret codes and understand the balance of all
dimensions. Let her watch all distortions, oh! Let it see
that scarlet planet, that looks different from each angle:
that Blue, White, Purple, Golden Planet.

I saw how my mind engorges with the blood of dawn
Let its Time stop.
Let its Space finish as well.
Let its eyes see and note the secret signs.
Let it comprehend the balance
Of all dimensions
That disappeared in the exact moment of creation.
Let it see the spectacle of this scarlet planet
And this purple planet.

Let time
Look and let it see
Secret signs. Arriving
in the shadow of the bright ray
long-awaited by icebound eyes, blind
in one direction. Arriving radiantly, its image
shimmering, embracing the dark. He knew the sound of water
the joy of the forest trees. In what seas then is man's life advancing
and retreating on the beach. Listen, you can hear his pulse – it's fast.

Sunny and azure, pale and pure, the start of his poetic life shone through the moist mists of England – both naturally and mystically – and his small throne room in London's bohemian Soho, where we used to visit, always felt exotic, bathed in a soft, quietly reverential light – especially when endless drizzling rain glowed grey through the windows, and glimmering drops gathered and ran down the panes in their ancient metal frames of style long-abandoned in England. This is not surprising – his study was located in a garret in a narrow and old mansion in the heart of Soho near Chinatown.

So-ho! Was the cry of the hunters in the sixteenth century, when they pursued rabbits with beagles on the local commonland, of which but a few reminders remain in ancient plane trees and the name of the old church of St Martin's-in-the-Fields on Trafalgar Square. The Soho quarter grew across the fields soon after the Great Fire of London in 1666 – when first began the regulated planning of London, and the idea of neat rows of houses surrounding garden squares guarded by iron railings that even today bring the green breath of rural England into the city's bustle.

One door in Osman Türkai's cell led out to a flat roof, from which in clear weather you could see all the tumble of roofs and attics across Soho, which was once a creative bohemia, with many houses plain externally but inside a strange brick anthill of narrow passages and stairways that appear out of nowhere and lead on and on up to reveal yet another tiny room – each one somehow separate from the whole architectural scheme, as if floating in a separate universe from the ordered world outside and populated by dreams, mirages and strange ideas created by the lodger's personality.

By the eighteenth century, the aristocracy were already suffering from the influx of vulgar foreigners of numerous races and languages, decamping here in ever-rising numbers as the British Empire strode out into the world. In later times, John Galsworthy complained in *The Forsyte Saga*, that Soho was 'Untidy, full of Greeks, Ishmaelites, cats, Italians, tomatoes, restaurants, organs, coloured stuffs, queer names.' And even Galsworthy didn't live until the times when London's dockland exoticism shifted west to Soho to create Chinatown, whose residents moved energetically beyond the laundry business to create restaurants that filled the heart of London with the savoury aromas of oriental cuisine.

Back in those heady early days of new, aristocratic Soho, the noble ladies and gentlemen, the statesmen, lawyers and high churchmen who lived here encountered strange and unsavoury arrivals from the continent: French, Dutch and Italian courtesans – and adventurers like Giacomo Casanova and his flame Marianne de Charpillon[72] who drove the seducer so mad with her flirtation that he almost burned down Soho in the fire of his unsatisfied lust.

It was here on Greek Street that the tragicomedy played out, that squalid melodrama about which Casanova later wrote, when a recluse in the Czech castle of Duchcov, 'the day I met Charpillon in London, I felt the approach of death...'

---

[72] In sixteen-year-old French-born Marianne, Casanova met his match. Raised among courtesans who specialized in fleecing rich men, she teased and tormented him as he lavished gifts and attention on her – raising his ardour to such a point as she played the part of his lover but refused to go to bed with him that he smashed up her house in frustration. After Marianne had him arrested, he taught a parrot to say 'Miss Charpillon is more of a whore than her mother' and put it on sale in the Royal Exchange. But the affair wrecked his confidence as a womanizer, and he abandoned his life of seduction to live in poverty as a librarian.

The year was 1763, the month September and Casanova was thirty-eight years old, a sad mediocrity in everything but a natural actor's ability to play a part and shed a tear on demand – still goaded to new adventures and so dogged by that eternal male fear of impotence that he often bought a few moments satisfied lust with pounds, sovereigns, shillings, pence and farthings, because even then sex was available for sale in Soho...

Poor Casanova! How hard he tried to imitate the aristocrats and celebrities of his time, desperate to prove to himself and to future generatons that he was the equal of Voltaire and Rousseau, of Goethe and Mozart, who just a year after Casanova left arrived in Soho as an eight year-old, already famous all over Europe, for a series of concerts in London. Ah Mozart, in whose company Casanova might have been noticed twenty-three years later at the premier of Mozart's *Don Giovanni*...[73]

But what did he think in those moments of silence, since he wasn't devoid of conscience nor totally overwhelmed by jealousy of his fellow Venetian Canaletto, who had returned from Soho to the radiant canals of his native Venice seven years earlier?

---

[73] After the opera, Casanova was apparently asked by a friend if he had seen it, to which he allegedly replied, 'Seen it? I practically lived it.' It was just a year later that Casanova began writing his own memoirs in Castle Duchcov. Some experts believe Casanova may not just have been an inspiration for this operatic tale of the great lover, but actually collaborated with Mozart on the libretto in the last days before the premiere, when the librettist, Casanova's fellow Venetian da Ponte, was away in Italy. Casanova's memoirs from Duchcov include pages from the libretto of *Don Giovanni* that he seems to have been working on.

How could Casanova compete? Casanova, laughed at by both Voltaire and Rousseau as if a monkey dressed in camisole and curls as if in revenge for his inability to discern a soul in women. How could poor Casanova's story compete with the steady, hard-working genius of his compatriot, except by stirring up the embers of his baccanalian fire and blowing on the fading glow of mostly invented scandal: a sad litany of female conquests, some deceived by the sentimental flattery common to torturers, others bought like cattle and some even taken by force.

It's so easy to become a scoundrel. You just need to go a little further each day than your conscience allows, and find each day new justifications for this little trifle.

But having never conquered himself and his petty lusts, nor created anything but a sanctimonious life story, this lecher, poseur, minimus, philanderer, buffoon and child molester cannot rise even to the doomed passions of a Don Giovanni, and so becomes the butt of farce and low comedy as the wilful womanizer who if he can't seduce buys, and if he can't buy plunders by force. So he is plummeted into the abyss of terror by the appalling recognition of the meaninglessness of existence if neither the first, the second nor the third succeed.

Yet Casanova, King of Flaneurs, can grin from his portraits because the memory of his idle pursuits has indeed dallied until our modern era of entertainment, when fools and sensualists triumph over the seduced and deceived world.

Of course, painters and poets, writers and philosophers did until recently inhabit the secret cells of Soho, but long ago the area turned into the habitat of prostitutes, and the proliferation of sex shops long ago exceeded demand. All the same, tucked away in some tiny cafes amid the hidden labyrinth of Soho's narrow byways, there are no doubt mighty young geniuses, subversives and know-alls – whose poetry is as low as the life of the area glorifying not the secret but the visible.

Türkai knew, of course, that ordinary beings must always be captives of their own spiritual comfort, prisoners of simple passions and desires – and to them the revelation of the cosmos may be utterly terrifying. Yet there is still a power in poetry and Türkai believed poetry can indeed raise people to new levels – because a person is not only comfortable in his imagination, but may create entirely new spaces and times that in time become new homes.

Türkai was a poet of the cosmos not because he left his native soil but because he knew intimately the myths of Ancient Greece and Egypt. And woven into the very fabric of his poetry too is the stellar, celestial myth of the origins of his ancestors, the blue Turks, and the Turkish language was always for him, who spoke English with equal grace and power, a language of heaven. At the time the scope of his enthusiasm was far from limited to Anatolian Turkey; the Altai Turks inspired him just as Egyptian hieroglyphs and Sumerian cuneiform, just as the legends of London and the Babylonian dreams of New York. All these civilizations merged in his soul and consciousness, joining in a polyphonic symphony of the world's continents. Yet the music of history didn't simply create spectacular images, it welled into the music of his poetic emotion, recognizable both in English and Turkish.

Recognizable, yes, but who truly penetrates its ecumenical core?

It was said of him, 'Türkai admits the gods and goddesses of mythology to his heart, yet remains neutral about the universal God. Instead, he expresses quasi-religious faith in the final triumph of the human will...'

Yet the time of Miezelaitis[74] and belief in the super-man has gone, and it seems unlikely to be right to assume Osman Türkai's starry poetic symphonies are rooted only in the intellectual energy and musical power of his earthly talent. Say what you will about its Sufi origins or the fact that Türkai was never seen praying in a public mosque, but the constant and eternal presence of the One God is unmistakable – it is the core that links, marries and welds into one all the astonishing variety of forms, metaphors and insights of his cosmic verse.

The unfathomable core of Türkai's poetry – the restless fiery crown of the universal tree, bristling with newborn branches and rooted in dying worlds – is the natural world view of a Turk and a Muslim, springing spontaneously from the recognition of the world's unity – that unity which is being greedily ripped into national shreds and fictional factions by avaricious politicians and the rage of the selfish.

Unlike other poets of Soho and other quarters of humanity, Türkai never found his place within Earth's co-ordinates. The terrible, unstoppable slide of civilization to its final destruction awoke no cynical interest in him. He remained tortured and tormented all his life, locked in an alien reach of space and time. Yet this lonely torment never distorted his poetic face nor cast a shadow on the noble dignity of his life. His agony, just as it once signified true art, transformed

---

[74] Eduardas Miezelaitis (1919-1997) was one of the most leading authors and poets of Soviet Lithuania, emerging in the 1940s and creating poems that explored the meaning and purpose of art and the relationship between the artist and reality.

into a unique creativity that neither patronized with pity nor condescended with cheap compassion, but instead delighted in the resilience of the human soul that lives on in the face of everything that would kill or corrupt it.

He left this life the way he lived – not belonging to any-one nor anything but his own special calling. Poets of the West could not understand his eastern roots and could not forgive his rejection of his own civilization – because they regard the business of rejection as their own. Poets of the East were alienated, too, because he absorbed the cultures of the West into his blood. On Türkai fell the thankless task of becoming the bridge between East and West over which others tramp.

But is it possible to unite humanity without lying down beneath its feet? Or will blindly partisan passions and the myriad divisive minutiae of life crush you?

Yet on Taiwan – on the lake of the Moon and the Sun, near spiked temples and pagodas topped with flat hats and curving brims, and in the Kenting National Park in the south where moist and gloomy monsoon forests nurture astound-ing butterflies that weave and flutter above the orchids – on Taiwan, we were still alive in this world and Osman Türkai smiled on us from the next in his steel green habit, and we should have lived and been happy ...

Somehow, though, we managed to get into an argument here – once more because of the trouble that circled your keenness to imprint the rough, honest and clear flow of exis-tence.

'A man, my good Sir, has seldom an offer of kindness to make to a woman, but she has a presentiment of it some moments before,' noted Laurence Sterne in his *Sentimental Journey*, that is likewise devoid of external action, yet is a ravishingly detailed narration of what is happening when nothing is happening but a heart feeling deeply about everyday life.

I was guilty then, like so many men when they don't understand, don't understand that even the rice drawing paper of those luminous scrolls on which Chinese painters, alive to the unity of the world, can picture a white lotus on the white ground, and the invisible autumn wind in canes and leaves and hair. They don't understand that even this paper, made for the imprint of ink and watercolour, can be of two kinds: the male yin that repels the wet colours and the female yang that readily absorbs their moisture.

I still think that the soul's action must be like the glide and hover of an unseen bird in the sky of universal existence, because only this subtle movement that relies on air currents and so merges with the movement of the world as a whole – only this movement makes plain the beautiful, ambiguous meaning of earthly existence, only this movement suddenly unites the chaotic gusts of high wind and brings together streams with mountains and the ever-chattering brook with the eternally silent cliff, and conjugates the brief glory of the spring flower with the long winter nakedness of undistinguished branches.

But I was forever straining, it would seem, the last powers of my heart to understand life as it happens and see behind the stillness of natural things the invisible growth and processes of life with such intensity that I cruelly failed to notice the impulses and flights of your nearby being and equally restless soul.

Forgive me, because even in the small variegated jasper vase brought from Taiwan – even in its visible airy stillness – through the sintered blotches and layered veins of the sharp green borders and soft chrome transitions glows and flickers the colour of its secret soul. For isn't it true that everything beautiful has a soul?

I look at it, and again become convinced that nothing in the world remains fixed and any Allah-given movement can just possibly become form, but can not possibly be stopped or imprinted. Yet it is equally impossible to decide something absolutely and forever, because such rigidity is much worse than the desire to imprint a moment; the imprinting serves only to deceive, while absoluteness kills receptivity to subtler meanings and compassionate hints of the Unity.

After all, you know that some instant meanings remain with us for many years, and, returning by chance, always present to a person his true, not imagined, face. And so, in Amsterdam airport on the way to London from Taiwan, we bought a few souvenir delft tiles more variegated in colour than the traditional blue, tiles on which now I see not the ice-bound canals, nor the unchanging windmills overlooking sun-shimmering fields of red and yellow tulips, nor even the elderly Dutchman who diligently carves out the wooden blanks of clogs, but instead a melancholy stork, that was not present on these bought souvenirs.

This stork lives on the Russian tiles covering the old Dutch oven from the time of Peter the Great in a Moscow museum, where it stands in a shallow marsh among spiked reeds. I remember how struck I was by the sign above it when I saw it thirty years ago: 'Not always flying' – that is how the words were written, with the old syllables including a pot-bellied yat[75]

---

[75] In other words, the Russian spelling includes a 'yat'. The 'yat' is a letter once used in the Russian alphabet that caused Russian children

– and its inner meaning chimed with the longing of my spirit and lingered with me.

Even the stork, born as regal inspiration for every soul as it glides in the sky, must humbly justify itself as it sojourns among the tussocks of the marsh. And didn't my penitence come because I felt myself right and so was everywhere wrong?

...in Taiwan, where you demanded that I fall out of my imagination and photograph you near the lone rock running out into the sea – and I just couldn't understand then why you needed it, so especially and persistently...

...in Kyoto in Japan, above the imperial pond with the copper-bronze, blanched-red and variegated carp in the green shadow of the curly branches hanging over the water, on an isle on which shone the soft gold patterned pavilion made for quiet reflection on the dream of every carp to become a sacred dragon, as only one in millions does, as if it will somehow overcome the raging rocky rapids of the great river.

...in Venice, when we for the first time emerged from the maze of side streets on to the Piazza San Marco to see the importunate pigeons swooping through the sunny sea-breeze sky, and you were overwhelmed with the joy of existence and simply begged to be photographed as you were then and as you will never be again...

...in your beautiful fullness and triumphant femininity that had lasted long but were slipping away, flowing through time's fingers like the reality of the canals streaming past the arched bridges and palazzos, like the reality of the club-shaped insets

---

spelling nightmares. It's a sound a little like an 'e' or 'ieh' that's the equivalent of digraphs in English, such as the 'æ' in encyclopædia.

in the gothic windows of the Doge's Palace, and the murmuring of the surf that musically knocks the roped gondolas on the waterfront on the Riva degli Schiavoni, where a chance breath of the sea wind cleared the view for us across the shining space of the blue-blue green lagoon to the islet of San Giorgio with its ochre monastery housing the Cini Foundation, and its soaring terracotta belfry, and, closer by, the Basilica of Maria Della Salute between the waters of the Grand and Giudecca Canals, with the Lido on the horizon.

The low sun raked across the flood-washed slabs and the Byzantine horses of San Marco as they strained to fly into the open space with sheer muscular effort. In that happening moment of truth you began to whirl with happiness, and I honestly but mistakenly imagined that you too felt the complete unstoppability of such moments, and I hesitated to capture you in that flow of happiness – but only because I couldn't see you in some sort of photographic frame, frozen in the flight of the soul.

Beyond the swish of the surf, the light-dance on the lagoon, the sweep of the skies. Beyond the caress of the sea breeze and the embrace of the eddies, beyond the transparency of the water that reveals the still submerged cathedral mosaics, without the movement and immortality of life, beyond yesterday and beyond tomorrow. Beyond the unity of everything that was then the continuity and durability of our shared happiness...

If I were a master – if I could catch the wind in a photo – I might be zealous in this art, but, sadly with my own poor hand, how could I hope in a single click to pause existence and joy that happen continuously? And doesn't only a child try to catch the fluttering butterfly, never fretting about crumpling its delicate wings.

The Chinese know how with exquisite moderation to do the minimum, to turn a tiny detail into a reflection of the entire universe – but what long diligence of spirit, what immense patience is required to achieve it! Only after realizing time doesn't exist, can you finally see it. Only by heeding the thread that binds the pale mist on the lake and the white shroud curling round the far mountain. Only by feeling deeply the loneliness of the weeping willows, the rippling weeds and the lotus blossom without the small fisherman in his boat in the middle of this universe – can you, oh no, not capture but *peep* into the eternal happening of life, like Tan Yuan, the artist, poet and calligrapher of the fifteenth century, whose picture 'Gathering lotus flowers' on a huge horizontal scroll is displayed on a wall in the National Palace Museum in Taipei...

And in that museum, too – do you remember? Of course you remember – through the delicate carved ivory latticework ball inside of which, like a Russian *matriushka* but with Chinese wit and diligence, is another perforated ball, with yet another inside, and another inside that – until you get to a tiny one barely visible in the heart of the others and only reachable with the most ingeniously curved needle – all carved from a single piece of ivory. For 300 years, the same family, under the aegis of the same imperial dynasty, patiently carved this extraordinary masterpiece until one of the descendants finally said, 'Well, our long task is done, and a new one must be started straightaway ready to pass on to our sons.'

Happy is the person who can pass a life's work on to a son or daughter! As the centuries flowed, the work became more and more painstaking, and a single wrong, rushed movement, made in irritation or momentary carelessness, could have ruined the work of many generations in an instant...

Yet what a sadness the completion of the task must have been to the craftsman who made the final incision on the last and tiniest sphere. Wisdom comes with the continuity of work, though, and that master knew that true labour never ends and runs on like the clouds that make stars, the creation of which Allah is rarely thanked for...

So forgive me for the way such small details and the general impatience of life drove us apart so that the gap between our perceptions was suddenly widened, and stretched ghastly and bleak in all directions...

It is meaningless to build bridges across this chasm of rejection; any artificial bridge constructed to span the secret abyss is all too easy to destroy.

Something very different is needed – a conscientious vision of the heart. Vision is needed, eyes uplifted in search of God-Unity, for only he can tie the threads of mutual knowledge, teaching empathy and compassion, in which there is no room for indulging other's grievances.

So now I know, on that accidental cliff in Taiwan, that untimely rock in the foam of the ocean, near which you sought so hard to be imprinted, distracting me from my accidental philosophizing – now I know it was not at all accidental for you.

I understood this only later, when I saw that small, old, yellowing photo in which your young father in his pilot's uniform is standing next to a similar foam-bound rock in the Arctic seas – and the reason for your impatience became all too obvious to me, because I as well, after taking a step away from myself, suddenly heard within my soul the howling in the long dark night of the eternal blizzard as it hurled bitter snow against the remote polar hut – heard a soul impatient to meet her father in the Arctic darkness of a daughter's expectations...

This is your childhood's and also your temporal shelter, and the white bearskin rug and the woven bedspread on the iron bed overwhelm me with their silence amid the ticking clocks that urge a time of separation, and I with the vision of your young days gaze at the sun-flooded bedspread, where among the palms and sand, three lanced horsemen, three burnous-clad Bedouins battle with lions, and you have a brave favourite who, as a true knight of the desert, meets the golden fury of the lion without a shadow of fear...

And so will your father, fighting his way back from the heavens through the blizzard, drive out all your childish fear. But the minutes pass, and hours, days, months and years, and still he does not return, and his plane above the white polar desert, above the endless ice and the black rocks smothered by the frozen sea, burns on, vivifying the dark and starry abyss with its blazing light as it spirals downward.

But I understood this only later – and learned with my heart through your writing. Will others ever understand how meaningless stars are, how desperate the icy void of space, how sad the infinite abyss of the heavens – if there is not alive among them your father's heart? They are so plunged in grief that one might even feel pity for their emptiness.

Deep void beyond the sky, beyond our sight:
Oh poor Abyss! Is there no end to your dark night?

The Moon, out of the mist, unsheathed its blade.
Where can it, its raging grief displace
If there's no bottom, no bounds to empty space?

The storms of time uproot the oaken tree.
The Moon-slayer sees just infinity.

No pen stroke delineates the space.
The black hole stretches limitless away...
Not for nothing in this way does pitch dark hold sway.

Oh it's black in Rus – it's time to save the saints![76]
Tendons tremble at the horror – someone faints.

'Come on, let's play hide and seek now, kids!
But where, when there is neither base nor lids?'

The Moon's shift rips and with the lashing rain
Fear comes down like some sly thug again.

Don't look back now you've begun – just flash your heels
and run.

'Bare boards squeaking – where's a hiding place,
Where's the game end, when there's no end to space?
No cupboard, chest nor some concealing nook.
In all nature, darkness everywhere you look.
But some malicious hunger drives you on;
It whips you, and beats you on and on.'

And in the boundless dark, beyond all sight –
Children cry 'Father' pitifully through the night.[77]

How much the isolated heart suffers the scorch of separation
in the hellish abyss that carries away solitary stars screaming

---

[76] An old Russian idiom says when disaster strikes, you must evacuate
the icons from the house (most Russian houses used to have icons).
[77] Poem by Lydia Grigoryeva.

and weeping. How much the loneliness of a girl became the eternal loneliness of a woman, and engulfed you ever in the vast chasm of orphanhood – in the warmth of Arctic Igarka[78] even with your mother and on the chill steppe of Krasnodon[79] without her; in Lugansk-Voroshilovgrad;[80] and in Kosovo – in the sanatorium for tubercular children among the profuse Carpathian gardens scented with honey and the exhaled rose juice from constellations of apples; among the yellow, spacious and lofty beech trees that rise as one with the mountains into that abyss of space mercifully veiled by the sunny skies, and blanket the ground with their russet fallen leaves...

These piles of fallen leaves, dry and fluffy, offered to the feet a featherbed, and the mysterious rustling and crystal freshness of the place brought back from childhood another starched snow-linen purity – when your Ma was bathing you before bedtime in the silvery trough filled with buckets of water splashed from the pump and boiled in the pan, then swaddled you in a sheet and carried you across the painted floorboards to the crisp delight of the freshest down-bed to be under the same honey bedspread of the lion fight to leave you blissfully dreaming – about what? – and behind the dark windows of your white-winged house the high, lush crowns of blizzard-white acacia shushed in the rain until this soft noise suddenly and mysteriously retreated from the windowsill, to leave a

---

[78] Igarka was the first city built on permafrost, far inside the Arctic Circle on the banks of the Yenisei river, with an average annual temperature of 10.5°C below zero.

[79] A city on the steppes of south-eastern Ukraine.

[80] Lugansk is a city in southeastern Ukraine known in the Soviet era as Voroshilovgrad, and originating in 1795 when British industrialist Charles Gascoigne established a metal factory here.

glowing green eye and the buzz of a radio, sending a story on invisible waves, piercing the dark like angels of light, time and space, with the sound of a huge, infinitely beautiful orchestra, so familiar, a passport to the kingdom of happiness.

And what was it, anyway, nagging with anxiety your child's heart, and awakened in your dreams?

Dvorak's 'Slavonic Dances', Smetana's 'Vltava', Mozart, Tchaikovsky, Beethoven…yes, but often, like an omen of inescapable love and separation, the Polonaise of Michael-Ceophas Oginski, once accompanied by the lyric tale of the woman he dedicated it to as Farewell to the Homeland.[81]

That beautiful tale of love, that forgotten dream of chivalry of the heart – it disturbed your soul in that small house, where in the black polish of the silent piano were reflected the lacy Chinese tablecloth of fanza and junks and, like a white cloud, the polar bearskin rug, dug out of the Arctic ice by your father; in that house, cloaked in the steady whispering of rain in the billows of blizzard-white acacia that was interrupted continually by the clear clip-clop drops from the mulberry and cherry, apricot and apple branches; in that abandoned Eden garden, where instead of cucumbers and tomatoes there bloomed dahlias with chornobryvtsi,[82] where along the fence sprouted glowing emerald shoots of oat and peacock flowers and the smoky-red or soft pink hollyhocks

---

[81] The Polonaise in A minor is the most famous piece by Polish composer Michael Ceophas Oginski (1765-1833), written after he was forced into exile after the failure of the Kosciusko Uprising of Polish patriots against Russia in 1794. Ironically, Oginski later became a Russian senator, and the Polonaise is much loved in Russia.

[82] Marigolds – a national symbol in Ukraine and often mentioned in songs.

of the Donbass steppe. It disturbed your soul and flung it high into the infinite flight and float of this blissful dream – fine as the spun gold of your hair, a shimmering mist of illusions – that immortality is possible in love…

Coming back in a hurry on those dark evenings along unpaved Shkolnaya street, between the unnerving, eerily gurgling honeysuckle bushes – each one a launchpad for a mugging, each hiding myriad weird faces and lost souls – you dreamed and you dreamed and your soul rose to those places where a man's love is calibrated not by his readiness to buy a fur coat and deliver worldly wealth but by his capacity to immortalize love, dedicating it to the creation of the heart, which is destined to suffer and lose time and even its homeland which once seemed unalterable.

Only in that heart-creation that conquered the grief of all betrayals would you become the One, as I feel you outside time and distance, outside the burdens of life and outside the attraction of death…

Yet heart-creation happens only in separation – and if in future I should be remote, then all my torment before God, all possibilities of flight and all the wonder of the world will merge in this creation, that brought all the sadness and pain of dying – and you should know that it is yours, because it is light as a soul, and as tender as that longing for home which you can never satisfy no matter how much you cry or call.

But if it happens, peace will come, the peace in which in the unity of love you're my wife, my daughter and the glow of home, and the memory of life in the desert of every-day where West tussles with East and on opposite sides of a shared Heaven that humbly opens only for the pure light of love and compassion.

CHESTNUT NEAR KARLOVY BRIDGE

Whether you glance at the clock, or close your eyes for a while to lie back in the brief sweetness of the hydrocarbon bath that wraps the body in tiny bubbles, the therapeutic bell will still suddenly ring, and the morning's procedure will come to an end. The sanatorium sister, Yarmila or Dana, will gently drape your shoulders with a clean white robe, and you'll have to go and dress to go outside.

Yet while the bliss lasts, it seems eternal, and Sonya, with her eyes closed, was really trying with all her being to give herself up to the moment, to dissolve in it her natural nakedness so chastely covered by the soft green fluid in the silky smooth bath.

She didn't want to move, just making the water murmur as she wafted the bubbles from her arms, stomach and hips; the circling hands of time were already lost, and she was floating in the fount of memory back to the mountains near the Ingush village of Nevinnomyssk, to the sunny, sandy pool near the dam, already warm from the sun of an August morning.

It was a Sunday, long ago, and their small expedition was wandering all over the North Caucasus in a small canvassed pick-up truck in search of grey layered clay for household stoves, lingering here and there to idle in the sun or kick a football with local geologists. Her father, the leader of the expedition, went on reading the newspapers, discussing the Situation in Czechoslovakia and suspecting Dubcek to be in the pay of the CIA. Meanwhile she, blonde Sonya, after soaking up the sun strolled down to the pool and stepped into the warm, clear water – and found it full of young fish fry, so hungry, trusting or foolish that they brushed against her bare feet and nibbled at her toes.

Enticed by the sensation, she lay down in the shallow water as she was in her red cotton bikini while the fish swarmed around her in silvery clouds, tickling and tingling with their mouths her entire body from her pink shoulders to her thin hips and slender teenage knees. The pleasure was both excruciating and rather guilty, even looking back; no man's touch had since given her such delicately perfect caresses or so opened her hot inner darkness.

Only now, lying in the Karlovy Bath with its silvery carbonate bubbles, did she imagine how it might have been to lie among the fish completely naked...and then suddenly the alarm rings and the fish scatter, and her life is back in real time, the time in which that absurd hourglass-bearing puppet skeleton of Death strikes the hour to set the silver bell ringing in that ancient clocktower in Prague – parading along with the figures of Vanity with his mirror, the Miser with his bags of gold and Pleasure's Turk with his lute, while below the polyglot tourists cheerfully follow the centuries-old performance every hour and clap as the twelve painted wooden apostles spin like a carousel in the windows of the intricate clocks until a golden cock signals the striking of the chime with a mechanical 'cock-a-doodle-doo' intelligible in all languages.

Before this current visit to Karlovy Vary, Sonya had been delayed in Prague and spent a leisurely day walking from the Old Town to the Castle over the famous Karlovy Bridge. Fortunately, even the workaholic and highly cash-conscious technical consultancy she worked for were obliged to allow forced deviations from the timetables of life every now and then.

The day turned out to be wonderful. The sun, slipping down like caviar from the crowned fantasy spires of Tyn cathedral, spilled across cobbles polished by countless feet in the medieval square. A gentle breeze wafted in from the river. And throughout the city, chestnuts blossomed, sending their fresh and unformed buds forth as if trying to soar into the sky after the thrusting cones of their blooms – so abundant and white, like those on the Sparrow Hills around Moscow. And there was pink blossom, too, in Prague, in pink candles that always reminded Sonya of that special patterned Karlovy Vary porcelain that consoled the eyes and heart with its beauty.

Declining the offers of flyers from a dozen street peddlers to the conveyor belt of tourist concerts – Mozart, and Mozart again, and of course Vivaldi – she settled under the parasols of a café right by the clock tower and ordered coffee, sipping until Death rang the bell, then ambled through the narrow streets towards the Vltava, navigating her way through throngs of tourists, past chattering women who she tried to meet forehead to forehead to avoid being bumped, elbowed or even scratched with a stray handbag.

Unlike others, Sonya was in no rush; she always gave way, or even just waited for the noisy stream to swirl past while she gazed into the shop windows decked with Bohemian crystal or antiques whose intricate displays she loved so in Karlovy Vary too. And so that's how she was delayed near the marionette seller right by the Karlovy bridge, pausing not just for the Czech dolls in the shop-cave but the music which rolled out into the street – the seductive and sweet sound of Julio Iglesias.

Sonya loved that song – the gypsy song 'Dark Eyes' but sung in French and called 'Nostalgie'. It would be so wonderful, she thought, to dance with someone here to that alluring voice, not to just embrace awkwardly, but to dance, dance like her father and other forty-year-old men who knew just when to lead their partner to one side or another, and spun her not just clockwise but anticlockwise too...

Forty years didn't seem old any more, but those here, both single and married, just wanted to get her into bed without even a preliminary dance – probably because none of them knew how to spin her the other way. And none of them were there when needed – even just to support her under the arm when she was lost in contemplation of the chestnut bloom above the river and stumbled on one of the famous cobbles on the bridge.

The chestnut, though, deserved a sympathetic glance, unnoticed as it was by the people who stared in the souvenir shops, listened to the street musicians and took pictures of the decorative statues on the bridge, or maybe peered admiringly into the distance to the castle on the hill with its cathedral over the wide and flowing waters of the Vltava. The living chestnut, rising right by the parapet, seemed lost to them despite its lush blooms, as if it was simply a background for the statues. Then, she realized, there was another invisible chestnut at the far end of the bridge, blooming over the water with similar neglect.

Her father had especially taught her to see living nature more than inanimate objects – her father who was always dragging her off on his field trips and turning her, unwillingly, into a complete tomboy because he so wanted a son. Instead of playing mothers and daughters, Sonya had learned to shoot ducks and fish, to kindle a fire in heavy rain, to pitch a tent and sleep on damp ground in complete disregard for the girlish need for mirrors and informative gossip with her peers. This singular upbringing persisted so long that it almost missed her awakening femininity – but then she woke with a start, tried to catch the departing train, scraped her knees, got out of breath, and missed it entirely.

Maybe, if she hadn't been weighed down by her ideals, she would've run faster, especially without that ideal of a man who burdened her romantic dreams. But then if she had caught that train, it wouldn't have been hers, and would be bound for the wrong destination...

Sometimes, Sonya thought, it might be better if she didn't dream at all, and just became a bluestocking with library glasses – but what can a person do, especially a woman who's very well educated? There were always plenty of people, like the tourists on Karlovy bridge, but they were all paired off – and of course in such a crowd the well-read, thoughtful man would think himself special, and that medieval Prague, its gothic churches, the chestnut trees by the Vltava and even the Death ring were meant for him – well, a fig to him! And now the tourists are thronging in and money can't buy anything exceptional, now or ever – only in the unreachable mountains, where money has no value. And the anomalous person may see the solitude of nature even in a crowd, and may become so absorbed in their dreams that you just have to bump into them to bring them back to reality.

But in Karlovy Vary, Sonya always felt good. She regretted wasting even a day in Prague. In that little toy town, which originated in the fourteenth century where a hot spring bubbles into a gorge in the mountains, it seemed as if the present was locked in its unforgettable nineteenth century glamour; nothing had changed to disturb the eyes and soul and it remained frozen in the picturesque finery of the empire-style sanatoriums, hotels and mansions that ran up the mountains each side of the bubbling Tepla river.

The twentieth century with its McDonald's and shiny porn magazines seemed arrested in indecision at the entrance to the dark glass multi-storey Hotel Thermal, a massive monument of shame to its Soviet architects – its slab shape pressing into the hill surmounted by a belvedere housing a camera obscura on a site that was once a gallows. Beyond the belvedere, the hill becomes a mountain, and steps ascend through pine and beech heavens via snaking *terrenkura*[83] to the crowning heights of Eternal Life where a pseudo-gothic castle tower, the Goethe Belvedere, rises amid dark firs.

Sonya had been coming to Karlovy Vary for several years now, ever since she developed liver problems and arthritic pain from too much sleeping outdoors – and always in spring at the start of the season when there was just enough room here. Tourists flocked in on buses at the weekends and it was very noisy, but even then you could walk away along the *terrenkura*. Maybe if you started on the Beethoven track past the Postal Court and the riverside bird-cherries which were already exuding their heady clouds of scent above the Tepla, you could wander far up into the mountains and while away the day with a book at the Goethe Belvedere until the invading tide ebbed.

Clearly, Sonya's dislike of idle interaction and absence of feminine emotion were rooted in the past and painful experiences, but to the Russian habituées of Karlovy Vary it looked a bit too much like foolish pride, stuck-up nonsense or plain rudeness – and Sonya was regarded here as something of a weirdo.

---

[83] Terrenkura are special winding tracks in the mountains designed for blood pressure exercises.

After a blue and clear beginning, May quickly clouded over as soon as the bird-cherry bloomed. Sodden gusts of northern wind stripped the pink and white blossom from the trees, and tore off young leaves and twigs still in their infant weakness. Rebellious eddies whipped the young whiteness and pinkness and green up into the sky, toyed with it a while then dumped them on the wet and cold paving stones and tarmac.

Emerging through the sliding doors of the old bath-house close to the Mill Colonnade, Sonya saw that the sun was hidden, but at least the rain that had raged all night against her window had stopped. Discarded red tulip bulbs were studded in rain dew. Black-pearl snails clung to the pine needles still soft from the damp morning warmth and seemed to move without caution, but were ready of course to retreat into their shells at any sign of danger and pretend to be dead.

From her interest in dead-seeming snails and weakly sprouting tulip bulbs, you might think Sonya had little concern for living beings, like that one walking along the promenade now, sipping from one of those little porcelain jugs designed for taking the mineral waters – a handsome man with stooped shoulders named Viktor Mikhailovich, with whom she had managed to dance yesterday at the Postal Court.

And if a woman is so surly, who needs her?

Of course, if life and so-called reality were like a play for the stage, which is only partially true, then according to the rules of the genre the characters must experience all kinds of visible incidents of interest to outsiders. But what happens if these outsiders actually incite others' crimes, betrayals and lies, and also, and especially, provoke chance romances and random relationships which for some reason are considered not just interesting but important events (although any third party's curiosity simply flatters and humours them before burying them entirely to avoid the smell...).

If a person's entire life is thus to be viewed as a series of adventures, interesting only to those sweating with the trembling lust of teenagers spying on the girls' showers through a scratch in the glass made with a nail – then what can we do with someone who refuses to be a monkey for others fun?

We are all well-educated people. Sonya and I myself both used to read a lot of Freud, who was yet another character in Karlovy Vary's past. But what is for one man a victorious finish, winning the woman of his dreams, is for another just the beginning. So how can we combine this denouement with the beginning of a new short drama, and also bring in the spectators, who are always curious to watch, especially if it's free.

Not just to be witty, or just plain curious, though, we should record a single blending and distortion of the flesh, savouring the moment when a face turns into a gargoyle in that hot two-way exchange in the dark. Or we should risk being laughed at to remember that not the intercourse itself but only death-anticipating love can melt the icy darkness of lust, only the warmth of love can remelt the lure of sensuality into the lasting honey-flow of light. And maybe that afterglow is like the glow of the chestnut near Karlovy bridge, or the fragrance of the bird-cherries by the purling river that shines and sparkles even in cloudy weather, just as love may glow in the mind even when its hidden.

The previous day in Karlovy Vary, the sun had shone, gilding the stream under the bridge near the Thermal, where green-feathered ducks splashed and bobbed for the crumbs of breakfast bagels, and wild carp, both big and small, held their place with their heads upstream. In the nearby Dvořák

Gardens, the blooms of lush, violet-white magnolia were just coming to an end in crumbling bowls; tight inflorescences of dwarf rhododendrons were just blueing; while in the sun-dappled shade beneath a two-hundred year-old plane-tree were clumps of yellowing and blueing heartsease, and under the yellow-flecked streamers of weeping willow, on a stone by the empty concrete pond, sat a completely naked mermaid.

Despite its open pose, this sculpture never awoke any bodily desires with its chaste nakedness, and nor did that other nude on the lawn next to the blooming azaleas – sitting naked and holding to her bent knees a clay pitcher which spouted water so clear it was almost invisible...

'How then, how?' thought Sonya entirely dissolving in that blend of sun and bloom, 'How can you preserve this moment, without dying in it, or imprinting it? How can you begin to feel time without stopping it, but letting it run on with the sun and the flowers and the breeze? How can you learn not to be saddened by the loss yet prolong the joy of that moment when the lawns glow with the gloss of wet magnolia petals? Can you lodge in your memory the pure pink foam of bird-cherry blossom, and the drooping emerald branches, and the astonishing freshness of the grass? It seems, then, all you can do is learn it by heart, like a lesson – store in the memory the new beech blossom aflame next to neat green firs around the blazing buds of azalea, which will against expectation yield white flowers. Otherwise, what else is there but to wait and hope that this festival of nature will begin again, and will fulfil that childhood promise of lasting happiness.'

And was it because she had no-one to share that delight, so beautiful and so sad, that she had decided to join the holiday celebrations at the old Postal Court where rustic sausages sprinkled with juices were baked on an open fire, where dark beer foamed and the locals danced to a small brass folk band that played only the old marches old Czech men and women love to dance to.

This Viktor Mikhailovich was probably not a bad man, though rather full of himself — and as the saying goes he knew his worth. That worth, though, no-one saw back in his native Russia where back in his youth he had married his classmate at the medical institute, then moved to Israel, where he now lived alone, divorced long ago, after going through dozens of flats and jobs.

'Don't you miss Russia?' Sonya asked him at the table on the Postal Court's patterned verandah, from where it is just a short step to the mountain that rose almost sheer to the sky, swathed in different shades of green, from the bird-cherried Tepla that gurgled over white stones.

'Not really,' he replied after a moment's thought, 'I haven't been back once since I got away from the bolsheviks. Why spoil the mood? I remember it, of course — my friends, my relatives. And nature... It would just upset me to go there, so why bother?'

Silence.

'But you probably miss the Russian outdoors, don't you? The real Russian wilderness. When I first lived in Jerusalem, I had a penthouse flat. From there, up in the attic, you could see a long way — almost all the way to the Dead Sea. My mates — both Jews and Arabs — whenever they visited, they'd sigh: what a landscape! What a view! But why would I care for those scorched hills. How boring! So I planted tubs across the entire terrace to block the view and felt much better. Now I live in a different area on the second floor — and I open the window and there are pine trees...'

'Do you like it here?'

'Yes. It's green. People speak Russian. It looks like Russia, but without the rudeness. And I'm my own boss.'

'Will you come here again?'

'Yes, I'll be coming here regularly.'

'Don't you feel lonely in Israel?'

'I've a lot of work. Though why work when so much is taken for the social? How many idlers do I have to feed from my own pocket? In the West, Sonya, if anyone lives well – then it's only either the very rich or the very poor. We middle-class take the rap for everyone else – toiling and sweating like a bum…it's a nightmare.'

And, after a break, the band started to play again, with a thump of the tuba, and Czech and German couples dressed up for the occasion stood up from their tables and, holding hands, joined in the dance. So did Sonya and Viktor Mikhailovich.

Viktor Mikhailovich was an experienced dancer – an enviable partner. He could lead anti-clockwise, and out either side. But either his palm was too damp, it seemed to Sonya, or with his other hand he held too tightly, trying to press her against him. Then in the middle of the dances, she suddenly remembered she was due for a treatment and left the Postal Courts. But instead of going into town, she went straight to the green mountain after briefly running down to wash her hands and face in the icy water of the Tepla.

The climb up the path past the Beethoven statue was steep and long, and Sonya had to stop to catch her breath a couple of times on the thoughtfully placed benches. Once she was at the top, she strode without stopping through the beeches and pines, and flushed with effort, kept entirely quiet.

Blue tits chirruped, warblers warbled and blackbirds whistled in the branches. The cascading brooks murmured. A woodpecker knocked its beak against a trunk, and its intermittent clatter echoed in the sunlit groves. Through openings in the tree canopy, the sky was turning blue, and you could see the discarded golden seed of buds floating in the air, and fluffy petals of maple blossom drifting to the ground. The path wound on, but everything comes to an end, and eventually Sonya turned to walk down from the solitude of the mountain heights to the familiar bustle of the town.

About half way down, she saw a red beech[84] she'd never seen before – deep crimson and vivid scarlet, with flecks of burnished gold, blazing against the cyan sky near a blue-and-white empire style mansion.

That extraordinary fiery glow, whose flames engulfed every twig and branch, faded in an instant as the sun vanished behind a rare cloud – then blazed up again so brightly its red leaves shone like a furnace against the lazuli blue sky.

Sonya stopped, unable to take her eyes off this surprise beauty, flickering and flaming in the wind as if with an impulse to fly into the heavens. And the amazing truth was that in this single tree the spring of fresh new green leaves was rich with an anticipation of maturity – a harbinger of a resonant summer and a true autumn, when other green trees finally match them in their red and gold. This tree remains the same throughout and will not betray itself in any way.

So why is Sonya so quiet as she emerges from the bathhouse and shivers in the moist air to look at the red tulips,

---

[84] The red beech (*Nothofagus fusca*) is a native of New Zealand, named for its foliage which can become bright red in winter. In spring, the leaves are green fringed with red.

and why does she ignore other people in the resort crowding around the sixth spring, including the tall figure of Viktor Mikhailovich, who is walking with a steady step and a watchful eye, looking for another dancing partner?

Is it impossible, Oh Lord, to keep silent about the fact that someone simply wants to live, and not die at someone else's beck and call; that no matter how long you live, it is still not enough that the future, in opposition to the present, exudes the wonderful scent of bird-cherry and is easily recognized in the glow of the red beech? If there is beauty, there must be justice, and there must be hope – and the most important thing is not the passing of clock time, but the dream and need of love. Blessed is the man in whom childhood does not die, but a woman's loneliness is an unjust thing.

6

A PRAYER IN BEECH FORESTS

ଚଠ

I ARRIVED IN Karlovy Vary in a somnambulant state. That's how I looked, you might remember, feeling nothing but cross after dragging the heavy suitcases for miles. But after we both made our little shelter in the old Wolker hotel comfortable, I decided to try and write something...as if it wasn't enough that our names were scattered like diligent ants on the sheets of books, newspapers and magazines. But staring stunned at the blankly glowing computer screen, I latched on to the insect tiredness of a thought that there really does come a time when our schedule-exhausted souls don't need the abstraction of words, but the materiality of walking, either together or separately.

After this amazing revelation hit me, I actually managed to do a little writing, taking my work-shy nature by the throat. Better to work than walk... Yet really my nature was just sleepy because of all those pre-dawn starts – and lusted after one thing: to snooze away on the hotel's bed.

And so it was dreaming of dozing, drifting away, dropping off, dissolving into sleep, slumbering, snoozing, snoring, taking a nap, catching forty winks, getting a little shut-eye, conking out and thoroughly and shamelessly abandoning itself to the all-too-willing arms of Morpheus...

The thing is that once I drop out of my daily routine, one thought keeps coming back; the fear that there won't be time to do everything, that I won't ever be able to keep up with the express train of fate. Maybe it's just me but, from a young age, of all the pleasures of leisure, the sweetest was not football but sleep.

Even dazed awakenings in the middle of the day or, more depressingly at sunset, even the deadly gloom that stuck to me like a cobweb after a snooze, making me as grumpy as my mother and younger brother knew so well — even that dependable despondency couldn't quite inure me to the temptation of a little catnap. I was a loafer first-class, a topnotch sluggard, an idler supreme, a lazybones of the first water... Whenever I could find a minute, I'd lie down on the sofa with the beautifully wise tale of Hodja Nasreddin[85] by Leonid Solovyov, read-out to me as an infant, always reaching the following, beloved, closing words:

'Life!' he declared, quivering and shaking, not noticing the tears streaming down his face.

And everything around him quivered and shook, responding to him — the wind and the leaves, and the grass, and the distant stars...

---

[85] Nasreddin Hodja is Islam's most famous trickster, celebrated for his wit and drollery, about who many funny anecdotes are told. The character is based on an imam who lived in Turkey in the thirteenth century. Solovyov's tale is translated as *The Tale of Hodja Nasreddin; Disturber of the Peace* by Michael Karpelson (Translit, 2009).

And with this call to action, I would gratefully drop off to sleep, lost in the peaceful immensity and boundlessness of time, which could not be counted nor recovered. Unlimited light flowed in through the wide windows, one of which opened on to a balcony, where the railings were touched by the spilling green lava of the branches of a giant, yellow-blossoming oak which rose from a hollow in that unchanging Kazan courtyard with its sheds and garages.

I'll never again sleep quite so blissfully and serenely as I did to the gentle whisper of those green, breeze-blown branches of oak – just as I can't wake up without sadness. But in Karlovy Vary, in those first days after sleep-deprived London, I didn't hope for the same – just a deliverance from obligations as I strove with all my being to plunge into sleep, at least for an hour or so, to put aside my worries, all the things that needed thinking about and finishing – to forget about them for a while, if only to start worrying about something else.

Sleeping without interruption, shame or reproach was easy in Karlovy Vary – and so I slept. The door to the balcony was slightly open. The May wind, curling through, swayed the white net curtains and carried with it not just the free, fresh air of the resort but the clatter and squeal of a saw cutting shiny paving stones – on the market square near the Plague column, a new marble-look stairway, bordered by flowerbeds and trees brought from the mountains, was being constructed to take people down to the healing spring.

Yet the noise didn't disturb me. As I dozed, my head was already so full of anxiety and unfinished responsibilities, regrets and accumulated sorrows, that I, like a witness to a crime, was constantly watching as my soul kept breaking into my sleep, muddling me and bewildering me again and again, and kept praying – in a naïve plea for redemption for something that was not given in full, it seems, to the Unity. I, from the outside, understood that I was the cause of these interruptions, these failings before Allah, these abbreviated prayers said with a strangers' words in the haste of everyday life – as if in this dream I owed this unpayable, inescapable, ever-increasing debt of gratitude and repentance. And my soul, separate from my exhausted body, kept on whispering and praying, in fear of God and, even in my sleep, terrified of being alone.

So what misconduct lost among all the pressing duties of the centuries would not let me hide in slumber? What guilt blocked my conscience from everything else? Why was it that, in the outdoors, in reality, in the acceptance of invisible life and in bright temptations, my soul could never sleep off freely in peace?

I know the answer – don't I know it!

'Life!' It is, after all, simply the visible outcome – a feast for the senses. Leaves and stars, flowers and winds, branches and grasses, beautiful animals and the variety of people, birds and ants, unity, indivisibility, completeness – all gain their meaning and purpose, like love, only in the light of the Unity of Allah.

But I know that just this, as simple as the glow of daylight through closed eyelids, is the original, primal and joyous truth that I didn't open to you, couldn't reveal. And in the confusion of a little sleep, inexpiable guilt murmured again and again in the name of Allah, Grace and Mercy:

Say: 'I seek refuge with the Master of the Human Race
King of the Human Race

God of the Human Race
From the mischief of the sneaking evil tongue
From the one who whispers in people's hearts:
Evil tongued to the djinns and the Human Race.'[86]

How could I say that in such a way – so that you would
know that this last *sura* of the Koran tells about everything,
everything that really exists, and may become visible? In
these sparse words, flickering with innumerable silences,
there permeates the core of the Unity – and the fate of people who look at the granite Plague monument amid the
noise, and, as they move on, barely discern the stone figures
of the Holy Trinity – the Lord God, the young King Jesus,
and the Dove (the Holy Spirit) – in a lattice of baroque rays,
then raise their eyes to the sun and briefly close their eyes,
before the glow of the day returns to give him or her a sense
of the Unity in which the Trinity are not separate and not
hypostases,[87] but just different titles reflecting the united and
invisible nature of Allah.

---

[86] As the author explains, this is the final sura (chapter 114) of the Qur'an,
in which Mohammed advises mankind to seek refuge from the wiles
of the devil with Allah. Different authorities translate it differently.
This is a translation of the Russian version in *Letters to Another Room*:
Qul Audhu bi-rabbi 'n-naas,
Maliki 'n-naas, Ilahi 'n-naas
Min sharri 'l-waswaasi 'l-khanaas
Alladhee yuwaswisu fee sudoori 'n-naas
Min al-jinnati wa 'n-naas

[87] In Christian theology, a hypostasis is separate person, one of the three
elements of the Trinity. It comes from the Greek for standing beneath
– or underpinning – existence. It was a controversial idea, since it
seemed to violate the idea of monotheism, but as the author here says,
can be reconciled by seeing them as three parts of a whole.

I am not the keeper of my brothers and sisters – but the soul who in my whole life never managed to share with you the one thing that is truly worth sharing, who still frantically begs forgiveness – who was praying for time, whispering in my sleep for both of us:

Say: He is Allah, the One,
Allah, the independent, the one all seek;
He does not bear offspring, nor was He born
And there is nothing equal to Him.[88]

This truth, as clear as water in the desert and as laden as the word 'love' with proof of the heart at work, I give thanks for because it reveals existence beyond and greater than all, and I realized through your proximity and unashamed tears that even during sleep I would not let go of the until–now futile ordeal and anguish. Everything visible is uncertain. Everything audible is misleading. And who doesn't know that in the eyes of a stranger, love cannot be explained – love that has no form that can be seen or heard, but is felt only by the soul and remembered in the heart?

But there is no need to be sad. You should rise and lurch to your knees like those saddled dromedaries that once did battle in the holy Sinai desert.

Not a camel like those snow-white fluffy plumed, double-humped toys with their elaborate gold-bridle and wedding

---

[88] This *sura* is 112, the *sura al-ikhlas*, which proclaims the oneness and absolute nature of Allah.
Qul huwa Allah hu ahad
Allah hu 's-samad
Lam yalid wa lam yulad
Wa lam yakun lahu kufuwan ahad

harness. Not, in other words, like the camel that was delivered from Alma-Ata and now lies serenely on the glass coffee table like a hillock in the Chimkent steppe. Not like that, but a camel of dark bay, lean and athletic, rampant and rippling with muscles.

One such camel, with moist-looking eyelashes, is there in our hall near the red frog from Taiwan, reflected in the mirror along with its anthropoid, smiling face and the variegated jasper vase, united in their mutually-mirrored worlds.

I bargained for it in jest in a gloomy shop on the Tunisian island of Djerba, as if passing through. The dealer in his red knitted hat caught my sleeve excitedly and swore that he recognized his long-lost brother, saying the price tag was just for American tourists and he would drop this exhorbitant price by a quarter, then half. To no avail. Why would I want a dewy-eyed Tunisian souvenir when for the same price I could buy a sturdy horse in the Urals or in the market at Krasny Bor?

'Then tell me your price!' screamed the dealer and I, just to get away, suggested a price ten times smaller than the original. 'Ah, do you want to kill me?' moaned this robust Tunisian, clutching his heart and wailing, before agreeing to the deal, without, I'm sure, being the loser.

Hued like a dark nut and sculpted from glossy leather, this camel was poised for a tough trek. It will always remind me of the Mediterranean Sea and the island with the oldest synagogue in all Arabian Maghreb;[89] of the ancient cities of

---

[89] The El Ghriba synagogue is thought to have been founded in the sixth century BCE when Jews fled to the island after the destruction of the Temple of Jerusalem by the Babylonians. It was the scene of a murder of three of the congregation by a security guard in 1985, and an Al Qaeda suicide bomb in 2002 which killed twenty-one people.

Sousse, Kairouan and Tunis, with their great mosques and forts, their stucco houses stippled with gold and glass, and their mazelike bazaars; of the desert home of the wild camel-herders, open to the sun and stars, with their cave houses honeycombed into the yellow sandstone, converging on a central funnel to the sky.

I vividly remember the road across the dry, sparkling salt of the Lake of Ghost Palms, with its shimmering mirages and huge sand roses of red, black, blue and precious green, its bubbling springs that feed the irrigation channels with singing, crystal water to sustain the amber dates and wild oranges ripening under the canopy of palm leaves. But maybe this memory is a mirage, too, a mirror of the senses, a wishful flash in the eye in hazy heat of the imagination that for centuries sought lush gardens and breezy oases to console its gaze.

Only the heart knows how honest and truthful the desert is, so kindred in life to the space between sleep and work...

Do you remember dismounting from those real rough and warm single-humped camels on the fringes of the vast Sahara, and sitting down on the barchan? Beyond this dune were countless dunes of white sand stretching on and on to the horizon, ever-shifting like waves in the sea as the sand moved in the tireless desert wind. We gaped at the vast, empty expanse, astonished by the clarity and completeness of the view in the mercifully early morning air – the constant movement of the desert, the light, ghostly touch of the wind, the arabesques of the sand, the fierce distance and, close to, the high, thin, crystal clear singing of the sand, which streamed through our fingers and flowed down the dune like an image of the water so longed for by the parched.

I still hear the whisper of the desert breeze, reminding my timid soul of the authenticity of this world in which the green of foliage and blooming flowers and springs are but accidental and sudden apparitions that miraculously bring life and soul to the desert whose grateful tears comprehend the green goodness of Allah.

Without being able to see and feel the desert with your soul, how can you hope for transformation? The thought that a primal Garden of Eden could be a perpetual oasis is meaningless. And so, in Oman's south there is the ferocious terrain of Dhofar...

It is a vast, arid place — a huge plateau etched with rocky ridges and fragmented by wind-scoured, needle-like rocks: a fatal wasteland seared by the sun and withered by the hot and blinding wind to its last grain of sand, its last dead stone in dried-up valleys and its last naked gorges.

All year round, among rare ossified strumps of trees and skeletal bushes, this is death's dominion, its arena of triumph over life, where the bony hand of the wind simply mixes sand from one barren waste to another. Everything here is an omen, a sign for the heart — even death and its imprint, the absence of life.

And this is because once a year, just as all hope evaporates in the scorching heat, so everything changes in an instant. The blazing wind, harbinger of Allah's word, suddenly stops, and invisibly another starts to blow — the moist life-giving ocean wind that Arabs here call the 'Wind of Plenty'.

'Be!' will utter Allah, and across the scorched and lifeless plateau and along the dead gulleys, thick wads of cumulus clouds will gather in the air, curling dark, grey and moist — and down will come the monsoon rains, crashing to the ground like waterfalls, transforming the desert in just a few days into a blooming Eden filled with murmuring rivers, swooping birds, fluttering moths and buzzing dragonflies – and from the desert sands of Arabia will race herds of gazelles.

Above, in the rain-washed crystal radiance, the leaves will rustle to reveal the gift of the all-encompassing, high green mercy of the Unity, resurrected and excruciatingly alive. Sacral, aromatic resins will move in the channels of Abyssinian myrrh trees, their notches oozing thick, pink-yellow myrrh; of balm of Gilead *Commiphora gileadensis,* that wonderful bush that exudes pure, golden tears, the forerunner of the healing balm of Mecca; and of the frankincense tree *Boswellia sacra,* created by the will of Allah alone, whose lingering incense, grey pearl copal gum, fragrant resin and soft oil of Allah will later burn around countless icons and crucifixes – in Buddhist temples in Kyoto and churches in Jerusalem, in Hindu ashrams and the monastery cloister of Saint Catherine under Mount Sinai, in Moscow's churches and in the orthodox cathedral in London's Ennismore Gardens.

The bounty of the Dhofar monsoons lasts just three months, but, like true love in a human life, is sufficient to sustain happiness and hope. Anyone who foresees with the heart the bloom and green of the rocky, waterless desert also anticipates the meaning of their existence – before and after the brief accident of death.

...forgive and have mercy...what delight and what sadness there is in this suspended promise of the Garden! Like the grace and complaisance of loose sand – like the liquid freshness of your flowing wind that cools your cheeks and brow with angels' caresses – and makes you believe in the changeability of fate...

White sand streaming down the face of the dune portends the peace to come; the soothing desert wind fans the face and allows the heart to see that the scope of existence may be born, granting a moment of bliss in the blistering wilderness, a moment that invisibly concentrates the entire green flow of eternity – and that verdant Garden may be seen by the heart amid the dry sands, where the traveller, with nothing to obstruct his path, needs only the will, the prayer and the way...

I know no other hint of Paradise as strong as these yearly resurrections in the desert – reminding us that hope alone can be transformed into a gift of heaven. Everything that exists is a sign for us, but it requires not patience to understand their primary meaning but the imperceptible triumph over oneself.

After making up for my lost sleep and pulling myself together, I began to venture out along the pavement by the man-made channel of the river, which appears to flow straight through the town but in fact meanders, twists and turns, so that the gingerbread mansions on their green heights seem to spin around the crowning vertex of the Hotel Imperial.

This gyre of old houses, hotels, spas, churches, colonnades, pillars, monuments, bridges and gardens is striking when you walk not staring at your feet but with eyes uplifted to the colourful clutter of plastered masonry that steps its way up the steep slopes of the green river gorge – and that stubborn mutual dejection and heaviness of the heart is transformed by the ever-shifting perspective of Karlovy Vary into the ghostly

and wearying fantasy of the classic erstwhile Carlsbad, redolent with the presence of Goethe, yes Goethe and Beethoven... and Casanova, because even he fits into the dictionary of characters and life stories conjured by foreign words:

Allegro ...Jacobin...[90]

Unseduced by the idleness of the baths, I walked all through the steep little streets of Carlsbad, visited every park and garden, every museum and every church; viewed every shop window display, where the consoling allure of dark-cherry and flame-coloured garnets in gold and silver filigree lodged in my memory – the allure, too, of bracelets, pendants and necklaces, ear-rings and rings, colourful porcelain ladies and cavaliers, of crystal vases and their sparkling traceries of misty blue glass giving the impression of eternal summer, and incomparable crimson birds, flowers and dragonflies.

But more than any of these temptations with which I could have comforted you when your heart was oppressed, I remember the blue and green gem-like cameos in miniature oval mountings, in the milky purity of which one could see limitless perspectives and hidden distances in weightless stone. Their subtle carved curves caught in an enchanted mist every detail of antique hairstyles and silvery, snowy, angelic female heads, and the innocence of youth and icy purity of perfection glowed within the stone's depths to reveal not the beautiful image of a woman's face, but the incorporeal, fleeting impression in blue and green of the unattainable, softly shimmering essence of a woman's soul...

---

[90] Here the author includes a long, alphabetical list of foreign words that have been imported into everyday Russian.

This was the pure ideal, beyond adornment, of the Immortal Beloved, a mental image of perfection so transformed that any person, having taken the healing waters and looking nowhere in particular, might consider it unattainable and, so, unnecessary, as they strolled on doctor's orders past the displays on Laznenskaya Street and the Staroluzhskyi waterfront to the luxurious Hotel Pupp – unaware that on the site of this grand hotel was an ancient house nicknamed 'God's Eye on the Old Meadow' and it was to these now vanished rooms that Beethoven wrote hastily from a cottage in the Austrian-Czech town of Teplice, goading the paper with wild flourishes and curlicues:

6th July [1812], in the morning

My angel, my all, my very self – Only a few words today and at that in pencil (yours) – I shall not be certain of my rooms here until tomorrow – what a useless waste of time – Why this deep grief when necessity speaks – can our love endure except through sacrifices, through not demanding everything. Can you change it, that you are not wholly mine, I not wholly yours – Oh God, look out on the beauties of nature and comfort your heart with what must be – Love demands everything and with good reason – that's how it is with me to you, and with you to me. Only you forget so easily that I must live for me and for you as well; if we were wholly united you would feel the pain as little as I – My journey was a fearful one; I did not arrive here until 4 o'clock yesterday morning. Short of horses the post-coach chose another route, but what an awful one; at the stage before the last I was warned not to travel at

night; they tried to frightened me about a forest, but
that only made me more eager – and I was wrong.
The coach broke down on the wretched road, a bottomless mud road. If the coachmen hadn't been with
me I would have got bogged down on the way. Ester-
hazy, travelling the usual road here, had the same fate
with eight horses that I had with four – Yet I got some
pleasure out of it, as I always do when I successfully
overcome difficulties – Now a quick leap from internal
things to external. We'll surely see each other soon; and
today I cannot share with you the thoughts I have had
during these last few days aboutg my own life – If our
hearts were always close together, I would have none
of these. My heart is full of so many things to say to
you – ah – there are moments when I feel that speech
amounts to nothing at all – Cheer up – remain my true,
my only treasure, my all as I am yours. The gods must
send us the rest, what for us must and shall be –

Your faithful
LUDWIG.

Evening, Monday, 6th July

You are suffering, my dearest creature – only now have
I learned that letters must be posted very early in the
morning on Mondays to Thursdays – the only days on
which the mail-coach goes from here to K. – You are
suffering – Oh, wherever I am, you are with me, I talk
to myself and to you[,] arrange [it] that I can live with
you, what a life!!!! as it is!!!! without you – pursued by
the goodness of mankind hither and thither – which

I as little want to deserve as I deserve it – Humility of man towards man – it pains me – and when I consider myself in relation to the universe, what am I and what is He – whom we call the greatest – and yet – herein lies the divine in man – I weep when I reflect that you will probably not receive the first report from me until Saturday – Much as you love me – I love you more – But do not ever conceal yourself from me – good night – As I am taking the baths I must go to bed – Oh God – so near! so far! Is not our love truly a heavenly structure, and also as firm as the vault of heaven?

Good Morning, On 7th July

Though still in bed, my thoughts go out to you, my Immortal Beloved, now and then joyfully, then sadly, waiting to learn whether or not fate will hear us – I can live only wholly with you or not at all – Yes, I am resolved to wander so long away from you until I can fly to your arms and say that I am really at home with you, and can send my soul enwrapped in you into the land of spirits – Yes, unhappily it must be so – You will be the more contained since you know my fidelity to you. No one else can ever possess my heart – never – never – Oh God, why must one be parted from someone I so love? And yet my life in V[ienna] is now a wretched life – Your love makes me at once the happiest and the unhappiest of men – At my age I need a steady, quiet life – can that be so in our connection? My angel, I have just been told that the mailcoach goes every day – therefore I must close at once so that you may receive the letter at once – Be calm, only by a calm consideration of our existence can we achieve our purpose to live together – Be calm – love me – today – yesterday – what tearful longings for you – you – you – my life – my all – farewell. Oh continue to love me – never misjudge the most faithful heart of your beloved.

forever yours
forever mine
forever ours

What an unquenchable authenticity of feeling, what an explosion of mute silence – but how much analysis, how many guesses have been expended on these letters!

Julie Guicciardi, whose name is forever tied to the Moonlight Sonata; Therese von Brunswick, for who Beethoven wrote *Für Elise*: neither of these he called Immortal Beloved – and only Antonia Brentano, a married woman and mother of four, who Beethoven met in Vienna, could have received these letters in Carlsbad.[91] Earlier that same summer there was a famous scandal in Teplice, where a moody Beethoven was walking with Goethe, who lightly touched his hat as they passed through a thicket of Austrian imperial high-society, obliging the great poet to slow down politely. Waiting for Goethe further on, away from the aristocratic melee, Beethoven declared: 'I waited for you because I honour and revere you as you deserve, but you showed those gentleman far too much respect!'

---

[91] As the author says, there has been endless speculation on the identity of Beethoven's Immortal Beloved, but the candidate who now has the most widespread support is actually Josephine von Brunswick, the recipient of other love letters in which she is referred to as Only Beloved.

Such intemperateness jarred with Goethe and persuaded him thereafter to write of Beethoven's 'unbridled' nature. But just how much drama can a man fit into two months?

On 25 July, on the way to a concert set for 6 August, Beethoved stayed at the same 'God's Eye' guest house as the Brentano family. On 7 August, he went with the family to the Frantiskovy Baths, where they all spent the night in the Two Golden Lions hotel. On 8 September, Beethoven returned alone to Carlsbad and again met Goethe.

Antonia 'Tonie' Brentano, about whom very little is known, left Vienna at the end of that year 1812, and she and Beethoven never met again.

Is this sad? Maybe, but could any woman alive have born such immense passion and such despair? And was it really to her, a woman so different from those Beethoven shared his philosophical thoughts that he wrote so from the tempest of his silence? With others, and even with Antonia's sister-in-law Bettina Brentano, a beauty and intellectual who later became famous through the publication of her letters to Goethe and inspired Marina Tsvetaeva,[92] Beethoven engaged in very different conversations, as recorded in one of Bettina's letters.

When I open my eyes I must sigh, for what I see is contrary to my religion, and I must despise the world which does not know that music is a higher revelation than all wisdom and philosophy.

God, what heights do exist! What a blaze of understanding is possible! Yet it seems always, always to happen in the immense

---

[92] Marina Tsvetaeva (1892-1941) one of the greatest Russian poets of the early Soviet Era.

loneliness of glistening icy peaks surrounded only by sky. How can you call from this cold and lofty remoteness to an earthly woman who, to anyone that aspires, is nothing else but the unattainable incarnation of the divine peace of creation? But this peace is in the Unity of God. Yet through which woman – in the mutual and only mutual sacrifice – will the rising God be visible? About Beethoven it was said he was constantly in love, but isn't it strange that only to this woman, little known to historians and uncelebrated by fame, only to this woman belonged the authentic, true cry of his great spirit and child's soul, unseasoned by philosophy or music?

Of course, you can speculate, guess or invent endlessly about this impossible passion – but I will not: its rare authenticity will not be marred by some accidental intervention. Let the name of the Immortal Beloved shine in mystery, like the shining green veil, the yashmak over the earthly features, of the perfect cameo – like the faint murmur of the eternal music of the leaves and opaline springs of Karlovy Vary…

That authenticity, suddenly appearing out of the despair of a man's silence, goes on independently of time, circumstances and sights. In the outsider's eyes the Immortal Beloved doesn't need a name, and to the woman is due, as to the soul, the deference, reticence and undisclosure. Let her shimmer, like a brief glance from beneath the pearl-grey veil, a magical flash through the fine muslin of a yashmak, that guards the heart and maintains the mystery of the soul.

After all, there is that distant secret of the ideal, the beckoning secret that I cannot touch even partly by writing – the secret hieroglyphs of the heart are beautiful, like the cryptic reality of the world. Any passer-by, walking along the old meadow – even the one that cannot see the now vanished bridges with their sculptures of Czech saints and the lost summer houses with their antique columns and the ghosts of houses long gone – even he carries in his heart at least the vestiges, the fine ash of his original dreams, and his face, if you look closely, holds the faint glow and radiant reflections of long-ago-constricted or vainly-wasted aspirations. And it seems to him sometimes that the inexpressible is preferable to words, as the authentic is preferable to replicas – and that everything that is too obvious steals from the soul the golden mystery of life, giving in return only what easily fades, like torn-off flowers.

So the notion of the yashmak and veil is an opportunity to keep the ideal, stolen from the people, who have forgotten that a woman is a soul, and for a person's soul, exposure leads to vulnerability. The mystery shields the naked tenderness – it is an intercession and protection given by Allah to those who protect themselves in order to find their place in the Unity without fear.

But Beethoven, whose green patina-ed bronze monument has found its place in a mountain ravine near a bend of the Tepla surrounded by red-leaved silver birches and exquisite bird-cherries, keeps walking in his masculine way, keeps clenching his fist and hunching beneath the sombre rain, keeps walking in the direction of the vanished 'God's Eye' hotel, his doom-laden soul emerging as the storm turns his awkward tenderness to despair – the inevitable music of frenzied and unanswered love to the world and to sacrificial wisdom, granted instead of simple human happiness...

You saw him so well, striding to the Immortal and Nameless Beloved, but after getting lost, walking on – into the eternity of the Unity...

Pity Beethoven — as he, grim-faced,
Through the vile and dark night raced.
Heedless of the waters' roar,
Through Carlsbad's sleeping streets he tore.

His speech was slurred and not quite sane.
He sped on through the gloom. In vain,
He clutched the air and clenched his fist
To crush to nought the damp night mist.

The awful storm brooks no escape.
The lightning twists into the shape
Of a vast tornado's maw —
No mortal can pass through this war.

Cold rain rams his massive brow.
Balls of lightning hunt him now.
Sharp whips of wind about him lay.
Fate drives him on; he must obey.

His green frock-coat is soaking wet.
But he cannot hear it yet!
The crash, the floods, land going under…
And then the booming claps of thunder.

Oh yes, wake up, and clap the sight:
Beethoven striding through the night![93]

In the meanwhile, the mountain groves of Carlsbad are green
with oak and chestnut, both of the beech family, with leaves

---

[93] Poem by Lydia Grigorieva.

that can be plain or pinnate – a sweet-sounding word – and shade-tolerant maple with its palmate or compound-pinnate leaves and flowers in hanging yellow racemes and seeds with wings like dragonflies called samaras.[94]

After climbing close to the town, I woke up and became bold enough to venture deeper into the mountains by steep paths I hadn't previously trod. Starting out from his monument, one of those trails, known as Beethoven's Path, runs away alongside the Tepla clinging to the mountain foot, then curls under a bridge before winding up Beech Mountain by what I must stay is a pretty stiff climb.

But climbing is good for you, the more so if at the top, amid young firs and pines, soft green mosses and blueberry bushes, you can catch your breath on the kindly provided bench in the sun-dappled shade beneath the beeches. From here the path beckons you on around the mountain, running almost level, with each new bend revealing gaps through which are visible tall silver-birch groves on the lower slope and wonderful views over Carlsbad to distant vales and hills, swathed in the unity of infinitely varied shades of spring green – dark pines and darker spruce, light birch and lighter limes and brightest of all the beeches in their quiet motley hues, rising amid a green mist of bushes.

Recovering my composure, I find a handy stick and set off – rather proud of myself, in a very human way, of achieving such an ascent. A man needs solitary moments like this, like this elevated walk among the peaks, like a fleeting moment of mundane heroism, to verify the power of love. Long may they last, the satisfactions of slight achievements. And already my legs are carrying me on, my heart has stopped thump-

---

[94] Or more simply maple 'keys'.

ing and I am striding on along this broad path, perhaps trod many times over the centuries, yet for me it's the first time, and I have no idea where it leads.

The pale trunks of beeches glow inwardly and each is like Lady Godiva in their silent chiaroscuro, in their veils of golden light. Streams tumble from the heights over steps of mossy riffles. Chirruping tits and cooing doves. The hollow tremolo of a woodpecker rings out in the forest.

Walk – and the fresh mountain dew drips from the branches and scatters into a soft golden rain that moistens the soil. Yellow-green racemes of maples are already shedding their covers to reveal those seed carriers or keys that will whirl away on the wind, a harbinger of the time when the trees will lose their leaves too. But even in this loss, they reveal their vigorous growth and life.

You know how in these forests the azure of the broad sky glows through the green canopy and topmost branches – it seems in these blue depths shines the path to happiness, the sense of overcoming your own flesh in the ascent to the Unity as you feel with your whole being the forest, the mountains and the air – that every-instant, never-ending, manifold life completion. Along the path, dandelions ripen with greenness and lily of the valley[95] shyly hide.

And to top it all, there in the middle of the path is a stone recess from which issue crystal clear drops of water – a tiny spring called 'Lifewater', unexpected, long-awaited, like a joyful awakening. The drops splash into a battered aluminium saucepan brimful with pure water shimmering with the reflection of the bright sky.

---

[95] The lily of the valley is often considered a symbol of man's power to envision a better world.

Then with a cautious touch to the lips, the icy, vivifying water is swallowed in a single gulp with childish delight, unearned but so utterly gratifying that it seems to merge entirely with all those quenching consolations of the past – the water bought in plastic jugs on the dunes of the Tunisian Sahara; the monsoon rains in arid Dhofar; the sudden meadows along the dry courses of the Volga and Kama; the autumn freshness of the Ilet and the radiance of the Mari lakes; the vivid aquamarine of Teletskoye and the sheer, snowy bliss of the Altai cascades on the ascent to the Altyn-tuu plateau; the deep, cold blue flow of the Rhone beneath the Pope's Palace at Avignon; the ancient well of the Cordoba mosque in whose subtle mirror of the centuries is reflected the sun moving in the swaying branches of orange and lemon trees; and the silvery murmur of the amazing fountains and carved channels in the Spanish Alhambra Palace with its arches spun with fine stone tracery that signify there is no winner on the Earth but Allah.

That small gulp yields the simple, great truth of the path and clarifies the authenticity of memorable existences – merging in living conjugation the past, future and present, since this is the same earthly water that in its timeless cycle is not separated into wells and springs, rivers and lakes, oceans, clouds and rain, but bound as a whole in the service of Allah to the continuing path of immortal, challenging and conscientious life.

After splashing my face with water, I finally woke from my slumber and once more I wanted to share between us this simple moment of thirst-quenching and consoling ablution and compliance with Allah that brought so much alive the Unity of Islam. So, no longer feeling lonely, I bravely prayed amid the rustling Bohemian forest, prayed and believed that one day I will be heard, because around me all was so ineffably bright and fresh that to feel and understand the point and meaning of the slightest action of life was, God, so easy – like drinking water from joined palms, like breathing out thanksgiving for the truth of human destiny. In dreams, and work, in torment and debt, in love and in freedom: let it be Thy will.

ABOUT THE FISHING ROD

It wasn't long after Masha Baratynskaya's husband died that she remembered a day from her childhood when she caught a small fish on a handmade fishing rod. Her husband had been ill for a long time, and in his last years he had needed continual, daily care. Nobody ever took such care of me, Masha was saying during the wake, and it was true. Her husband had lived for fifteen years with a kidney machine until a transplant was finally found. The transplant had worked remarkably well – until he suddenly had a stroke and died. It was so infuriating it would make anyone cry!

But she remembered that long ago day. It was October, just when it all starts dripping and drizzling – and out of nowhere come gusts of chilly air that whip up the yellow and blushed leaves, and make the grass shiver. But this time the trees were calm after Moscow's bustling summer; they'd ceased to rustle and glow, since their leaves had drifted down on to the asphalt and were lying flat so they might be examined in all their vivid beauty. At first they looked like a school herbarium, and then, by chance, the goose's webbed feet that seemed so big when back in her infant days at the dacha near Zvenigorod.

There was a pond, overgrown around the edge by thick growths of herbs. On one side, there stood a copse of ancient maples and there huge leaves dropped off the

branches and whirled down to lay on the grass. Girls were
expected to gather these leaves to make natural wreathes to
wear on their heads, like some of Masha's friends did. Girls
were also expected to play dolls, but Masha didn't care to
do that either. Masha wanted to go fishing, like all the village boys. But to go with them would have been awkward
and they would have teased her. So she made a fishing rod
for herself.

First she cut off a walnut branch to make stick. Found a
goose feather to be her bobber. Found a rusty old nut to be
her sinker. Easy. The fishing line was harder. But she found an
old nylon string bag on the fence. Masha cut it up with scissors and knotted the lengths together to make her line. Then
she made a hook for herself out of a scrap of wire. Found a
worm. And went to the pond, to the far side where there still
spreading maples and undergrowth – and no people.

She threw out her arm to cast the line. The nut plunged in
with a plop, but the goose feather settled nicely afloat on the
water surface. Silence fell. It was mid-afternoon. The deep
shadows of the maples extended to the middle of the pond,
where the sun shone silver on the blue water between the
floating cumulus clouds. It was like a second sky in which,
every now and then, pond skaters scuttered – and you didn't
have to lift your head to see there would be no rain today,
and that the evening would be warm and filled with the
rich scent of phloxes. Phloxes smelled especially sweet after
the banya, when Masha wrapped her fair hair in a wet towel
and ran like some Little Muck[96] back to the wooden cottage, its windows shining in the dark. The fragrance of the

---

[96] Little Muck is a mischievous character in an Arabian nights kind of
cartoon who wears a very oversize turban.

phloxes was so heady then she wanted to stop and breath it in and bathe her entire soul in that intoxicating, lazy scent that came with neither end nor explanation, but that she just wanted to go on for ever and ever so today and tomorrow and always she could inhale such fragrance under the twinkling stars of Moscow's suburban summer night.

Then the goose feather suddenly flicked and sank below the surface. Masha tugged sharply – and out on the end of her makeshift line came a fish! A silvery fish with eyes like beads and red fins and tail. And it was alive. It wriggled off the hook and dropped glistening on the grass. Masha was startled. She hadn't expected to actually catch anything!

She cupped her hands around the fish, around its silvery, shimmering scales on which stuck bits of dry, golden grass. She carefully picked off some of the grass and lowered the fish back into the water between her palms. The fish was motionless for a while, then writhed and twisted its back and propelled itself from her hands out into the smoky, secret depths of the pond. So Masha had let her fish go, and she never went fishing again – in case she accidentally caught another.

Masha Baratynskaya was moving on down the avenue, trying not to step on wet leaves, trying not to slip. And she suddenly realized that autumn had already begun – and she, just her luck, had left her umbrella behind in her empty home, and so now shining drops ran down her cheeks, like the gathered drops that fall from the tips of leaves when it drizzles. She had forgotten how to cry at least ten years ago.

THE DOROTHEAN FIELDS

෬

HE DIDN'T UNDERSTAND HER – that will surely be written about us later as well, and will be as much right as wrong.

Of course, trying to understand you, a woman, is like trying to guess the future, a hopeless undertaking. You can say only one thing about the future: that with or without us it will go on, it will happen, it will carry forward the momentum of the world plan where opposites attract and things alike repel in accordance with the predestined balance of instantaneous mechanics of starry spheres and self-less hearts.

And so I, too, persisting in my daily exercise in an effort not to lose the rhythm of the vividly happening Carlsbad spring, kept on walking the surrounding highlands, a little slower as I ascended some of the steeper heights. In the end – on my third expedition – I finally climbed up to the high, spruce-covered summit known locally as the mountain of Eternal Life.

I reached it from the Thermal, from the bridge over the Tepla beneath which barely moving carp feed in the dark amber flow. Nearby, under the old silver birch leaves of the

Dvorak garden, a man often sits, who will for a fee cut out a paper silhouette of anyone walking along the promenade.

Luring passers-by to his subtle craft with a display of his best shadows, he works intently to capture each sitter, selecting key features, so that the difference between people's silhouettes gradually emerges, unique and distinct, caught with a single deft cut of the scissors.

But I can see that what once was an art becomes just entertainment. Remember that square Weimar album of silhouettes from the time of Goethe, that pantheon of past shadows. The skilful precision of those contours and configurations reveal with just a white background the perfect substance of a person, meeting it seems Goethe's yearning for an ancient harmony in life, for a kind of cosmic balance in which you can escape the day-to-day trifles in the simple and secret perfection of art's eloquent excision to the truth.

Such a theatre of silhouettes, which in Goethe's time were of the blue-blooded or of the outstanding minds of that classic age, long ago became commonplace, just like the wonderful Russian film animations of the fifties for which artists deftly cut characters from the shadows in the fashion of the day, now abandoned but will surely appear again sometime.

Of course, it's tempting for anyone to see their own existence as complete and exact, compositionally balanced and meaningful in content, like the graceful life of those paper shadows among the black trees, Greek busts and antique furniture of the Duke Karl-August von Saxe-Weimar[97] and his

---

[97] Charles Augustus was one of the key figures of the Germany enlightenment, and his court was renowned for its intellectual brilliance. One of his first acts on becoming Duke of Saxe-Weimar in 1775 was to bring Goethe to court and make him a privy councillor: 'People of

august family which so generously supported Goethe. But
in that now ghostly and charmed time, in which Casanova
appeared like an omen of the final death of the imprinted
god and all harmony, which not even those zealous Germans
Nietzsche and Schopenhauer could bring back. What can
you say of those others, those no more commonplace but
less gifted Werthers[98] who struggle with the grand illusions
of youth and plunge into pursuit of the sensual disappointment of things that can not only be seen but also touched.

The Unity cannot be seen, but if you look closely at the
silhouettes, shadows and contours of the age, then you may
see on the map leading away from this golden century, a fork
in the road where the ways of Casanova and Goethe entirely
diverge – to follow two different routes, two forever alien
perceptions of the world. And the life path of Casanova will
entirely melt away in the official chambers of ochre-walled
Duchcov, along echoing corridors hung with engravings
of long past places of sojourn – Venice, London, Paris and
other now redundant capitals – to the melancholy rooms of

---

discernment,' he said, 'congratulate me on possessing this man. His
intellect, his genius is known. It makes no difference if the world
is offended because I have made Dr Goethe a member of my most
important collegium without his having passed through the stages
of minor official professor and councillor of state.' Goethe's 'Sturm
and Drang' movement changed the stiffly classical Weimar court to a
youthful party.

[98] Goethe's *Sorrows of Young Werther* (1774) is the story of a romantic young man who shoots himself after his love Charlotte marries
another. It was one of the first best-sellers and made Goethe famous,
though later in life he regretted its youthful indulgence, only admit-
ting that: 'It must be bad, if not everybody was to have a time in his
life, when he felt as though Werther had been written exclusively for
him.'

that ageing resident where now stare portraits of the true celebrities of the age and silhouettes of lovers seduced and seducing turn sideways, along with various objects whose only essence is possession: blue and white Chinese vases, a clock with a moustached figure of a Turk with a chibouk pipe.[99] Those melancholy rooms with windows that now open towards the gates of this Baroque castle next to which is now pinned the indispensable-in-Europe commemorative plaque.

The creator of his own life story, how he strove in the silence, seeing only the divine view over the castle park to the distant Krusne mountains – and Casanova, as Voltaire witnessed, always hated mountains, just as he hated other views of nature, preoccupied it seems only with himself, like a man who stares at the calm waters of a lake and sees only his own reflection.

That's why I don't think that, while staying in Karlovy Vary, he could have climbed the slopes of the mountain of Eternal Life to see the surrounding vista, nor paused on the way up at that belvedere with the camera obscura, nor at that next stage where three crosses stand in proud commemoration of the victorious return of Catholicism to the fold of the Czech Hussites[100] which inspired Smetana with the idea

---

[99] In fact, none of these objects belonged to Casanova, but have been lent by Prague's Museum of Decorative Arts. The only object which did belong to him is the gilded, spindly-legged Rococo chair in which he died on 4 June 1798, at the age of seventy-three.

[100] In 1415, the judicial murder of Bohemian religious reformer Jan Hus sparked a Hussite revolution against the monarch, German aristocracy and the established Catholic church. For two decades, they defied international 'crusades', owing many victories to their charismatic general Jan Zizka and his novel 'war wagons'. The episode

for the national anthem Vltava. It is unlikely Casanova ever reached this place – perhaps because of his old age, perhaps because of his dislike of nature, or maybe just because the first stage was the site of the town's gibbet. I don't know. Anyway, he was always drawn to another arbour, rather lower down, near the river cliff that even now seems to attract lovers.

Erected by Duke Christian Clam-Gallas in honour of his love for Princess Dorothea of Courland,[101] this gloriette[102] above the Tepla gave its name to a wonderful little valley that connects old Carlsbad (and the God's Eye house) to the Postal Court. Since 1791, it has been called the Dorothean Fields. In just that year, Mozart died and was buried hurriedly in a pauper's grave; Schiller came to Carlsbad; Goethe, after an official trip to Venice, became director of the Duke of Weimar's library and museum, and Casanova, that arch-sponger, was beaten up on a Duchcov street – and maybe he brought it on himself with his conceit and truculence.

Perhaps you see him above the Fields of Dorothea, between the columns of the ancient rotunda, sitting crookedly with his hooked chin resting on his cane: Girolama Giacomo, once the luscious-lipped Jacobus Casanova de

---

became the basis for a Czech national epic and a forerunner of the Reformation.

[101] Dorothea von Medem (1761-1821) was a German noblewoman famous for her intellectual salons and also her romantic affairs with men like Talleyrand and the great Finnish statesman Count Gustaf Mauritz Armfelt while on diplomatic missions to places like Karlovy Vary and St Petersburg for the Polish court on behalf of her husband Peter von Biron, Duke of Courland.

[102] A rotunda on a high point in a landscaped park.

Seingalt – poor Giacomo, who was never much loved by his actress mother and took revenge on all women through the tragicomedy of his life, who wasted a faint sparkle of talent in attempts to shine next to true genius – a sad and bitter egotist, whose much vaunted romancing didn't leave in the world even an arbour for a couple to linger, just the solitary, shabby striped armchair in the Duchcov Castle in which he died as he lived, alone.

Yet how many multilingual tourists, how many men, visiting Duchcov, strive superstitiously to touch the arm-rest of that death's chair, in the hope that some of that legendary monkey knack might rub off – and the seducer's ghost has escaped these baroque chambers to seduce the Christian world into his delusion of life more persuasively than the authentic, but almost forgotten, voice of Goethe. Casanova's shade triumphs as self-obsession and the lure of bodily temptations now trample on the spirit, and on any understanding of each other that is not rooted in simple desire.

Casanova's way...wasn't it the high road to unbelief and mortality, the road that leads the whole sensual world back-wards from the Unity to a momentary hysteria of the flesh – flesh orphaned without its soul. This way is so different from the way drawn by Goethe, the origins of which he ascribes, with the humility of genius, not to himself but to the Sufi path of feelings described by Laurence Sterne: 'Everything that is happening, derived in the present, seems quite natural and inevitable, but we find ourselves at a crossroads and it is because we are losing sight of those who sent us on the right path. That's why I want to draw your attention to the man who ... initiated and facilitated the further development of the great era of cleaner understanding of the human soul, the noble era of tolerance and tender love.'[103] And remember that Radishchev,[104] too, owes his journey to Sterne – and so all the primary works of Russian prose seem to merge two great spiritual movements, two great prototypes, in their memory of Habbakuk[105] and Sterne.

But what a bitter joke it is that in the Duchcov library, which Casanova, regardless of his role as librarian, was too self-occupied to organize, the tourists are regaled with the emotive sound of Mozart's *Lacrimosa*[106]...as if Mozart is the sun to compassionately spread the warmth of life, like the rays of the natural sun that penetrate the oak, the birch, the pine and the clumps of spruce that cast a dappled shade on the sandy trail rising through the forests up the mountain of Eternal Life on past the Three Crosses.

I walked all the way up here, too, and the tall crosses rose like man-made trees, surprising in their bareness, as if expecting new crucifixes. Pausing a while for reflection (and

---

[103] Goethe was a great admirer of Sterne. As he says, 'Yorick Sterne was the finest spirit that ever worked. To read him is to attain a fine feeling of freedom; his humour is inimitable, and it is not every kind of humour that frees the soul.'

[104] Alexander Radishchev (1749-1802) was the first great radical of Russian literature, whose famous Journey from St. Petersburg to Moscow (1790), describing conditions in Russia, earned him exile to Siberia and the admiration of Pushkin and many others.

[105] This is not the Biblical prophet but Petrov Habbakuk, a recalcitrant seventeenth-century village priest who was martyred for his opposition to the religious reforms of Nikon and for his championing of Old Beliefs. His prose work Avakum's Life is said by some to have inspired the long tradition of tragic and rebellious holy men in Russian literature, as the author is saying here.

[106] From the *Requiem*.

wanting a drink after the climb), I imagined that if I was climbing just to see these Carlsbad crosses, to see at the end their bareness on the waterless peak, my soul and heart might have been overwhelmed with disappointment – so true were they to the Islamic unity of other trees in their bareness, their stark silhouettes a simplification of existence – like a deliberate ellipsis in the silent grammar of nature; like the surety that everything is said by God with a single, balanced silence; like art that reduces to human level already perfect and independently immortal life.

However purposefully these crosses stood in my Muslim path to the Unity, though, they did not signify the end but another stage on the ascending route to understanding.

The present, in which we lament so many imperfections, is all too often built on a foundation of superstition and partial conceptions, on the idolization of our own nationality and the differences between cultures that are insidiously transformed to unquestioned fact.

But what really is indisputable fact today – when the whole world has been turned upside down and legends depart even as we desperately try to catch them flapping away like unpegged clothes in the wind of history? We are scared to lose our central myth – for what are we left with? But the truth is the truth only when it is common to all; and isn't the cure just, when it returns the joy of unity?

Yet how hard it is for us to accept that our sense of history is so often coloured by myths that the resulting moral culture may have very strange roots. Even recently it has been possible to insist, like the Greeks who condemned Socrates and the Romans who were obsessed with order, that a myth is more important than the truth because it provides peace and continuity and keeps the common people in the grip of custom. So a legend, sanctified over time, reaches beyond the hearts and minds it originally served, and some of the best human minds become convinced that the national or traditional sense of morality is the ultimate truth. Was it this sense of morality the historic Goethe meant when he responded to Eckermann a year before his death?

> 'Altogether,' said I [Eckermann], 'the Evangelists, if you look closely into them, are full of differences and contradictions; and the books must have gone through strange revolutions of destiny before they were brought together in the form in which we have them now.'
>
> 'It is like trying to drink out at sea,' said Goethe, 'to enter into an historical and critical examination of them. It is the best way, without farther ado, to adhere to that which is set down, and to appropriate to oneself so much as one can use for one's moral strengthening and culture. However, it is pleasant to get a clear notion of the localities...'[107]

Yes, the locality... Whoever is thirsty won't forget the existence of the desert where wells and springs are Allah's reminder of Him. Thus, in the Land of Midian,[108] in the middle of the rocky desert mountains, is the ancient monastery of St Catherine, founded in the sixth century around an

---

[107] Goethe's conversations with Eckerman, 1831, 335. All the translations quoted in this chapter from the Conversations are from the HXA version available online.

[108] Either a place or a people (or both) mentioned in the Bible and the Qur'an, and thought by some to be in northwest Arabian peninsular on the shores of the Red Sea. Midian is said to be the son of Abraham.

even more ancient shepherd's well, which even today supplies water to the monks and keeps the olive garden green in an arid valley under Sinai mountain. This is said to be the life-giving well by which Musa-Moses settled long ago after fleeing Egypt for the first time. It was by this well that, according to monastery legend, Moses defended the seven daughters of Jethro from attack by shepherds – and was given Jethro's daughter Zipporah as a wife in gratitude. Legend has it too that, nearby, Allah appeared to Moses in the burning bush,[109] that is now hidden in the stone grotto of the chapel, sheltered from the weather and the polyglot tourists, in the midst of who we submissively wandered up and down the stairs of the sacred precincts, trying to hear through the babel of tongues the quiet voice of Silence uniting us all:

O People of the Scripture, why do you argue about Abraham while the Torah and the Gospel were not revealed until after him? Then will you not reason? (The Holy Qur'an, 3:65)

So how do join in unity a feeling that looks sacred only when it's divided? In this Sinai monastery are still held many priceless treasures – Arabian mosaics, Byzantine icons,

---

[109] The holiest part of the monastery is the Chapel of the Burning Bush, often barred to visitors. Beneath the chapel's altar is a silver star reputed to mark the site of the flaming bush in which God appeared to Moses. The bush was said to have been transplanted a little way away and is still alive today, carefully tended by the monks. The Bible says the bush was not consumed by the flames, so the Orthodox name for it in the author's Russian original is the Unburnt Bush. The bush is a bramble of the rose family called Rubus sanctus, which includes the raspberry and blackberry.

Russian and Greek manuscripts, chalices and goblets studded with gems and, above all, a collection matched only by the Vatican of illuminated manuscripts in Greek, Coptic, Arabic, Armenian, Hebrew, Church Slavonic,[110] Syriac, Georgian and other languages.

Also there in St. Catherine's monastery hanging on the walls of the ancient stone chambers in the sacred gloom is a copy of the Charter of Privileges, bestowed on the monastery by the Holy Mohammed – Prophet of Islam:[111]

This is a message from Muhammad ibn Abdullah, as a covenant to those who adopt Christianity, near and far, we are with them.

Verily I, the servants, the helpers, and my followers defend them, because Christians are my citizens; and by Allah! I hold out against anything that displeases them.

No compulsion is to be on them.

---

[110] The primary language of the Orthodox Church in Russia.

[111] Author's footnote: The Orthodox writer Valerii Alfeeva writes in her book *The Pilgrimage to Sinai*: 'A large sheet with frayed edges and ragged around the corners is a copy of the famous Charter of Privileges, granted to the monastery in the year 624 (622 – Ravil Bukharaev) by Mohammed – who at that time, some evidence suggests, lived in the mountains of the Sinai desert. This pledge from the founder of Islam and its prophet is an amazing testament to his religious tolerance: his promise to monasteries, monks and Christians to not only protect their integrity and guarantee their freedom in the Sinai desert (and beyond right across the world – RB), but also to provide special benefits, such as exemption from taxes, even in wartime, security holdings and by updating the temples. The original Charter has a patterned small mosque in the margin, and the signatures in Arabic script of 21 approved witnesses, and is now kept in the treasury of the sultan in Constantinople.'

Neither are their judges to be removed from their jobs nor their monks from their monasteries.

No one is to destroy a house of their religion, to damage it, or to carry anything from it to the Muslims' houses.

Should anyone take any of these, he would spoil God's covenant and disobey His Prophet. Verily, they are my allies and have my secure charter against all that they hate.

No one is to force them to travel or to oblige them to fight.

The Muslims are to fight for them.

If a female Christian is married to a Muslim, it is not to take place without her approval. She is not to be prevented from visiting her church to pray.

Their churches are to be respected. They are neither to be prevented from repairing them nor the sacredness of their covenants.

No one of the (Muslim) nation is to disobey the covenant until the Day of Judgement.

> Mohammed, the Herald of Allah

This covenant was written in Medina during the Prophet's submortem year (a year before the death), the year of his final pilgrimage to Mecca, when he spoke from Mount Arafat to all who could hear then and in hope that all of us will hear now:

And remember – you are all equal. All people, no matter to what family, tribe or race they belong to and no matter what position they hold, are equal... Nobody has a right and superiority over others. From now on you're like brothers, and everything that was said by me, you must spread to all the lands of the world. Maybe, someone who didn't hear me today will extract from what I said more grace, than those who did hear.[112]

Within the bounds of St Catherine's monastery from time immemorial has stood a small mosque for those Muslims who protected the monastic caravans from bandits as they trailed across the desert. In the flurry of the visit and throngs of people, I failed to make it into that mosque, which was converted to a warehouse long ago, and so I made my wanderer's prayer on the side of the gorge on Moses mountain, with a view over the monastery with its high, fortified walls, and over the olive groves and vineyards watered by the holy well, around which rise spikes of cypress – *that noble tree of victory over death, the regal tree of silences* – and all amid a hubbub of tourists, waiting their turn to walk on the time-polished tiles, have a peek here and there, take a photo next to the Burning Bush Chapel – and then return to their air-conditioned coaches, not forgetting a quick ride for five Egyptian dollars on the ochre Bedouin camel, just to make sure they get the authentic feel, of which they will remember everything but the keen voice and music of Silence.

It's impossible to hear Allah through the chatter.

Yet don't words themselves hold their own sacraments? Sometimes, one word in a hundred touches a hidden string – and sets off the living vibration of some aching need or revelation from the past. And so the cypress, that living utterance, with its invisible voice that in the gentle motion of the wind

---

[112] Mohammed's Farewell Sermon, the Khutbah, given on 9 March 632 in the Uranah valley of Mount Arafat near Mecca in Saudi Arabia. This wording is from the author. Other sources translate it differently.

merges colours and patterns, and the sinews of its trunk and branches, into a single flesh which rises to a slowly sweeping, sky-steep pinnacle – so this magical cypress becomes a spectacle that lodges in the heart. Then, wherever you are, however you are accomplishing the feat of living every day – you'll hear the spiced silence of the cypress avenues that embroider the mountain slopes in lost New Athos in Abkhazian,[113] or maybe the noble cypresses that answer without a sound to the distant whisper of the Mediterranean in the ruins of Carthage – or those elegant cypress exclamation marks in precious conversation with the gardens of the Alhambra and Cordoba. But that's later and in mind-wearying tears.

For now, just one utterance: the expression of undying and time-conquering love, the love that is dissolved in the Unity, the love for which a single word can be enough – because in that word, as in the tiniest atom of creation, is concentrated the white energy of the entire world, bound by the fateful bonds of heart and heart. And without that all too hasty worldly cleverness, it becomes clear that it is not the person but their unselfishness and their love for God that leaves traces behind on Earth.

And to avoid leaving those footprints in vain, one should stay on the path – even it is one of those *terrenkur* exercise paths winding through the densely growing pines and spruces on top of the mountain of Eternal Life – the path to

---

[113] Abkhazian is a territory on the southwestern slopes of the Caucasus bordering the Black Sea that's a major source of dispute between Russia and Georgia. New Athos is an ancient coastal town, once settled by the Genoese, and renowned for its beautiful landscape of cypress avenues, lemon, orange, tangerine and olive groves and its gardens of palms, laurels, magnolias, oleander and eucalyptus.

the place known as Goethe's Belvedere. A *terrenkur*, especially in a mountain area, is never a trifle; if you try to climb straight across the bends, apart from the effort, you are confronted with another hazard. Fallen, smooth, glossy brown leaves carpeting the ground beneath the silver birches look completely harmless from a distance, but as you hurry on to them off the path, these dry leaves will slip under your foot, and even if you don't tumble and injure yourself then you'll lose two things: the goodness of the path and your natural balance.

You know of course that I'm not advocating being bound to the beaten path – only for the feeling and understanding of the path when it's under your feet.

Walking up to Goethe's Belvedere, I once turned off the path, easily tempted by a forest knoll on which there seemed to be a some kind of Roman temple with a wreckage of fluted columns that turned out to be the ruins of an old arbour. I was thinking about Goethe, whose favourite place in Karlovy Vary was neither this hill, nor even the peak of Eternal Life, but amid the wide open rustle of leaves and the purl of the river in the Dorothean Fields, where even now one path to the Beethoven statue is called Goethe's Path. I kept thinking that in the unity understood by the heart, there is nothing alien, if 'alien' is simply part of the progressive search for meaning. Clambering up over the slippery, tricksy leaves, I was pleasantly imagining sitting down on one of those fallen columns and taking a quiet puff on my pipe. But, here as well, life intervened in my plans – for there among the ruins, like a recurring story from an old Carlsbad engraving, a pair of young lovers were lying in each other's arms, and I, chancing upon them, was obliged to look away and hurry down the opposite slope, which was so steep and treacherous that I began to lament yielding to my temptation to leave the path.

The summit of Eternal Life was a disappointment. The site was planted with huge spreading dusky black spruces – like those in the paintings of Caspar David Friedrich – in which domes and spires suddenly shook and spiralled down to the ground in the wind. In the middle was an empty tower in amusing Gothic style with a café that was locked because of the rarity of pedestrians, so any hope of refreshment was quashed. The melancholy of emptiness blew upon me too, as I lingered at the pinnacle of Eternal Life among the darkling spruces rustling in the fading light.

As the twilight spread, the gothic outline of Goethe's Belvedere, the fruit of some architect's fancy, mingled its meaningless silence and desolation with the growing darkness of this kingdom of the shadows that drains the colour from the daylit world glowing with emerald leaves and sun-glinting green needles to leave an absolute and limitless greyness that was utterly assimilated into the imagination of those for who even Goethe who once walked here is a classic, completely western gothic ghost – a paper shadow, a phantom of the past, a silhouette in a frock coat framed by fluted pillars and allegorical statues...spare us! Was the purpose of the climb simply to rescue banale phrases and concepts?

God, what do we know, what do we remember about Goethe if we are spellbound by the magic of his name alone?

'Mountain peaks slumber in the dark of the night...'[114]

---

[114] This from Lermontov's famous short poem 'To Goethe':
Mountain peaks slumber
In the dark of the night;
Still valleys down under
Fill with misty grey light;
Nothing stirs on the road,

'Werther has been written already!'[115]
'This is stronger than Goethe's *Faust*...'[116]

And what if Goethe was a Muslim in spirit? Doesn't that sound crazy? Or an ancient pagan? That might sound sweeter to another heart. Yet – a collector of stones, plaster medallions and commemorative medals, copies of ancient sculptures; a connoisseur of engravings and picturesque landscapes; but an owner of a house so plain it looked like a pauper's – what did Goethe believe in?

29 July 1782: Goethe writes to Lavater, the author of a treatise on Pontius Pilate:

> Although I am neither an opponent of Christianity nor anti-Christian, I am determinedly not a Christian, so your Pilate and all that made a bad impression on me.

Not a Christian – an unbeliever then? No, I don't think so. One of Goethe's most diligent disciples, Eckermann suggests Goethe was a deeply religious man, writing on Sunday 4 January 1824:

No breeze shakes the trees...
You may set down your load
And rest if you please.

[115] The title of a story by Valentin Kataev (1897-1986) a Soviet novel whose entertaining approach to Soviet conditions transcended the officialese of so much socialist realist work.

[116] This is Stalin's famous comment added to the last page of Maxim Gorky's fairy tale A Girl and Death after hearing the author read it on 11 October 1931. The phrase has often since been used as an ironic complement on any literary work.

I believe in God, in nature and in the victory of good over evil, but my devotion was not enough, I still had to know that the trinity is one, and one in three ways – but it was at odds with my love of truth, in addition, I did not understand how I can be in any way useful.

Goethe, some say, believed in mind. Did his faith, like the Roman stoics, rest upon the confidence that a soul, relieved from passion, is blessed and immortal, while zeal is death to immortality? This is how the great Roman emperor-philosopher Marcus Aurelius wrote in his note books from 173 to 180 AD:

> What a soul is that which is ready to renounce its body at any moment, ready either to be extinguished or dispersed or to continue to exist; but this readiness must come from a man's own judgement, not from mere obstinacy, as with Christians, but considerately, with dignity and persuasively, without a show of tragedy.[117]

For Marcus Aurelius, stoicism worked well with the polytheism of the Roman pantheon. Goethe, who even in old age fell prey to the passion of his poetic heart, was a monotheist. Yet even he, with all his moral respect for Christianity, found church dogma too crowded, just as it was later for Leo Tolstoi, who also read Marcus Aurelius.

For Goethe, just as for Tolstoi, Jesus is human in his idealism:

Monday, 28th February 1831

Christ thought of a God, comprising all in one, to whom he ascribed all qualities which he found excel-

---

[117] Marcus Aurelius *The Meditations* Book 11.

lent in himself. This God was the essence of his own beautiful soul; full of love and goodness, like himself: and every way suited to induce good men to give themselves up trustingly to him, and to receive this Idea, as the sweetest connection with a higher sphere. But, as the great Being whom we name the Deity manifests himself not only in man, but in a rich, powerful nature, and in mighty world-events, a representation of him, framed from human qualities, cannot of course be adequate, and the attentive observer will soon come to imperfections and contradictions, which will drive him to doubt, nay, to despair, unless he be either little enough to let himself be soothed by an artful evasion, or great enough to rise to a higher point of view.[118]

But any Muslim will agree with these words with an easy heart, since the Christianity of Jesus himself, who never mentioned the Trinity, is an integral part of the Muslim's spiritual vision. Honest, Germanly-proper Eckermann continues:

> His opponents have often accused him of having no faith; but he merely had not theirs, because it was too small for him. If he spoke out his own, they would be astonished; but they would not be able to comprehend him.

But what sort of faith was it? Worldly and wise in the politics of life, Goethe never spoke of it openly, but that faith was – Islam. In his Weimar conversations, he again and again speaks of the Prophet and the vision of Islam, which he studied deeply when writing *West-Eastern Divan*. In the very

---

[118] *Conversations of Goethe* by Johann Peter Eckermann.

name of Goethe's last great poetic creation, there is a clear bond drawn between Islamic ideas and those of Western Christians.

Monday, 11ᵗʰ April 1827

It is very interesting to see with what doctrines the Mahometans start the work of education. As a religious foundation, they confirm their youth in the conviction that nothing can happen to man, except what was long since decreed by an all-ruling divinity. With this they are prepared and satisfied for a whole life, and scarce need anything further.

I will not inquire what is true or false, useful or pernicious, in this doctrine; but really something of this faith is held in us all, even without being taught. 'The ball on which my name is not written, cannot hit me,' says the soldier in the battlefield; and, without such a belief, how could he maintain such courage and cheerfulness in the most imminent perils? The Christian doctrine, 'No sparrow falls to the ground without the consent of our Father,' comes from the same source, intimating that there is a Providence, which keeps in its eye the smallest things, and without whose will and permission nothing can happen.

Then the Mahometans begin their instruction in philosophy, with the doctrine that nothing exists of which the contrary may not be affirmed. Thus they practise the minds of youth, by giving them the task of detecting and expressing the opposite of every proposition; from which great adroitness in thinking and speaking is sure to arise.

Certainly, after the contrary of any proposition has been maintained, doubt arises as to which is really true. But there is no permanence in doubt; it incites the mind to closer inquiry and experiment, from which, if rightly managed, certainty proceeds, and in this alone can man find thorough satisfaction.

You see that nothing is wanting in this doctrine; that with all our systems, we have got no further; and that, generally speaking, no one can get further.

In Goethe's comments here, there is the gist of Islam, and even if not expressed by a Muslim they show the mind of an Islamic philosopher. Yes, Goethe, for who the culture of Islam lay more in the field of ethnography, didn't really hide his concordance with the spiritual core of the Muslim faith, which began to deepen in 1813 after a German soldier brought him an ancient Arabian manuscript from Spain with the final sura of the Qur'an.

In the name of Gracious Allah the Merciful,
Say: 'I seek refuge with the Master of the Human Race
King of the Human Race
God of the Human Race
From the mischief of the sneaking evil tongue
From the one who whispers in people's hearts:
Evil tongued to the djinns and the Human Race.'[119]

This sura, which concludes the miracle of Qur'anic revelation, confirms the Unity of God, who holds all the names that in Christianity belong to the hypostases of the Trinity.

---

[119] See note 86 on page 149.

Why separate these Three, asks the Qur'an, if Allah in his sheltering Unity and mind-corresponding is at once God the Father, God the King that the church call Jesus and God the Holy Spirit – the One Holiness in the world? But whispering, whispering into the hearts of men are the djinns whose main purpose is to divide the world, and subvert the inseparability of God's Existence. This is what Goethe was thinking about, copying down this sura and believing its appearance in Weimar a divine omen. Only someone of his stature could see within his own little native Duchy things common to all mankind, the universal core of the good news of Islam that is so often overwhelmed by the brilliantly colourful folk culture of the visible material world.

5 January 1814. Goethe wrote to Trebur:

> Talking about the prophecies, I must tell you that today such things are happening that earlier prophets would not even allow to be spoken. Who a few years ago would suggest that our Protestant school would permit a Muslim to read verses from the Qur'an in the sacred liturgy? Yet it happened, and we also attended a church service in Bashkir and saw their Mullah and welcomed their Prince in the theatre. As a special favour to me, I was presented with a bow and arrows, which I will hang over the fireplace in eternal memory.

And several days later:

> Some of our particular religious ladies even ordered a translation of the Qur'an from the library.

A true Muslim is not someone who wears a gown and a skullcap for anyone to see, but one who acknowledges and glorifies the Unity of Allah, which, in accordance with God's creation, must be reflected in the unity of his soul and the unity of the world. This is Islam, and this Islam, which calls upon the mind and heart to perceive nature and believe in the complete logic of God's creation, Johann Wolfgang von Goethe clearly and unconditionally acknowledged:

'Närrisch, daß jede in seinem Falle
Seine besondere Meinung preist!
Wenn Islam Gott ergeben heißt,
In Islam leben und sterben wir alle.'[120]

Foolish, that each should testify
To praise their own especial view!
If Islam means give God his due,
In Islam we all live and die.

How well this sits with the words of the Prophet of Islam who said that every child is born in Islam, and it is parents and surroundings that make a Christian or Jew.

Goethe, who in 1772, even before *Werther*, tried but failed to complete a play about Mohammed,[121] was not simply try-

---

[120] This is from Goethe's poetic sequence *The West-Eastern Divan* written between 1814 and 1818. This life-affirming poetic cycle is a love poem to the fourteenth-century Persian poet Hafiz but also mirrored his romance with a young married woman, Marianne von Willemer – the subject of the sensual 'Suleika' poems.

[121] Based on a translation of the *Sura Al An'am*, the sixth chapter of the Qur'an which tells the story of Abraham who, by using his own rea-

ing pastiche in his Islamic poems; he lived in Islam's spiritual reality.

19 September 1831, Goethe writing to Louise Adele Schopenhauer:

We all live in Islam, no matter what form we have chosen to reassure ourselves.

1816, Goethe to Marianne von Willemer:

So we must remain in Islam (in complete subjection to God's will)...

20 September 1820, Goethe writing to Zelter:

And I cannot say anything else except I am here to hold on to Islam.

It is possible to quote many more examples of Goethe's spiritual closeness to Islam. They inevitably destroy the myth about the great citizen of the world as purely an admirer of the human mind, as well as many other ideas about him – for example, the fact that Goethe thought the duchy of Karl August, where he lived, a perfectly ordered state. Only one who agrees with Goethe's Islamic views can comprehend the depth of his attitude to the infinite problems of momentary politics. His words ring like a tocsin in the ruins of ours:

Sunday, 4th January 1824:

'Because I hated the Revolution, the name of the 'Friend of the powers that be' was bestowed upon me.

---

son, stops worshipping celestial bodies and turns towards Allah so that he could receive revelation.

That is, however, a very ambiguous title, which I would beg to decline. If the 'powers that be' were all that is excellent, good, and just, I should have no objection to the title; but, since with much that is good there is also much that is bad, unjust, and imperfect, a friend of the 'powers that be' means often little less than the friend of the obsolete and bad.'

'... nothing is good for a nation but that which arises from its own core and its own general wants, without apish imitation of another; since what to one race of people, of a certain age, is a wholesome nutriment, may perhaps prove a poison for another. All endeavours to introduce any foreign innovation, the necessity for which is not rooted in the core of the nation itself, are therefore foolish; and all premeditated revolutions of the kind are unsuccessful, for they are without God, who keeps aloof from such bungling. If, however, there exists an actual necessity for a great reform amongst a people, God is with it, and it prospers. He was visibly with Christ and his first adherents; for the appearance of the new doctrine of love was a necessity to the people. He was also visibly with Luther; for the purification of the doctrine corrupted by the priests was no less a necessity. Neither of the great powers whom I have named was, however, a friend of the permanent; much more were both of them convinced that the old leaven must be got rid of, and that it would be impossible to go on and remain in the untrue, unjust, and defective way.'

What a blessing that the true thoughts of Goethe were captured on paper! Re-reading them now, it's as if I'm reading a modern book by an Ahmedian Muslim, of which many are native Germans. But still, even with the availability of many complete biographies, books and manuscripts, the myth still lives of Goethe as a giant who Europe can oppose to the 'dark power of Islam'... But there is no darker force in the world than the dark callousness of an ignorant heart, and such a heart is alien to any faith: 'the eyes are not blind, but hearts in chests are blind', the Qur'an says bitterly.

Sullen and bearded *neomuslims* think that Allah is on their side – on the side of principled aversion to other cultures. But there is not and cannot be ignorance in Islam: for it leaves only a shell and a ritual – and the spirit that leads the world to the Unity disappears.

So, why are nations are different? Why do their moral cultures become so separate? The God of Islam, Christianity and Judaism, God of Buddha, Krishna, Confucius and of Socrates replies – and it is an irrefutable answer:

Al-Hujurat: 49:13
Oh human race, We created you from a man and a woman and made you nations and tribes, so that you could know each other. Truly, the most worthy among you in the eyes of Allah is the one who is the most pious. Truly, Allah – is All-Knowing, All-Aware.

Who, disappointed by the world's ways, will sense with the sighted heart and mind the time of judgement – the Epoch of Knowledge? If we won't start to know in love – we will learn in blood and sorrow. But we will know, because that is God's destiny for us.

No hero or knight will gain victory if he is not righteous, and to be righteous is to aspire to the Unity through knowledge and compassion. Who doesn't understand this is condemned to stray in the vicious circle of history – with a weapon of vengeance and his own code of honour, like the code of the Bedouins in the time of the Prophet. Allah knew that in our time there will be militant and intolerable *pseudo-islam*; isn't this why straight after verse about knowledge, He said:

Al-Hujurat: 49:15
Nomads say: 'We believe.' Say: 'You don't believe; better say, 'we adopted Islam', for the Faith hasn't entered your hearts yet. But if you obey Allah and His Messenger, He will not belittle anything from your deeds. Truly, Allah is Greatest-Forgiving, Merciful.

And straight afterwards:

Al-Hujurat: 49:16
Believers are only those who believe in Allah and in His Messenger, then have no doubts, but are active with their wealth and in their life in the name of Allah. Such people – are sincere.

Believe in Allah – in Grace and Mercy. Believe in the Prophet – who was sent as a 'mercy for the whole of humanity', calling for the mutual knowledge of love. You say – Wahhabism; Taliban, you say – that Islam will strengthen itself by the force of weapons and by the epic strength of blood feuds. And at once in the next verse Allah answers to His Prophet:

Al-Hujurat: 49:17

Tell them: 'Do you want to introduce Allah to your faith, when Allah knows everything that exists in the heavens, and about everything that exists on earth, and knows everything existing?

For those who bend Islam to themselves, for those who use Islam for secular purposes are most of all directed to the words of Al-Hujurat's sura – a sura of the Epoch of Knowledge. You raise Islam as a political banner in defence of your own tribal myths? Do you think that it's acceptable to sacrifice people in the name of your faith?

Al-Hujurat: 49:18 – 19
They think they do you a favour by adopting Islam. Say: 'Do you not consider the adoption of Islam as a favour to me.' No, it's Allah who gave you a favour when He guided you to the Faith, if you are truthful.
Truly, Allah knows the secrets of heavens and of the earth. And Allah sees all that you do.

Faith comes into sincere and innocent hearts, like the heart of a child. Ignorance engenders only callousness. But it's in the nature of people to become attached to myths, and even the ruins of a myth can be sweeter to them than an unrecognized truth and God's vision that leads to the Unity – the innermost meaning of all movements great and small.

STAIRWAY TO HEAVEN
(*To Shavkat Abdusalamov, the hermit Takvash*[122])

---

[122] An artist, writer and film director born on 28 April 1939 or 1936 in Tashkent.

...my brother, I sincerely tried but have finally given up my attempts to describe you in words. Share the silence with me. I cannot explain what is contained in the mute concord between brothers.

People imagine you a prophet. People join the bitter words of your parables to the delicate precision of your verses, and cry with compassion from which there is no shelter in a desert.

People are surprised. People tell you where you are from, as if they know it.

But I don't know where you're from, and I will never find out, but I know that you're my brother, and through many deserts I see your creative loneliness, salved with heaven's light. I see you and your labour, the work of a Master, to whom consolation is given grace, and ordeal a sighted heart. I see you by the light:

> Allah is the Light of heaven and of the earth.
> Its light is like a niche, in which a lamp is placed.
> The lamp shines inside the glass.
> The glass is like a sparkling star.
> It's lit from the holy tree, an olive tree,
> Not from the East, not from the West,
> The oil of the tree burns almost without fire.
> Light on the light (Light in the world).

People tell you where you're from, as if they know. I want to love them, just like you, but I am afraid of the heavy imprint of their opinions. Can they see, do they recognize that on your canvases, in the full and painful details of earthly existence, nothing is stopped and everything moves and flows to the limit — then back again?

Not everyone who tries to leave knows that he has already
returned from his flight. Everything exists here and now, but
everything exists in eternity, too, and in the desert of life
there is no East or West. There is only light and a painstaking
work by the light.

Your canvases are full of light, Shavkat. Those who once
touched God for their whole life look for the touch of His
hand among humans and think that it is people who make
us orphans. How little do we have in this desert, but what we
do have is the most necessary – a ladder to heaven, without
a handrail to help you, and our wooden wings which pull us
down to the earth.

The weight of symbols. The inanity of earth coordinates.
The scream of the train that leaves for the West, only to
appear from the East straight away. You know it's the same
train, brother, on which you can't go anywhere without
coming back at once. And you know that the only person
who truly moves is the one who knows where exactly he is
at peace.

But how hard it is to stay in one place like the mountain that ever waits for the Prophet![123] He never comes, but

---

[123] An allusion to the saying: 'If the mountain won't come to the Mohammed, Mohammed must go to the mountain.' The legend goes that
when the founder of Islam was asked to give proofs of his teaching,
he ordered Mount Safa to come to him. When the mountain did not
comply, Mohammed raised his hands towards heaven and said, 'God
is merciful. Had it obeyed my words, it would have fallen on us to
our destruction. I will therefore go to the mountain and thank God
that he has had mercy on a stiff-necked generation.' The saying has
been traced back in English to 'Essays', (1625) by English philosopher
Frances Bacon (1561-1626).' From *Random House Dictionary of Popu-
lar Proverbs and Sayings* (1996) by Gregory Y. Titelman.

appears in the forbidding loneliness of other guests – in ghosts, myths, legends and other sad inventions of gullible humanity, lit by the reflected light of Allah. You ask them to settle on your vacant ground and, like mirages, they stay with you a while so that you can see yourself in them.

But, tiring of human chatter, they always go back where they've come from, because they are like the Magi who follow the star that never stays in one place.

And only the holy mother Mariam lingers with her child, the only essence among multiple mirages who lives, and keeps living, on the edge of the stony waste of alienation that begins and ends all deserts of the world. There, where wayward biblical hoopoes and heaven's fragile butterflies flit among the sparse bushes and lonely grasses, she stays on in her shelter of reeds and bent poles blown through by the wind – for if she'd got fed up and walked off beyond the horizon, taking her son with her, who else would have kept purity and chastity alive in the world?

And where do we go from here, from this scanty shelter, the only authenticity in human life? Only a mother knows that it is pointless to chase a butterfly in the desert, that it must fly to you of its own accord from heaven's meadows that bloom imperishably, like your heart, like a Silence that is mute only because it doesn't want to spill the water of truth in vain.

And her boy, her bare-browed boy with his soft halo of fresh morning sun, after clambering up the ladder on to the low reed roof, is sitting weightless, dangling his feet and smiling, and his smile, like a butterfly of the desert, is accidental and immortal.

Wherever he looks from his perch, hoping to guess where his father is coming from, he sees only the horizon everywhere, and everywhere the unmerciful expanses from which ever emerge and retreat the Magi and the round-the-world train, those itinerants always off searching for new stars and mirages, but always returning to your waste ground of alienation.

Among the desert travellers there is never a father, and yet somebody must wait for him – otherwise for what purpose is the shelter that stands in the wind, and the *tandur* made from stones where the rough bread of life is baking?

But wisdom always comes late and childhood never dies. Whoever inherits a shelter in a desert inherits a ladder and knocks together wings for himself out of empty boxes, fallen off a train.

If there's no father on earth, then he's certainly in the heavens; it's just necessary to find him and set up a ladder for him – otherwise, how would he come down?

But the sky is vast, Shavkat, and in our desert the winter is longer than summer. And how hard it is on our wanderings to keep the fire in the *tandur* burning, so that the mother can keep warm, and the father, when he returns, can warm his hands on hot bread!

After all, everything comes back – even the father. Yes, he will one day return – and then the water murmuring in the springs of the heart will help bring back the earthly desert to life.

When I think about you, brother, I think about Allah, who made us orphans to continually remind us about Him.

Share your silence with me, Shavkat. Take me, to support your stairway to heaven.

For it is me walking from afar, fearing with a clumsy word to scare off the hoopoe sitting on its perch.

8

WHO CRIES

ಙ

WHEN THE HERMIT Takvash generously gave me his drawing, and added me to the Wanderers of the World in his own hand-written inscription, I acquired a very high opinion of myself! In an instant I became outrageously conceited. I was so swept up by this sudden gust of vainglory that I even wanted to give my portrait to a museum, to remind people what they are like, these Wanderers of the World.

There was no need to ask Takvash for such a portait. I already had such an image. And when you look at it, you get the impression the subject is crying. If you look closely, though, it's clear they are not tears; they are just raindrops running slantwise down my face. In the picture, it is forever raining, and the rain is whipped up by the whirlwind of a life out of control – a whirlwind that behind the rectangle of the picture frame stirs up, hurls down and bears away wet and shining living leaves, drops of water, and such a mixture of floral shreds it's impossible to guess what time it is outside: spring or autumn. It is a very vivid portrait, but you can only see yourself in it in a certain mood – like in any mirror.

WHO CRIES

Meanwhile who else if not Takvash-hermit would know how comforted I once was by my wandering – after the complete frenzy of the past? Living pictures slipped by either side of the long road; people filled out their own lives, passed through me without imprinting memories. I remembered almost nothing, imagining I would find another me and find the truth of life in these searches, unburdened by memory. But the Earth turned out to be round, just as everyone said, and I came back against my will. Then I realized that life in any form is a continuation – and it's impossible to deceive even yourself by deliberately obliterating the past.

That is why vanity is, like any consolation, ephemeral. Whatever people think, only the wanderer himself knows the purpose of his travels – the false and ever-elusive peace of the soul.

The man who is truly wise stays in one place and lets the truth come to him. But the wanderer gains nothing but regret what for is lost. Why does peace slip so from the soul? Why amid the clarity and certainty of life does a commotion often intrude on the soul that can only be escaped, it seems, in self-absorbed work, frequent travel or some other mind-less activity?

I once thought that in my wandering I was searching for home – not the place my portrait hangs nor that other, mysterious home yet to be, but one that was mine – mine to the very air contained in its walls. I imagined it on a high wooded hill, under the sun and stars – a place with wide windows to let me see forever those consoling distances. And so one day such a house was given to me with you, and with it came a garden, where on the ever-green grass in sunshine and shower walks a ginger cat...

In this garden, I planted a lilac bush, and found a cat to feed. And because our house, as fate has willed, happened to be in England never seen by the honest hermit Takvash except in his dreams and by many other people I in fits of tender loneliness call my friends — because it's in England, the cat's food must be bought once a week in a supermarket, which you have to drive to once a week. The food is in tins, and you take twelve straightaway and then one more — for The One Who Cries.

The One Who Cries is pictured on a special box near the till where you're asked to donate a tin for the home for abandoned cats. It's a black cat, drawn as if by a child, and it cries because it's lonely and has nothing to eat. Once a week, I give a tin to The One Who Cries, but it's little comfort to my soul, and I, who never quite recovered from my wanderings, always remember that feline. The One Who Cries.

After all, a cat, just like a human, can be upset. And not just our too-trusting ginger, who I named Mumzik, thinking when it was a kitten that it was a male cat. Or rather, a hundred grams of male cat, because when you picked up this lonely vagrant that meowed to you it was just a tiny, tiny scallywag — so tiny you thought its tail might not grow.

Its tail did grow, of course, very fluffy. The kitten also grew to be a cat, though only a small cat. In the evening, she sits on the wall and waits for me to come back from work. She mews when she wants something, but I don't always get what; one has to learn to understand even a cat.

You remember how we took Mumzik despite my doubts — we didn't have our own house, and who was to look after it when we went away as we so often did? But Mumzik stayed, because anybody might hurt a little cat. Even a cat like Dante.

Dante is a black cat, Italian. And not just a cat. Dante is black like resin, and humongous, weighing almost a *pood*.[124] Dante lives in Turin, in the three-star Hotel Astoria near Porta Nuova station and sleeps in one of the leather armchairs in the lobby. People come in and out, move in and move out, but even though he's here all the time still Dante looks at everybody apprehensively. That is how he looked at me as well, and during all our three days intercourse he didn't once drop his suspicious glare.

Once I went to Turin on business. I flew via Frankfurt am Main, whose international airport used to impress me but now reminds me all too plainly of Moscow's Domodedovo with its sea of stress-marked faces, suitcases, baggages and trunks. Alas! Everything seemed lost now in Frankfurt too. The sense of novelty and the foretaste of the unknown has gone, and with it the excitement that touched me on my first flight here – years and years ago. The gates to the once-closed world now let everyone through, and numerous refugees and wanderers pass through every day in search of happiness, which still cannot be found in people's homelands. Everybody is going somewhere, just as on the overcrowded Russian trains. Everybody is seeking happiness and prosperity – but nobody freedom or peace.

Behind the glass walls of that German airport it was spring then. I was looking at the pale-blue sky and thinking, what – what am I lacking now to be too sated to anticipate the unknown? Indeed, didn't I notice how, while I was pretending to be a mature soul, old age had crept up on me, swap-

---

[124] An old Russian measurement of 16.38 kg.

ping the silly happiness of constant amusement for the bland taste of knowingness and an indispensable human resentment that settled in my heart of the fact that life had passed so quickly?

What did this spring want for my heart to rejoice and sparkle as in the past?

I was steadily approaching my fifties, and the joy in novelty was gradually giving way to the mercy of sadness. Not the sadness that sweetly pains the heart with the autumn-wind-shivered splashes of gold and crimson in the forests, but a different sadness – the sadness of innumerable tirednesses, when even a final farewell from life seems like a relief from work – work that doesn't have a beginning or an end, or a border, or any obvious purpose.

I was bogged down in a multitude of work then, each task running into the next, so that there was never any end, or peace for my soul. These travails woke me at crack of dawn, like a persistent baby's cry, and it was impossible not to get up. And the worry continued throughout the day until in the evening my eyelids began to droop irresistibly, and my body turned to cotton wool. I was falling asleep, fainting away – becoming unconscious – and the worldly tiredness triumphed over me until the dawn's glimmer returned all too soon, so that everything started over again.

Sometimes, waking and rising before daybreak in a fit of momentary faintheartedness, I prayed for the beautiful unknown to somehow leave, to leap out from this learnt-by-heart vicious circle – to abandon me, and leave everything but the ringing emptiness and freedom of the primaeval, blank page of creation, a single thought that would finally push me forward to a single, authentic purpose on earth: work that would forever heal me with its incontestable necessity, giving me peace and the continuing happiness of accomplishment.

That is how I lived then, bending like a slave over my day work, and when I'd lift my head to look at passing life, it looked alien and strange, like my own name pronounced by a stranger amid utter silence. Through the living pictures of the surrounding alien reality – through the blooming and dying of seasonal flowers in the small garden rightfully belonging to that ginger English lady Mumzik – only the incomprehensible guilt for my visible prosperity penetrated the silence, along with those recurring melancholic memories of friends lost on my travels and of another life lost through hastiness. This looked very much like a sinful despondency so I prayed to God – at home, and in the white Ahmadian mosque, the oldest in London, around which even in January colourful roses bloomed with curling green leaves, and century-old pear trees stood in unashamed nakedness.

And in the mosque, there came an answer to the dreams of my dawn weakness. In the minutes of the evening prayer, when I was bending to the ground and stretched across the clean green carpet, some words came into my head out of the blue. 'A fortuitous guest,' they said. I repeated them straight away, so as not to forget them.

But whose fortuity was it? Was it mine? Where was I fortuitous – in the mosque? In the world? Yet I am a believer who knows for sure that nothing in the world is accidental. Everything is created to bear witness that the world is unified and its unity is made one by love.

Love?

Yes, and of course a person is never fortuitous if he can love, and everything that is neither love nor sacrifice is a needless waste of your powers. So hadn't Allah caught me in the vacancy of meaningless prosperity? Like Jesus and the fig tree,[125] hadn't he pointed out my mundane fortune and my stinginess in love.

And where there's too little love, dejection triumphs, and the sadness of the past smothers the future, which cannot be prompted. Yet how can you love without loving the Unity first? After all, love for a person and love for work as an act of sacrifice can be blind, and you can sometimes see clearly only with the light of love for the Creator. In this moment of revelation, I realized I did not have the nobility to love without fear, and though the world around me grew bright with this mysterious discovery, it weighed me down for some time.

And so, my new state, in which I forbade myself self-importance and narcissism, didn't relieve me from the duty to *witness*. The true was destined to come true so I, like a novice, gave myself once more to the road, despondent about my uselessness to myself, to God, to people...

I was flying to Turin. Pink Alps floated under the plane's wing through breaks in the cloud: alien mountains. Again, as on the flight over the poor and deceived Caucasus two months beforehand, snow whitened the ridges beneath me, and ice glistened in unexpected sunshine. Cloud shadows were drifting slowly over the rocky slopes, and as the shadows ended, the mountains showed dark patches of brown and green. The plane had already reached Piemonte, dusk

---

[125] This is a reference to the Biblical story that tells how Jesus, to demonstrate the power of prayer, cursed a fig-tree that had no fruit (because it was out of season) – then returned the next day to show how the tree had withered from the roots.

was rolling in – and then the flight was over, and I was sitting in the back of an Italian taxi moving across the floodplain of the river Po, level as the Ararat valley, in the vast semicircle of mountains to the west. As darkness fell we entered Turin, and only here, walking through the lofty Savoyard arcades that arched elegantly over all main the walkways of the city centre, I realized what I missed in this European spring.

The drip of thawing snow. The delicate, resonant music of my past springs. Not a single icicle hung from the roofs or the arches. Nothing dripped. There was neither ringing or murmuring in this beautiful, but silent spring.

And where there are no snowdrifts, there are no spring waters. But it's pointless to think about Kazan, about April in Aeropotovskaya Street, with its twinkling, finely spun crystals above the exuberantly gushing streams; God be with them, those massive icicles, that dropped like bombs under the feet of passers-by – and thank goodness if it's just under their feet! Obliging memory, which chooses only the brightest flashes from childhood. Sparkling streams, flowing in icy channels down Gastello street then, like the Volga itself, turning south almost at right angles to run past our 'Finnish' university house, and I run joyously with them, floating something in the stream – I don't even remember what, probably a hand-made wooden boat or that rubber squeaking clown that I named Parkhomenko, after the movie...

The houses here are like izbas, with carved blinds and wooden gates; it's a suburb, and it's a little creepy here at night. But when it's light, and the streams purl under the sun, it's not creepy at all, and even a coffin lid, resting on a neighbour's gates, doesn't scare me. There was a heavy black cross on the lid, and it's the first cross and the first death I remember. But I remember better the streams and their silver sparkle.

Grown-ups don't like these streams, just as they don't like the sagging, charred snowdrifts, because they can foresee all the dirt and slush. But as a child I couldn't see this. The streams murmured. The fragile ice floes glittered. And I have my whole life in front of me, to scrutinize these thin plates of ice that look so much like the wings of those giant dragon-flies that hover in the summer air above the white and pink clover of the green, oh so wide and green, airfield![126] I have all the time in the world, too, to scrutinize the icicles and see how water runs down towards the spikes to form a clear drop, and then breaks away and falls – providing, of course, it doesn't cool and freeze first. The icicles grow anew each night, and each morning starts with the murmur of dripping water.

Yes, that was Kazan, to which inevitably my memories return again and again – just as to other cornerstones of memory in these conscience-induced letters. I wonder sometimes if I am losing myself in the labyrinth of these selective moments of memory? But no – just as the human soul unconsciously keeps us on track, so nothing bequeathed by Goethe, Mozart and other true masters in the art of com-position is forgotten entirely. Nor is the primary motive lost forever beneath the authentic creative anxiety. Even though it sometimes drifts off into unrecognizable variations, it always comes back with a new look and a new development in the heart.

After all the heart lives and forces us to live, and the dry consistency and reason of preplanned ideas is alien to it. It is sighted in ways that are not always plain to us. Because it is always waiting and responding to life in the rhythm of its

---

[126] In Russian villages, aircraft land on grassy fields.

beat, the unfathomable heart lures you to journey to wherever to hear harmony once more and to recognize that it neither lives in vain nor completely selflessly.

Indeed, for the heart everything happens *here and now*. It feels no time nor spatial distance between the biblical truth and the news on the BBC. Any framing of conscious thought is just a picture frame, which can transform even the simplest landscape and most ordinary person into a work of art, rectangularly selecting and visually emphasizing their special quality from out of their commonplace surroundings. In this frame, the most prominent things can become minor details and trifles can acquire great significance, and it becomes clear, that nothing, yes nothing, is fortuitous in the world, apart from people themselves, when they cannot understand what they are alive for.

But me – am I not trying to understand it? And will I ever succeed, God? Will I finally find my destined place in the rapids of the Unity – in the rapids that sometimes flow calmly and sometimes writhe through the gorge of people's ideas to churn away any false peace – in the rapids that roar with the mysterious force of the heart that suddenly overturns life with the purifying and unbearable power of conscience, and chokes the repose of the soul with its stupid impetuosity – that mad intemperance which interferes with the soul's real need to share what it believes to be the truth, and deprives it of that peace for which, as it seems, it has been sent?

My love, who do I imagine explaining this all to? And where? In this world that slyly eludes us in its diversity, this world where I find myself to be here or there rather accidentally – everywhere I am hoping to substantiate my existence with my own memories of foreign lands, with my memories of people who with their touch and words confirmed my presence in the world, which I myself would not have been so much aware of in my travels.

It's a trifle sad to realize that your life is just part of someone else's and not yours at all – an unknown history which someone cannot fairly divide into dates and occasions yet can convincingly distort without you having any control at all. Why must a person be forced, even if he's an accidental occurrence, to fit his vital existence into a rigid sequence of events, when his whole being, in the inconceivable quivering of the authentic and unguessed life, is convinced that nothing in the world becomes rigid and ends, but stays ever in dynamic movement, like the autumn flocks of birds in the sunset sky over the wide river?

So what does change in existence, apart from the clear outlines of the bird flocks, wheeling in the sky before the winter frosts, turning with the wind and gliding on invisible air currents as if they are unable to decide which bank looks nicer? What changes with time if time doesn't exist?

Does everything that has at least some link with our still flowing presence in the world happen right *here and now*? Do memories exist that don't have the courage to be open and visible reality, but remain just the secret food of the unquenchable and all too diligent conscience? Especially when even Judgement seems just part of everyday experience.

And so Who Cries reminds me of how shameful it is to believe yourself kind, but doesn't remind me about compassion and sympathy, even though only compassion and conscientious sympathy still bind us to the otherwise aloof world. It's not pity for the living that drives my actions in vain dreams and attempts to dissolve in the invisible beauty of the world, but the constant guilt for someone else's grief and someone else's weakness — that childish guilt that during my life turned into inexpiable and unforgivable guilt. So I, just like any other human, added troubles and sorrow to this world. It may be blissful not to understand the pain you cause to others, but I am frequently tormented and tortured by it — that guilt, which people cannot let go of, and which only the Unity can forgive, if it wishes to.

And so Who Cries, with its childish naivety that so wounds me, each time brings to mind all kinds of forgotten things and forgotten people — like Kazan poet Gena Kapranov, killed in his forties fishing on the Volga by *a bolt of lighting to the heart* — and again, could I *invent* such a thing? And Gena did invent rather than just simply breathed out his conscientious confession, the secret sadness of which I couldn't understand back then:

Let me share with you this triviality:
True love only comes with sympathy?

Oh, I ceased to be embarrassed by my shifts across the world long ago, losing my exterior shame along the way when faced with the unfair but conscientious needs that tie another person to a place more strongly than any chain! The years go by — I succeed in it.

I'm in the past now, in the ninetieth year of the last century: Frankfurt am Main — the first time in my life a strawberry got stuck in my throat, a wild winter strawberry found blooming amid the yellow fluff willows of Tübingen above the ice-cold clear-flowing Neckar near Hölderlin's[127] tower — and

---

[127] The round yellow tower on the banks of the Neckar river where the poet Friedrich Hölderlin (1770-1843) lived alone, cared for by the

it called for immediate penance on bended knees. Just as Moscow's ineradicable penury had poisoned the view of that blissful sunset over the ocean from the rock on the shore near Sydney. It was in the past, but I was drained by the shame of mundane prosperity in the pink cherries of London, and any damp wind in foreign lands tormented and tortured me as an undeserved abundance.

It's even longer ago, in my early youth, that I was embarrassed before my less prosperous friends by how kind life was to me, ashamed of the unearned wealth of my parents' home. I invented misfortunes for myself and, forgive me God, I borrowed – just my luck – from my own distant future the frantic agonies of worldly abandonment, the bitterness of scanty bread and the dreariness of autumn – yet it still tormented me, the shame of obvious prosperity. After giving this shame such licence, I almost slipped down into pitch darkness, deliberately making up new torments for myself and wrapping myself in elaborate fetters of conscience, as if trying to damn myself for wasting the gift of simple human happiness. I didn't know then how to share happiness and thought it was much more natural and honest to share misery.

What has it done to me, this conscience and secret shame? Into what maze of unrepentant loneliness did it thrust me that to escape cost me half my life on earth – destined, as it turned out, for the invulnerable joy of work and the adequate wisdom of a guilty compassion? It is buried deeply now, that shame, in the thick chiaroscuro of the soul, and lives there, hiding and squinting in accidental rays of disinterested spring light, undimming rays that fall through the clouds and trees on this earthly paradise, cutting to the quick

carpenter Ernst Zimmer, for the last forty years of his life.

and illuminating the whole earth, regardless of nationality, state or native language. All earthly things must be shared fairly, and if there remains anything to share out, there is left a burden of undying shame.

Once all is shared, the rest, as before, is used in the present – and now I know how unfair it is to share debts.

So about 20 kilometres from Turin, on the mountain of San Giorgio, from whose rocky feet the green bends of the Po stretched far over the spring valley of Piemonte – on this alpine slope, without any unusual confusion or embarrassment, I indulged myself in a little philosophizing, which suited my Turinian affairs well. Among these affairs was a dinner party in the medieval castle of Piossasco, braided with ivy right up the russet walls of its square tower to the battlements. On the open terrace shaggy shadows of cypress and stone pines played, along with sharper shapes of greygreen magnolia on which bare twigs were already putting out pointed buds, hiding in their lilac secrecy the blindingly white, glossy flowers of yet another incomprehensible spring.

Neither you nor Mumzik were there when we walked up to the castle, with the company listening absently to the story of how this citadel came to be and how the restaurant here, *Nove Merli* (Nine Blackbirds) got its name. Once in the restaurant, I read the details of this tale in the sumptuously presented menu with its heraldic cover, which for this occasion had a little bouquet of fresh flowers attached. This long dinner was delivered to a round table with eight place settings and silvery cutlery:

Salad with chicken breast with artichoke, asparagus and
fresh tomatoes,
Salmon cutlet in pastry with a light anchovy sauce,

Ravioli with wild mushroom sauce, sprinkled with black
truffles,
Baked Piemontese veal with cauliflower garnish,
Lightly toasted fritters with sweet muscatel dressing,
Coffee and a choice of wines from the castle's cellars

I had plenty of time to enrich myself with speculative knowledge about the facts: that the first mention of the castle of
Piossasco dates back to 1090, when Marchesa Adelaida of the
Savoy royal family gave it away along with the surrounding
estate to the noble knight Merlo – who is thought to have
come from Lombardy. That's why by the time of the First
Crusade (1096-1099), this knight already had a coat of arms,
with a blackbird on a white field. The descendants of Merlo,
whose family name means blackbird, all laid claim to the
castle and not only battled with the house of Savoy to hold
on to it but feuded bitterly among themselves for centuries
until finally, in 1340, the family did a deal, and a new coat of
arms was created to represent those Merli who were in on it,
with nine blackbirds on a silver cross against a red oval field.
But the line of the counts of Piossasco was finally broken in
1933 with the death of the countess Gabriella di None, and
the much rebuilt castle is now owned by the local council
and is a tourist destination with a restaurant and hotel.

Once I reached this point about it being a tourist destination, I rather lost interest, and only the link to the First
Crusade stuck in my memory. After dinner and small talk,
I strolled out between the cypresses and magnolias on the
terrace and once more saw the snow-capped peaks of the
Alps rearing up in the distance and, nearer to, the wide open
spaces of Piemonte with its green vineyards, ochre houses
and lofty *campanile*.

How free seem the cypresses and magnolias, and even the burgeoning blooms of vines on the alpine slopes, with their unceasing growth to fulfilment, as if they know entirely all the motives they need in their own *here and now* – as if for them everything was mapped out long ago, and all they have to do is follow the plan.

But that is not how it was.

Of course, vineyards would run wild without the helping hand through history of man who, despite habit and the daily need to work, can't understand why he lives and suffers, and is frightened by idleness because that's when he starts to think, what's it all for? But that's where the vicar comes in; the vicar will explain, and the man will accept it, calm down and then labour on again for his daily bread. Then, walking out between the vines, as if for the first time, he will see that their thick and ancient whips are entwined in a level canopy above the ground so that their outlines look like a cruci-fix – and the beautiful swelling of black buds and inaudible rumble of reviving sap in the vine's woody flesh will bring comfort and strength for new torments.

The wind was blowing, and the air shivered and blurred in the fast-cooling light of the sinking sun. It was my last day in Piemonte. That unexpected celebration was unexpectedly finished, but what did I take with me, beyond the aftertaste of dinner and that iconic photo of the Icon of Turin I bought for you from the black-and-white-clad nuns in the catholic shop on the corner of Via Garibaldi and 20 Settembre? But then what was I supposed to take with me? Everything was inside me in that moment of farewell to wandering – a tired pleasure in existence and the memory of new sights, but, alas, no new sense of that *authentic* history that still troubled my imagination.

I already knew that it's pointless on anonymous human journeys to read thick and clever books and try to co-ordinate images, events and dates: all of these, whipped up with gusts of hasty inquisitiveness, settle quickly in the soul like the archival dust of immemorial centuries. Such long wished for knowledge flattered any mind, but didn't touch my fevered heart, which if it strives for anything then it's for the wholeness of feeling for the world. The easily acquired what, when and how of calculated erudition will just as eas-ily burn up in the blaze of the heart which burns only to know why.

Is it true, though, that nature never answers why? If so, then for what is that presentiment, premonition and pres-age carried on the spring wind that so quickly becomes an autumn wind? For what is that sense of prescience and abso-lute truth in your personal final materialization in nature? Confronted by these ineffable, patient expectations, despair seems false because if something seems impossible to achieve, you can always become part of the mystery and that is a comfort, if comfort is possible – and until then, you just have to breathe, breathe while you can fresh grass and new leaves and pure jets of air which alone, as they become winds, defy any human borders and always invite you beyond the bor-ders of your own existence.

In wonderful, limpid silence, the Piemonte valley filled with the scent of shooting grass. You could see clearly and far, and so the feel of solid calm was even stranger, refusing to answer direct questions – why do people suffer in the search for riches, why does the truth hide in inexplicable twists of history, lost in half-guesses about motives, with all brief successes remaining just that, no more than a promise of lasting fulfilment: a question and a prayer – a hope for a final and complete explanation of the world from the one true source?

Oh, to approach the meaning, to pour together the multiplicity of human truths – each one like a bird in a restless, ever-wheeling flock, like a bird that when caged loses the only purpose in its plumage – soaring flight. The flock whirls about in the wind, rising and falling on air currents, dividing and coming together again – and even though the purpose of their thoughtless movement remains a mystery, they undeniably retain their unity, their wholeness, outside of which the multiplicity of individual flights is just an idea, an invention of the mind, an optical illusion...

Yet is it only revelation that brings you nearer the meaning, only revelation that can answer the heart's 'why?' because the mind burdened with knowledge doesn't ask such unclever questions any more? But still...

Why can a man just abandon his vineyard to the mercy of the elements – leave it merely for an idea, for his own personal conception of the unity in reaction to somebody, because the idea got tired of waiting, and the true Unity is forgotten entirely? What was it that made the knight of Piossasco castle, along with hundreds of other blue-blooded crusaders from Lombardy, from Burgundy, from Languedoc set out to God knows where? What wind blew the farmer from his land, the foreman from his workshop, the merchants from the stalls? What made them leave all they had to liberate the tomb of Christ?

And what 150 years on drove the descendants of these knights and mendicants with the same fury of lawful faith to assault not the faraway faithless but the very local and glorious culture of Languedoc and Provence, destroying in a froth of blood that culture that gave Europe troubadours and minstrels, the ideals of chivalry, the cult of the Fair Lady and the legend of the Holy Grail – all of which sprang from the proximity of Muslim Spain, of El Andalus which for three centuries outshone the European Renaissance?

So why do people focus so stubbornly on their differences and senselessly disdain all that they have in common? Or is it just me, lucky enough to be unaware of proprieties, a childish guest in my naïve ignorance, who has a presentiment that in the study of these separate identities rooted in the past there may be reborn an era of mutual recognition, when joyful recognition of kindred spirits, recognition of yourself in another, is paramount and there is a natural understanding of the Unity's commonality?

Of course, not one of the dinner guests, with all their erudition, could answer the heart's questioning, because it is more exacting than the questioning of the mind. And so I refused to join with them in the nonsense of inappropriate brilliance.

The answer was Silence.

And the newly arrived spring air, wet with anticipation, streamed, flowed, shimmered in the sunset light in the interconnecting vessels of universal spaces. And the clear landscape of Savoy Piemonte responded to the call of the watchful imagination to bring to life those historic mirages of Lombardy, Avignon, Cordoba, Granada, Venice, Rome, faraway Sarajevo and Provence beyond the Alps. Continuing life and continuing history merged into one as the spring was accomplished – in the strong, protective arms of the Alps, the Alps that embrace northern Italy with the Appenines, leaving it alone to face the Adriatic and the ever-restless Balkans, yet binding it to Provence through winding gorges and the azure coast of the Mediterranean. The Alps called with the clarity of their skybound snowy crests – a single glance at which was enough to discourage any archival dogmatism that simply clouds the mind seeking for truth.

Only after revelation comes to the heart will the heart try to reconcile itself to the discoveries of the mind – and then any knowledge is just a verification of the revelation, not its basis.

Thus the Alps are not a barrier, but a seam.

Thus time is not a series of separate events, but a continuous whole.

Thus silence is more potent than speech.

If these Alpine vertices were saying anything with their shining silence, it was just one ineffable, authentic and therefore simple thing: we are always here, they say, and that is why everything about us and around us in the single air of humanity is always happening here and now, as in the human soul. All else is just a probability, an accident, a game of imagination and the ingenuity of historical science, the embellishments of those honestly bespectacled and stuffily impartial academics who have answered everything, but in progressing along their geometrically correct corridors have lost the feeling of the present witness.

And so, on the vaulted terrace of the castle of Piassosco, on that rocky spur of San Giorgio mountain capped by shining celestial snows, I simply breathed while I could – and I couldn't breathe enough. And silently I asked myself, as my own feelings faded away: what happens when nothing seems to be happening? How does one moment of visible existence differ from another? What secret, what enigma, what unscientific mystery spills so enticingly from picture postcard Piemonte, with its broad valley, its snowy crests and rocky crevices, its hidden caves and deep clefts, that are so thoroughly studied by tourists and wordsmiths?

For someone to realize what is happening, does he really need the vast and unexplainable movements of the masses, the great disasters and crashes, or the thundering horses of Apocalypse to burst from the snowy glaciers into the vineyard silence of the valley?

Or does he need an incredible miracle of existence thrust under his nose, and then straight away to be threatened with the loss of this miracle? Or does he need a succession of miracles and impossibilities to continually remind him what is happening so that he understands, that nothing happens in vain, even amid utter tranquillity?

Even if he doesn't believe in an Apocalyptic cavalry, in thunder and lightning rolling down from the high white peaks... what if the answer came to him not in the spring, but in the copious autumn? What if it came not just as a pack of horses, but as a force of terrifying fighting elephants charging down San Giorgio mountain with almighty bellows to trample and destroy the ripe grapes of careless Piemonte — would he finally believe that there's more to the world than just his own boredom?

Yet that too, in the invisible authenticity and unstoppability of life, happened for real and — like an avenging revelation from the heavens — struck the mind and the vision of ancient Roman winegrowers in the form of the Carthaginian armies of Hannibal, who crossed the Alps near here with his warrior elephants; and so in Piemonte, in that October of 218 BC, something happened in broad daylight that seemed completely, absolutely, heretically impossible ...

Those Carthaginian elephants, tamed somewhere in Morocco or Tunisia, could they really cross the Straits of

Gibraltar, stride across all Spain, tramp through the coastal gorges of the Pyrenean heights, force their way across the exuberant blue, untameable Rhone, then battle their way up across the savage rocks to the snowy wastes of Monginevra[128] – almost two kilometres above sea level – and then make the steep descent to the Piemonte valley not only alive, but ready to fight? Indeed, so ready that neither before nor after did anybody inflict such a defeat upon Rome as Hannibal did during that Second Punic War.

But it did happen. With just this difference – for there is a difference – that then nobody took the descent of the elephants from on high as the beginning of doomsday: nobody in ancient Piemonte imagined that the world would ever come to such an unusual end. The prophet Daniel wasn't yet born, nor was Jesus the Messiah – the Messiah, who in the heretical Gospel of Thomas so stunningly answers the apostles' question: 'Tell us, when will the End come?'

Have you found the Beginning then, that you are now looking for the End? You see, the End will be where the Beginning is.

And to another, he said:

If you are asked, 'What have you in yourself from the Father?' answer: 'Movement and peace.'

But these words will be forgotten for two thousand years, forgotten like so many other things from the first

---

[128] Monginevra or Montgenevre on the Italian-French border is just one of the possible routes Hannibal and his army took through the Alps.

centuries of Christianity. Forgotten not only because Hannibal's elephants and army crossed into Piemonte from the
Alps but because they were crossed, too, five hundred years
later by the British legions of emperor Constantine. With
them came the idea of the oblivion of the past, the new
truth of empire, that broke from the West and soon engaged
in the battle with the painful truths of the East. According
to legend, it was on the way from Britain to Rome, in Pro-
vençal Arles on the Rhone that there appeared to Constantine the sign of a Cross in the sky with the message: 'With
this sign, you will conquer!'[129] Here, in the moment of the
emperor's revelation, Catholicism began; from here, inter-
twined with the idea of a unified state, grew the new Rome
on the banks of the Golden Bosphorus, and then braided the
whole Roman empire with the crimson, lush, uniform vines
of the state canon.

But here's a paradox. After Constantine, Christianity
became a ruling idea and spread far and wide, travelling to
and fro across the Alps in conjunction with all the heresies
that shook Rome for centuries. And the people of the Muslim East whose name in Arabic sounds like 'sharykin' – those
saracens in the crusaders' legends – didn't pose for Catholic Rome even a small part of the alluring religious threat
blooming then along the border with Moorish Spain in the

---

[129] The author is here confusing two different Constantines. It was Constantine the Great (Constantine I) who crossed the Cottian Alps and,
according to the chronicler Eusebius, saw the sign of the cross and the
words In Hoc Signo Vinces but this vision happened on the shores of
the Tiber, as he was about to enter battle with the usurper Maxentius
to regain control of Rome in 312. He came from Britain six years
earlier. It was Constantine III who, a hundred years later, came from
Britain with a rebel army and made Arles his capital.

Albigensian countries – Aragon, Navarre, Toulouse, Provence and Languedoc.[130]

It turned out that all the truths of the East could arrive via the West – and not necessarily through the vineyards and olive groves of the Mediterranean north – for the sea's coasts that seem to divide in the end unite. And so the powerful ideas of the Christian gnostics travelled for centuries not just through the Balkans, but through northern Africa and Spain, washing up against the feet of the Alps and Pyrenees, going under various names – Manichaeism,[131] Arianism,[132] Bogomilism[133] and Albigensianism. These teachings all became overgrown with their own philosophies and ritu-

---

[130] The author is talking about the countries where the heretic cathar movement began to take hold in the eleventh century. Some of Catharism's roots are said to have been in Bulgaria as well as with the gnostics – hence the author's reference to the Balkans in the following paragraph. The cathars were in some ways forerunners of the Reformation, protesting against the corruption of the priesthood. They were also like the Quakers later against eating meat, war and capital punishment – and sex was for them a necessary evil. The cathars were brutally suppressed in the long Albigensian Crusade of the early thirteenth century led by Simon de Montfort, and the horrific persecution that followed.

[131] A Gnostic religion that originated with the prophet Mani in the third century AD in Sassanid era Babylon, and emphasized the struggle between good and evil.

[132] The teachings of Arius, a third century presbyter from Alexandria in Egypt, whose argument centred on the Trinity, saying that the Son of God was subordinate to God the Father, because he had not always existed.

[133] A Gnostic based heretic movement that began in tenth century Bulgaria in reaction to church and state oppression, owing its name to its reputed founder, the priest Bogomil. The Cathars and Patarenes, Waldenses, Anabaptists and in Russia the Strigolniki, Molokani and

als, but their prime inspiration, wherever they began, was that strong and original aspiration to understand the essence and nature of God. These gnostics, knowledge seekers, always found the canonical limits of faith too restrictive, and occupied themselves in all kinds of meditation, even if it ended in this life in the fire and other unspeakably cruel terrors of martyrdom.

It's all too easy to become confused by these early teachings, especially those that have reached us only in the scraps of apocryphal writings that avoided the flames of the Inquisition miraculously – those almost lost teachings that were only revealed more completely after the discovery in 1945 of a treasure trove of manuscripts near Nag Hammadi in Egypt. They were not found then by a questing knight, nor an earnest monk, nor even an inquisitive scientist, but by an ordinary Egyptian labourer. He was simply scraping around a boulder in a field when his mattock struck a big terracotta pitcher in which he found, to his disappointment, not coins or jewels, but a treasure whose worth he couldn't appreciate.[134]

Doukhobors, have all been either identified with the Bogomils or closely linked to them.

[134] The fifty-two texts discovered in Nag Hammadi, Egypt include 'secret' gospels, poems and myths attributing to Jesus sayings and beliefs very different from the New Testament. It's a miracle they ever got into the hands of researchers. After he dug them up, the finder Muhammad 'Alí al-Sammán dumped the contents of the jar by the oven at home, where his mother burned some of them on the fire. It was only after a blood feud in which Muhammad and his brothers hacked off his neighbour's limbs and ripped out his heart and ate it, that he decided to give the papers to a Coptic priest in case the police came looking. The priest then sold the papers on the black market so that they eventually found their way to the Coptic Museum in Cairo.

They were very ancient papyri covered in the text of ancient apocryphal writings. Nowadays, it is thought they were hidden in the year 390 by the monks of the nearby monastery of Saint Pachomius and so were saved from destruction of all non-canonical Christian texts that followed the council of Nicaea in 324, the first under the Emperor Constantine, who hereby canonized the idea of God's Trinity.

Soon after the thirteen Nag Hammadi papyri finally fell into the hands of researchers, it was found that written on them were fifty-two sacred texts many believe to be the lost Gnostic Gospels, the last clear evidence of that faith which was so mercilessly and high-handedly attacked by the Orthodox church.

Evidence: just like the Dead Sea Scrolls and the Turin Shroud.

So isn't evidence a key concept in spiritual trials? There is the genuine evidence of the church and personal historic culture which connects you indirectly to the source of the world – or there is your own direct proof of God, and here there can be no perjury.

How long ago people discovered this! Right from the start, Christians stood out as people who not only declared their faith in Jesus and his Gospel, but also that they were given, beyond the general communion, their own special 'evidential revelation', a direct feeling and knowledge of Divine Gnosis.

It was this 'personal feeling of the truth' that for them distinguished an authentic believer from the faithful crowd. They believed that such personal, direct and absolute knowledge of the Unity and the authentic truths of existence is available for ordinary people. Moreover, the acquistion of such knowledge and evidence has to be the most important achievement in anyone's life.

Oh God, isn't this the core of Islam too? Was it accidental that the lands where the Gnostic world-view was mostly rooted – the Near East, Iran, Afghanistan, Egypt and the countries of African Christianity – so naturally adopted the Islamic world-view, in which suddenly direct answers were found to all those ancient questions and mental struggles of Gnosticism. Such answers, which naturally knitted the ripped fabric of civilization and gave such a colossal impulse to the human mind to suddenly see a world in which Aristotle and Plato, Moses and Jesus became eloquent contemporaries of the first Umayyad Caliphate, not to mention those last great geniuses of the Muslim Renaissance in Spain.

So isn't Gnosticism – that spiritual, historic bridge from Christianity to Islam – isn't it just a link in the invisible evolution of the human spirit that leads into the universal evolution to Unity, which is the sole purpose of Faith? And so this discourse is not about the truth of contemporary religions. In the second half of the twentieth century, there wasn't a year when a new work wasn't born on the subject of Jesus's historicity and so, the spiritual truth of Christianity itself. The majority of these books, though, are terminally ill with the diseases of the age – sensationalism, pseudo-historicity and the desire to shake the basics.

But God spare us from shaking the basics, because the basics are not guilty of anything. What have sacred myths and lies to do with the real basics of faith? This is a rhetorical question that applies to all the world's religions, including modern Islam. In every age, there were more than enough people wanting to equate faith with dogma, but the authenticity of life sooner or later blows away any dogma with the fresh, purifying winds of the truth.

For each nation, there is a time.
And when their time will come,
They will not fall behind even for a minute,
But neither will they go ahead of their time.

The Holy Qur'an 7:35

The fresher the wind, the more it blows in your face and makes your eyes water, the quicker you get used to the view.
 Do you remember that wind on the greenstone hills of Andalusia, crowned since Muslim time by those shining white villages – the ones, that around Cordoba are called Alpujarras? *The sun sinks down in shining gold On Alpujarra's distant crest...*[135]

---

[135] This is from the Serenade from Alexei Tolstoy's *Don Juan*, set to music by Tchaikovksy:
 The sun sinks down in shining gold
 On Alpujarra's distant crest
 And my guitar will call you singing
 Oh come to me, my love, my best!
 If any men dare say another
 Could ever be the match of you:
 Then armed with flames of love, I'll fight them
 To the death, to prove what's true!

 In the red and dusky sky now
 The Moon's in all its majesty:
 Oh, my love, my dear Niseta,
 Hurry to your balcony!

 From Seville to old Granada
 In the silence of the night,
 All you hear is serenading
 And the ring of swords in fight –
 Full of blood and full of singing

How could Pushkin[136] have seen this in authentic, invisible reality?

Are we happier than Pushkin? We, whose faces were fanned not only by the frantic mistral of Avignon, but also by the calm, consoling wind, streaming from the hills with its own clear flow along the loamy waters of Guadalquivir and, whirling through narrow streets of the Jewish and Muslim quarters of historic Cordoba, then flying past the unmoving cypresses of eternity into the spacious courtyard of the Cordoba mosque to rustle the vivid green of the orange and lemon trees...

We two wandered together through Cordoba's ancient quarter, where once was born but also died the unity of humanity; walked past the white-walled Arabian and Jewish mansions curled with vines, ivy and other blooming woody climbers; walked under the arches into ancient yards with cool tiles and blooming pots around low circular fountains; looked into the craft shops, in one of which you bought that sacred, seedlike silver bracelet made in traditional Jewish style with its glowing purple-opal stone... We walked

---

For all those lovely ladies true!
Yet I'm the one who'll give my love.
My song, and all my blood for you!

In the red and dusky sky now
The Moon's in all its majesty:
Oh, my love, my dear Niseta,
Hurry to your balcony!

[136] The author is wrong in attributing these lines to Pushkin; they were written by Alexei Tolstoy, the cousin of the author of *War and Peace*, who could well have travelled to Spain. But the point about the power of Pushkin's creative imagination is apt.

along the 800 year-old city wall, near to which there are now monuments to Maimonides and Averroes, the geniuses of the lost civilization, which there was never and will never be another like on Earth.

From the eighth until the tenth centuries, Muslim Cordoba was the largest and most magnificent town in Europe – glorious not just for its palaces and neat streets ever lit by lanterns, but for its harmoniously organized civil life, based on the key right of any person, freedom of conscience, about which in 1930 British scientist Muhammad Marmaduke Pickthall[137] wrote:

In the eyes of history, religious toleration is the highest evidence of culture in a people. It was not until the Western nations broke away from their religious law that they became more tolerant, and it was only when the Muslims fell away from their religious law that they declined in tolerance and other evidences of the highest culture.

If Europe had known as much of Islam, as Muslims knew of Christendom, in those days, those mad, adventurous, occasionally chivalrous and heroic, but utterly fanatical outbreaks known as the Crusades could not have taken place, for they were based on a complete misapprehension...

Innumerable monasteries, with a wealth of treasure of which the worth has been calculated at not less than a hundred millions sterling, enjoyed the benefit of the Holy Prophet's Charter to the monks of Sinai and were reli-

---

[137] (Mohammad) Marmaduke Pickthall (1875-1936) was a famous British muslim scholar, novelist and translator of the Holy Qur'an.

giously respected by the Muslims. The various sects of Christians were represented in the Council of the Empire by their patriarchs, on the provincial and district council by their bishops, in the village council by their priests, whose word was always taken without question on things which were the sole concern of their community.

The tolerance within the body of Islam was, and is, something without parallel in history; class and race and colour ceasing altogether to be barriers...

In Spain under the Umayyads and in Baghdad under the Abbasid Khalifahs, Christians and Jews, equally with Muslims, were admitted to the schools and universities – not only that but were boarded and lodged in hostels at the cost of the Muslim state...

...For the Muslims of the past, the Qur'an was just encouragement. There is no compulsion in Religion. Men choose their path – in Islam or outside – and it is sufficient punishment for those who oppose that they draw further and further away from the light of truth.

What Muslims do not generally consider is that this law applies to our own community just as much as to the people outside, the laws of Allah being universal; and that intolerance of Muslims for other men's opinions and beliefs is evidence that they themselves have, at the moment, forgotten the vision of the majesty and mercy of Allah which the Qur'an presents to them.[138]

In faith there shouldn't be compulsion.

---

[138] This quote combines excerpts from several of Pickthall's commentaries, including his *Tolerance in Islam*.

Truly, the difference between good and evil has now become clear;

So the one who refuses to follow sinners and believes in Allah truly, he holds in his hands a strong handle which will never break.

And Allah is All-hearing, All-seeing.

The Holy Qur'an 2:256

And it is true that the Holy Prophet of Islam let a Christian delegation from Syria use his mosque when it was time for them to pray.

During the entry into Jerusalem, the second Rightly Guided Caliph of Islam Umar, who performed the Muslim prayer at all the sacred places of Christianity, refused to pray inside the Church of the Holy Sepulchre, saying that in future some ignorant Muslims would demand this church on the basis that the Rightly Guided Caliph of Islam once prayed here. So he performed the *Namaz* at the doorway.

Since then, the church of the Holy Sepulchre has remained a Christian church. Another thing the Muslims did for Christian freedom of conscience was that they ensured that any Christian sect was able to pray in this church, so that none would ever establish a monopoly over the empty tomb. The same was done for the Church of the Nativity in Bethlehem and for the other churches that had a special sanctity for all Christians.

When the crusaders took Jerusalem and inflicted their terrible slaughter, they committed Muslims to fire and sword, and Christians of the eastern sects too, indiscriminately — and those who didn't leave with the retreating Muslim army, were made religious renegades and heretics, and deprived of all the rights that Islam gave them.

The same happened in Spain, where to burn out the last spiritual traces of history's greatest civilization, the inquisition was raised and went on to consume the whole of Europe in with its furnace. And Granada was finally and mindlessly destroyed, together with its people and its common Muslim, Christian and Jewish culture that then gave back to unclean Europe the fundamental ideas of Classical and Islamic scholarship: philosophy, mathematics, geography, chemistry, medicine, botany, hygiene, the idea of science itself, town planning and navigation; and along with them the book shop, the library, hospitals and universities, and most importantly, the basic command of respect towards other's beliefs and freedom of conscience, and which I just remembered when, wiping away the tears from the Andalusian wind, I stepped with you into the great Cordoba mosque and happily lost myself in its astounding space...

...among its pillars and arches that looked like trees blooming in red-white, its ceilings of spun patterns, and the flickering gold paintings of its *mihrab*[139] ...And in the infinity of its inner world, that is like the outer one in everything, a person can likewise find peace and happiness in the exact realization of his place on earth in relation to the Unity of God.

In Cordoba mosque, *because it's a tourist attraction,* it's forbidden to pray, so I made my prayer secretly, as if I was doing something criminal. But I didn't complain – are complaints really needed for private moments?

In this architectural space that dissolved unity and equilibrium in its very air, I clearly remembered the Qur'anic

[139] A semicircular niche in a mosque that indicates the qibla; the direction of Mecca to which Muslims should pray.

motto of the Spanish dynasty of Nasrids. It was interwoven into the fine stone patterns of the niches with their stalactite pelmets and tracery and into the perforated palace walls, and it was repeated in the water that murmured in the infinitely happening Islamic gardens that never faded in my weeping soul in Granada, Cordoba and Seville. That motto, which the emir of Granada, Abu Abdullah, repeated as he yielded the city to the fervently Christian King Ferdinand V and his Catholic Queen Isabella in return for a promise that the Muslims of Granada would forever be allowed to keep their faith, customs and property:

There's no other winner, apart from Allah.

But soon after Granada was surrendered there were no living traces left of the Muslims or Jews in the whole of Spain, as they were executed or expelled and left behind only a memory of that glorious past and brilliant architecture that today attracts tourists from all over the world. The inquisition destroyed the people, but wasn't able to destroy the evidence, in which any searching eye even nowadays may foresee the proclamation of the Unified God's world.

In Cordoba, in 1523, the Dominicans were trying to end the architectural heritage of Muslim culture. After asking for permission from the king to build a church in the centre of the city, they destroyed the centre of the unique Cordoba mosque[140] and embedded in it a plateresque Catholic

---

[140] When the great Pakistani poet Muhammad Iqbal visited the mosque in the 1930s, he was so overwhelmed by it that he wrote a famous poem, which includes the lines:
Sacred for lovers of art, you are the glory of faith,

cathedral, which is still there, its domes and naves rising right through the heart of the mosque, striking into that empty violence of form for ideology's sake.

It said that when King Carlos V saw what the zealous builders had done to the pearl of Andalusian architecture, the Cordoba mosque, he grabbed his head in despair and exclaimed: 'God! You destroyed something that has no comparison in the world for the sake of something you could easily have built anywhere else!'

But let's not grieve any more over the past, when even a Catholic king is stung cruelly and irreparably.

And there is another image comes to me as I sit completing these long, unsent letters to nowhere: an image of a world in which a Christian church nestles inside the harmony and balance of an Islamic mosque, a mosque that in its great simplicity has survived centuries of assault. Doesn't it contain within the ovary of a single, united future, because it cannot be any other way?

And now, after looking as long as I can into the mirror of my own silence, I begin to guess the answer to the question that I have spilled so long into these sad and sadly joyful letters and collocations – these letters in which, oh God, didn't You find at least that honest and mirrored authenticity in which people immortal to me, familiar and unfamiliar, can recognize themselves?

If all the events in life and the reality to come (these events that bring tears or finally determine the heart) – if these

---

You have made Andalusia pure as a holy land!
Recently, Muslims have lobbied to be allowed to pray in the mosque and when two believers were prevented from praying in 2010, they violently attacked two security guards.

events are just small details of zeal in the universal Armageddon on Earth and in the Heavens, then do they really have any special meaning beyond the common, unimagined, uncomposed, invisible and solely authentic battle that happens in the honest silence of love and future deeds of penitence in the mutual comprehension of each other?

After all, everything authentic, as it turns out, really happens when it seems that nothing's happening at all...

...This eternal battle of love against multifaceted hypocrisy and debauchery; this deep, intimate and infinite drama of people, looking for Your truth and beating off in despair the most plausible lie!

And when nothing happens in visible reality, there is the invisible authenticity that underpins the neverending and wide-ranging drama of the search for the Unity, in which there is no past and no invented and edited history, but a continuity that will triumphantly happen on the one single and infinite Judgement Day. And all honest, great and non-accidental events in the here and now already contain in themselves all the deaths and all immortalities of the future and Your Silence, which is greater than any answer?

In the name of Allah, Most Gracious, Most Merciful.
When with the help of Allah the victory will come,
and you will see,
How the multitudes of people take the faith of Allah,
Exalt the glory of your Lord, praise Him
And seek His forgiveness.
Truly, He is the one who ever forgiving.

(The Holy Qur'an 110:1-4)

SECRET LILY OF THE VALLEY

She didn't understand him.

And that was a tragedy.

Not that she considered him ordinary, though that would've been unbearable for him too. But she, he imagined, considered him completely unremarkable – that is, completely non-existent. But he did exist surely! The striking, and to be honest, only proof was the obvious love for him of his parents and, at times, of other relatives. And then, he himself felt that he existed. In fact, he always thought and *felt* a little too much, and because of that he was rather quick to fall in love, but from feeling to melancholy understanding takes a lifetime, and life, he's been told, lies entirely in front of him, so why get so upset? Yet he, poor fellow, was upset, terribly, and he kept trying to sneak out from the sad ordinariness of his reality into wonderful dreams, in which appeared remarkable visions of the South Seas and life under sail, drawn maybe from Jack London, or maybe, the Voyage of Captain Blood – it's impossible to tell now.

Even then, long after he was twelve years old, when he had a chance to sit in a real paradise on white pearly sand in the shade of a spreading palm tree on the shores of the blue-green Caribbean, and look through half-closed eyelids at the buccaneer sea that slyly sparkled and gurgled between those black tidal islands of dead coral – as he sat there, the time came by chance for him to understand that there is no such thing as *the life ahead*: life can only be in the *present*, and strength to those who can feel it exactly in the moment it's given!

There and then, completely losing hope of realizing himself as the incarnation of a child's dream, he guessed that his present, if it ever existed, was happening in his *childish* upset and torment – the torment that, apart from family, nobody in the world seemed to recognize his presence in the world, and especially not the girl he loved unrequitedly and mindlessly and who was so maturely, painfully and so amazingly beautiful. He guessed that his entire future, as the saying goes, had become led by an inextinguishable feeling of inner inevitability.

After that unexpected revelation, the sudden sensation of his bare feet in the shade-cooled sand, the arbitrary spectacle of the iridescent sparkle of sea and the light touch of the sea breeze on sunburnt shoulders – all now coming together with the momentary movement in the night on the English provincial A3 road that was taking him home from work: all seemed to him infinitely accidental, not yielding to any awareness – unaccountable, causeless and still so hopelessly real that this totality of sensations couldn't be entwined with the delicate net of illusions with which he had tried to catch the present all his life – had hoped that he'd finally take it, like a living dragonfly, in his hands, to thoroughly examine it in all its secret details and, after thoroughly understanding it, let it go with a light heart into the blue sky which accepts everything that flies.

Nowadays, he didn't even really understand himself. The dreams that had come true, like the fortnight in piratical Barbados or those work trips abroad, couldn't – after they've joined the familiarity of life – sweeten that reality in which, submissive to the daily routine, he was coming back late on a wet January night from the old English town of Guildford where he worked in a Japanese-owned bioplastics laboratory to Petersfield where he lived and survived nowadays.

Survived? Well, maybe he would have chosen another word, but over the last few months, even alone with himself, he had got by even in the face of a lasting anxiety. The extension of his contract kept on being put back. It was due to run out in a year and he feared for his long-term future, so he was plunged in the bitter uncertainty of indecision, already imagining the future in which he lost his job and his mortgaged house and the hire-purchased car bought with such effort, along with all the other junk acquired in England – and at the end of it all there'd be just one ending: finally being tagged as a loser and slinking back to the broken trough[141] in Russia.

Desperate for a long-term contract, he often worked late in the laboratory, but his bosses, seeing how they got his talent for nothing, avoided giving him any promises or reward for all his hard work, even though of course they did pay by Russian standards well over the odds. He was quick and efficient, doing the work of three people if he was engaged on what he thought were simple tasks. This didn't endear him to his colleagues who between themselves called him *Rasshida* – an imperative form meaning *rush it!* Or rather, 'Come on, get moving!' The name also sounded way too much like 'Russia' with all its gloomy associations, but what can you do?

In the meanwhile, his Petersfield home, even though it was seventy miles from the incredibly expensive capital, was sucking away his earnings like a hoover, and the world-famous British cost-of-living left no hope of saving anything

---

[141] This is a Russian saying that means going back to square one.

for a rainy day. In other words, he was working just to be able to live in England, hand-to-mouth as the saying goes, and ahead, even if he ever got that unlikely permanent contract, there loomed only old age with a tiny pension, which wouldn't even be enough to keep paying for the house, let alone enjoy a well-earned rest. And so, back in the house that was his own in name but was in fact owned by the bank, his wife was waiting for him and preparing to shove into the microwave another frozen lasagne ready-meal...

She had refused to cook at all until she discovered those foreign meals in their frosted cellophane-covered foil dishes, but just one look at these chilly feasts was enough to give him stomach cramps.

And so his home and his lifestyle did little to make worthwhile that continual transfer of his salary and Christmas bonus, which flowed through his current account at the bank like water through the fingers.

But maybe he could have forgotten this in his work and thought of his luck compared to the half-dead friends he'd left behind at the Institute in Moscow, if it weren't for this terrible loneliness – and the smiling indifference of his colleagues to anything not the least related to the laboratory. While they were deeply inquisitive about the minute details of his scientific work, they showed him, an outsider, no personal warmth whatsoever – politely refusing his invitations and not inviting him anywhere with them either, not even to the local pub for a pint at the end of the week. Stuck in his memory was that scientific worker from Russia who went mad from the forced and extreme loneliness of these academic circles of exclusion – so deprived of soul-to-soul contact that he became thoroughly paranoid. But then in Russia, his scientific work would have been canned long ago, and he would have been stuck on a very sad salary in a two-roomed *khrushchyovka*.[142] So he did find some comfort in his favourite work and inwardly dubbed his colleagues 'biorobots', who outside the laboratory doors he wouldn't find anything in common with even if he tried.

That's why it was even more odd to hear on the car radio, forever tuned to Classic FM, requests for real concerts: British husbands were asking for something to be performed for their wives, British lovers called in for their loved ones, and British children dedicated music to their parents – proving incontrovertibly that beyond the edge of his own exclusion there still existed here a soulful life, in which feelings were present, and mutual love, and friendly involvement.

He was especially struck by one request, which the compere relayed with extreme politeness and engagement, because it was for, as he said, the secret love of a bank worker for his colleague, who not only didn't know that he loved her but mustn't find out. That wasn't a request, but a novel in a few sentences, completed by the stormy third part of Beethoven's 'Moonlight Sonata'. And the pale tragedy of this request from someone loving hopelessly disturbed many as much as him, I suppose, as he sat tiredly behind the steering wheel in the dark, swishing through the snowless wet-with-winter-fog night, on through the moving roadside flare of headlights. But if English drivers, likewise rushing home, thought about something theirs, something English, then his thought went the other way, and he, for some reason, didn't want to correct them as he corrected the car's course with a single mechanical movement of the sensitive steering wheel.

---

[142] Cheap, low-rise, cement-panelled apartment blocks put up in the Soviet Union in the 1960s when Khruschev was in power.

So, she didn't understand him.

But what was there to be understood, it could be logically asked? Yet he, like everything alive, already had his own history assembled from multiple encounters with reality. Who can make sense of it? That first love, for instance, why does it happen? Maybe it was exactly that unique personal history, that moneybox of the mind and heart stuffed with discoveries, inklings of the truth, agonizing expectations, honest delights and truthful feelings that demanded him to share his savings with someone? And then, isn't it the purpose of love to share the authenticities of life, which as they shine and sparkle in the memory, pump new blood into life and restore the meaning and joy to the darkness of existence? But if you keep them all completely secret, they will not be seen by anybody – unless you have the courage to share them.

In fact, any tiny entity, even if it's hidden from the world, trails behind it multiple life consequences – like that secret lily of the valley which did exist, did grow, bloomed and yet has remained undiscovered in the thick shadows, covered in small white stars and the moving reflections of a sunbeam, in the May grass of the city park, notched with deep narrow gullies and overgrown by ancient trees, where, in winter, spring or autumn, they were taken out for the gym classes…

God, how he dreamed to find that lily of the valley and stand out from the crowd of his classmates. How he dreamed she would suddenly see him clutching that vivid green stem and its snow-white, fragrant bells. How he dreamed that he would place in her hands that single pure lily of the valley embedded in those wide glossy leaves… But he never found the secret flower, God, even though others did. Others also jumped further, ran faster, were taller, understood life better and shone with their wit, too, finding just the right words at the right time, words that seemed and were so apt...while he, crop-headed and stocky, kept quiet, filling his mind with imaginary conversations and events, arranging them in his endless dreams inspired by books and history films.

So why did he think she has to understand him? Only because she too was tow-haired, and often blushed deeply from shyness or embarrassment. Or maybe because in the school essay on a free topic she wrote about hopscotch in such a way that for years to come he remembered that spring and the chalk white squares marked out on the asphalt; and the sparkling streams purling down from under the melting, sagging snowdrifts; the sky above the town, clear and blue, with fluffy clouds; and that extraordinary revelation that hopscotch should be played only during early spring when the city's trees, poplars and maples hadn't yet opened and stretched their bare branches into the clear air – that time when the city's gardeners, standing on the special towers on trucks, lopped off tall branches together with their swollen buds with their long-handled secateurs, so the branches were strewn on the pavements, and before they cleared them away, you could choose yourself a stick, then on the way from school thwack out a ringing beat as you ran it over those black, curled iron spear-like fences, of which there were so many in that old city of everyone's childhood.

Oh, he was so much inferior to her in observation! And is it so surprising that his life proceeded in the silence of his imagination – provoked sometimes by the most ordinary things, but more often by a book illustration or even those postcards which he bought at the newspaper kiosk near the school for three kopeks, taking it from the twenty kopeks he was given for school breakfast.

The kiosk was in the corner of a small square, in the centre of which there was a bust of a great writer. The pictures on the cards were magical scenes from fairy tales, and their colours, lines and silhouettes, skilfully depicting things that don't really exist, excited his ungrown soul and made it ache, as if behind them, behind these pictures and images, was something much larger, something all-encompassing, beautiful and wistful, something able to fill everyday – *to school, from school* – life with the extraordinary and sublime.

It was just this extraordinariness that tormented him who felt so ordinary in everything, so easily rejected and so grievously tortured by childish ambition, which gave him even more grief as he grew up.

When the fairy tale cards eventually bored him, he turned to scenes of distant mountains, seas and savannahs which for a long time seemed better than the view from the window. And it wasn't by chance, of course, that he then got obsessed with collecting stamps, in the perforated rectangles of one of which glowed the blue light of a tropical forest, with a fiery-yellow leopard in the hazy foreground, frozen mid-leap. That tiny picture wouldn't let him fall asleep and kept leaping in front of his eyes, making his heart beat faster, as if in love.

That was a leopard – but why was his imagination just as disturbed by the meticulously drawn thickets of misty green bamboo and other delicately painted bushes and trees from that colourful book about Chinese, or maybe Korean, partisans? Why did his mind quiver at the imprint of the coloured ink and the swirling coniferous branches, every needle of which felt far too real to be simply pen marks on paper? What was it striving to tell him? Why did it trouble him, as if he absolutely had to catch some hint to transform the ordinary into the utterly extraordinary?

He didn't understand what gave him such expectations and such untold hopes, and couldn't explain anything. But certain images seemed *scrumptious* to him and he wanted more and more, like that birthday cake with cream roses or that unforgettable fizzy drink, glowing brilliantly crimson in the crystal shot glass, that his parents had treated him to on his birthday – it was in the semidarkness of the boat-restaurant 'Mayak', moored on the Volga near a long bridge in view of the white-stone kremlin, and the wide river *ples* sparkled and glittered behind the lacy curtained windows. But that world, the world where his parents were, was an internal one – a world of forgiveness, peace and unselfish affection: into this world he could bring anything from outside and not be laughed at for being such a homebody, which is what he was really, even though infinitely embarrassed by that secret shameful circumstance.

Yet what could he tell her about his little world? Certainly not about the time early in his childhood when he was taken to the Black Sea, and how he ran completely naked along Batumi Beach through the warm, shallow water, and how, floundering and beating the water with his feet, he swam to and fro in his rubber ring, and how he ate golden, boiled sweet corn which, lacking salt, he simply rinsed in seawater, making it taste nasty? Nor about the time when he was taken for a walk to the famous botanic gardens, where it was hot, damp and stuffy, and he saw for the first time how bamboo grows and its thick, waxy-green joints, and he was horrified by the spiced and living darkness that seemed to swirl under the drooping creepers and tangled roots of unknown tropic bushes and at the feet of the coarse-haired palm trees that overgrew their pots. That was where too he was struck for life by leaves of the tropical water lily, *Victoria amazonica*, wide and round as restaurant trays, that floated on the black, smooth surface of their special pond.

His father, young as life itself, lifted him up and put him down right in the middle of one of those giant green trays. The leaf bore his small weight, and he, who joins this story for such unheroic ordinariness that he doesn't even deserve a separate surname let alone a patronymic, didn't even think about jumping from that green island to swim into the unknown – not just because he was really young, but because he was such a coward, too, as he had very recently proved, when his father decided to play a joke on him, leaving him by himself on the white gravel path of that celebrated botanic garden.

According to the story, the moment he looked around and realized he'd been left all alone, such perplexity and horror flooded across his round face that his father jumped out of his hiding place, just as the boy started to cry and let flow the tears of that momentary orphanhood.

Is that what he was supposed to talk to her about? But she herself, for sure, was filled with the same tiny, but still personal sadnesses and joys. And would he have really understood her, if she began to speak about them, these greatest secrets of the growing soul? But she was cleverer than him; she didn't confide in the wrong people, and could, when necessary, be proudly silent. Added to that she lived behind the high, fortified stone wall in the out-of-bounds regional artillery school, and so in his eyes she was like a real enchanted *tsarevna*, or maybe even a princess from a castle of knights like Ivanhoe.

So why destroy those enchantments?

Can anything be changed by extreme candour of the heart? The secret lily of the valley, which in the unfading past still waits for someone to find and appreciate it, has a name in English that may be even more lovely than the Russian *landysh*, yet doesn't awake in the local people any special emotions when planted in the tidy flower beds of private gardens. As a species, it's completely disappeared in the wild,[143] where alone May's brief and secret lily of the valley can truly bewitch with its fresh, nostalgic scent – and its heavy aroma of irrevocability.

So why didn't he find that lily of the valley? Why couldn't he find one to give to her, if only to create for him the same conversation about everything and nothing that worked so well with his more athletic peers? Maybe these light conversations could have soothed away that nagging feeling of rejection, and started a romantic friendship, a romantic friendship he could have forgotten in time. It never happened. But something did happen. Something completely different, much more painful. And if it wasn't a tragedy, it was certainly a drama – for isn't it dramatic when a secret is revealed, and one instance of brave candour fatally draws another in its wake?

Oh these Saratov sufferings in the emptiness of his parent's flat after school, the bitter-sweet torment of 'Moonlight Sonata', and later Gershwin's 'Rhapsody in Blue' which he played so many times that he knew every note well enough to conduct it from memory. He imagined himself being tall, handsome and famous, but couldn't find any special talents in himself, and so languished with inexpressible, gnawing

---

[143] The lily of the valley, *Convallaria majalis*, is actually still common in the wild, on grassy banks in ash woodlands.

ambition in his heart. His passion for postcards gave way to a yen for those newstyle ballpoint pens and little notebooks which he bought in the kiosks and central stationery shop, proud that he could buy them. In one of those notebooks, or rather organizers – small but thick, in a knobbly yellow cover made to look like leather – he even started a diary. Without any special persistence, he wrote in it from time to time in his childish scribble – his handwriting was really quite ugly – putting down on the geometrically lined and squared pages proof of his weird, private worries.

And then the day came when, exhausted by love, he determined to climb over the wall and lay all his feelings before her.

And so he took the most decisive step in his life, and no other step would ever in future match this in its desperate decision. It was late spring. The sky was blue with wispy clouds. Newly opened leaves were already rustling on the branches of poplars and maples. A gentle, moist breeze was curling up from the city's river. And a miracle which he could never have dreamed of has happened: she has agreed to go for a walk with him, intrigued by his threat to talk to her 'about something serious'.

Each one of them clutching their own anticipation, they walked *together* through the spring town, but not for long. Here too, he was destroyed by his impatient longing to free his emotions – that boyish impetuosity and hastiness which still overwhelmed him now, years and years later. 'Don't you know, that I am madly in love with you?!' he gabbled, or something like that – and for the rest of his life he was haunted by her bewildered look, astonished, it seemed, by that burst of absurd bravado, yet still secretly, absolutely unintentionally, shining with girlish delight.

But what was her surprise and her entirely reasonable reply that they were far too young to be in love – what was it next to the admiration that sang in his soul? What was it in the face of that puppyish rapture which in its ardour sees no obstacles, and revels only in its delight? Like the shining, sunlit new leaves, that bright fresh world and the feeling that all of life and all the people in it were created solely for these wonderful beautiful moments. And in the sudden fullness of existence, in the rush of trust he had waited and hoped for so long and so alone, he thrust his little yellow diary into her hands – and so spoilt everything, because you should never give too much at the same time, but he lacked that great practical wisdom.

They parted as friends, it seemed to him, agreeing not to tell anyone about it, but next morning the whole school knew all about his ridiculous confession and his diary. She, as he understood later, had revealed it not out of malice but because she couldn't bear the pushy questions of her girl-friends. It was they who talked her into handing the diary back to him, in public, administering such a humiliating shock after the sublime ecstasy of the previous day that he still flinched with the pain as he listened to Classic FM that night on the English road so many years later.

He became a laughing stock, yet his injured and reduced soul was not satisfied. He had to plumb the depths of humiliation, to drown in the foetid darkness down to its sticky bottom – in the wild pursuit of 'too much' and the faint hope that from there, from the bottom, there is only one way – back up, to the lost glow of cherished illusions.

And so, drawing pride from the humiliation itself, he started to give his small, yellow, hymenopterous diary to anyone who wanted to read it – and there were plenty. He saw them all, how these irrelevant people, his classmates, hastily read the badly formed scrawl of his innermost, painful, foolish lamentations, and he understood that maybe this exposure was not so frightening – but what was truly terrifying was something else, invisible and unavailable to them all: the irrevocability and isolation of the broken dream.

She didn't understand him.

Now, slightly embarrassed by the noble anonymity of the hopelessly in love bank clerk's musical request, he remembered how greedily and hastily those alien eyes had read his secret thoughts as he peered into the dust- and water-smeared windscreen – peered at that banal phrase as if into the mirror of his soul, until finally to his astonishment he understood, as an outsider, with what utterly plain and paltry despicableness his first love had ended, for the essence of it, of love, as it turned out, is not being understood, but trying to understand the one you love.

After all, not once had he thought about what she was feeling then, what she felt to suddenly find herself in the middle of events over which she had no control whatsoever – for it is true, you can't put a shawl over someone else's mouth.[144]

How could she know then, how could she guess even in her nightmares, that twenty years later, as if in some terrible romantic novel, that he, devastated and shredded by another difficult love and another woman's *misunderstanding*, would suddenly marry her, and then just as suddenly get divorced, and move to the end of the world, so that his life would once more be as ordinary as everyone else's: a new family and meetings once, or maybe even twice a year, with the

---

[144] A Russian phrase meaning you can't stop people talking.

son growing up without him, tow-haired and roundfaced, in whose eyes he sometimes saw the familiar bewilderment and in whose soul, he anxiously suspected, nested the same inherited volcano of painful pride, heart's anguishes and unquenchable passions?

But because it was so ordinary, so like everyone else, it didn't worry him that often – and any nostalgia or unsettling dissension slipped away. Only once, quite recently, had he dreamt, dreamt that he was jumping from a train on some vaguely familiar, wintry, snowdrift-cloaked halt, then plunging up to his waist in the white, fluffy, ardently and dazzlingly pure snow with its so bracingly fresh scent – and when he woke up, he realized he was crying.

But he put it down to nervous exhaustion and the general uncertainty of life, and waved away the memory of the snow, deciding that right now he wants just one thing – to drive further and further on the dark, wet, empty road, to drive infinitely, without stopping, in the naïve hope that the mechanical movement is the forward motion of life. But he knew that if he went too fast, he'd miss the slip road to Petersfield, where his wife, probably, was already taking yet another pizza out of the freezer to heat up – and he knew that quite soon the A3 road would come to an end in the dullness of Portsmouth and there terminate in the alien and always cold sea – in exactly that final end of the world about which he once so passionately dreamt.

POSTSCRIPT

&

I DREAM OF A HOUSE. In the dream, as it slips away, I don't see it in its longed for and beautiful entirety, but I know it is spacious and light, and its rough log walls smell of fresh pine, and the resinous aroma merges in the the dream with another fresh scent. I sense that this other freshness – emanating from the forest whispering nearby and from tirelessly moving wide water (though I don't know if it's a river or the sea) – is breathing beyond the doorstep. Yet in the dream I feel that comforting peace of being needed which always envelops you in the circle of family and dear friends, who don't ask for daily proof of your special gifts, abilities and general fitness for life.

So I don't really know how it happens, or if I'm leaving or coming back home, walking up at sunset through the dusky Dulwich forest to the top of Sydenham hill after a shift at the BBC spent chasing earnestly after the latest news on the planet. It's true that every day in the world happens loudly – and it happens more frighteningly, more noisily in the whole radio-world of schedules and broadcast networks, as if all that matters is to:

talk,

      talk,

           talk,

                talk,

                     talk,

                         talk...

...about things which already tomorrow no-one will remember, apart from those that these things have, unfortunately, happened to.

Yet, despite being interrupted by the *big* events of the world, about which I regularly broadcasted to invisible people, somehow these long letters got written as if by themselves, spring was imperceptibly accomplished and August was already coming to an end. Meanwhile, in our garden, which I'll again find in the thickening darkness, summer had brought its own events.

The jasmine bush had bloomed then wilted by the stone wall, and in the translucent twilight of the brightening dawn its tender-white, lightly-scented flowers – like large splashes of lime against the background of dark-green ivy – blended lightly but distinctly with deep red and soft yellow roses, and with the camellia bushes with their glossy, wet-looking leaves.

And in the morning, the bold squirrels that live in the sycamore, taking no notice of the statue in the Tashkent gown smoking a Czech pipe, pinch tubers of spring-withered tulips and hyacinth bulbs from the flower beds right under my nose, and Mumzik, the ginger cat with golden eyes, finds once, in a crevice in the old stump, a huge and very alive stag beetle.

I rescue that coleopterous insect from the cat. This huge beetle is a stag beetle, *Lucanus cervus*,[145] an insect warrior in articulated armour, with legs covered in strong prongs, predatory jaws and compound eyes. It was born just to scratch and crawl, yet resting on the palm of my hand, it is surprisingly beautiful, with the broad, rigid plates of its multicoloured elytra and its veinous muslin-like wings that it suddenly opened, heavily buzzing, to soar away – higher than the huge squirrel's sycamore – and so fast that it soon disappeared entirely.

As I walk up, after another day filled with worries about the Judgement day, the oakwood seems bigger in the dipping sun than in the morning. The sunset rays penetrate between the leaves, creating bright red flares and glimmers on the earth and grass and the wrinkled trunks of the widely spaced oaks, and I imagine dappled deer on the path, the bold deer of English parks. But the deer are only a mirage, and if there ever were deer in Dulwich wood, they have long since gone. Still, the jolly, silver-grey hedgehog, snuffling and shuffling, crosses the path for real, heading to its night work at the same time as I return home from mine.

Everything, happening without me, was changing – and now it has changed. The bushy thickets of poisonous–healing hemlock have withered, rusted and dried. The acorns have ripened on the oaks. And the smell of autumn is everywhere, though who knows why when radio forecasts in these areas say we are to expect a woman's summer, which in England is called 'Indian'. That name has come from America, where

---

[145] The best known of all stag beetle species, and sometimes called just the stag beetle. It is now a threatened species because of the clearance of its dead wood habitat from forests.

the first colonists considered everything Indian rather unreli-
able. In the past, before that pushiness from over the Atlantic,
the Indian summer was called here St Luke's summer or St
Martin's summer, and sometimes even All-Hallown summer:

Farewell,   thou   latter   spring;   farewell,   All-Hallown
summer![146]

So exclaimed William Shakespeare, saying goodbye to spring
and the woman's summer with this sublime line, but maybe
Shakespeare never existed, and maybe there'll be no us – but
will at least a single line remain of us in future silences?

Of course, I want something to remain, but everyone wants
something, heaven knows why – especially in those half-
imagined pre-autumn spaces on the way through the oaks,
the enigmatic grove to where, like a red reflection of the
sunset, a fox suddenly flashes between the bushes of barbed
mistletoe, and in the middle of the duckweed-greened small
pond fenced off by small logs, on the small island with its
shore of thickly growing sabre-leaved, yellow-flowered irises,
there are rooted two oaks, one living, and the other, with
peeling bark, dying in the uncomprehended fairnesses of the
world.
    Everything has its own fairness, and stepping past the red-
fruited hawthorn and the dense blackberry bushes studded
with daily-ripening red and bluish-black berries, stepping
on towards the only glade in the area, with its blooming
fireweed, pink dog rose and white feathered grasses glowing
in the farewell sun, I understand again that there is nothing

---

[146] Prince Henry to Falstaff in *Henry IV Part One*: Act One, Scene 2.

accidental in the Unity, and any categorical answer is empty and false simply because it's opposite to the Unity.

Walking on up past the glade, past the rustling August leaves and the grasses waving like ghosts in the sunset breeze, I confess to the old residents of the forest – confess that on the memorable wooden benches, I was thinking not about the Altai taiga, yet still for them another completely unreachable world. This world was not even seven hours continuous flight from here – but it was four persistent hours drive to the Welsh mountains, where this summer we once ran away to from alien schedules.

You remember how in the gathering dusk, on the narrow road, winding among the groves and mossy Welsh bogs, we suddenly saw a stone cottage – a lonely dwelling under the rising of the mountain. We stayed there and paid the cost, unable to leave such beautiful perfection: not only the walls of rough stone entwined with mauve wisteria, but also the heavenly garden, climbing up the slope on rocky steps by the murmuring, steeply falling creek, which charmed us in the gloaming.

On the advice of our hosts Anna and Alan, we went for a walk straight away, already hearing the roar of a strong flowing river in the nearby ravine. And truly the river, Afon Glaslyn, was surging powerfully over the mottled yellow pebbles of the riverbed between the boulders, under the drooping eaves of the conifers that clung to the gorge's steep sides. In some places, it writhed and squirted, oppressed by the rock; in others it flowed freely away from waterfalls in glassy jets, driven by the vertical plunge of raging foam. And we, making our way gingerly along the bank, understood that in remote Wales too we were caught up by the visible feeling of our unforgotten homeland. My soul was pierced with such a furious memory at that moment that I prayed to Allah – prayed to be in Altai, fully aware that with my submission to the alien timetables it was absolutely impossible.

Impossibility – indisputability – distrust – naïve stupidity. If something is needed from the Unity – it happens and is accomplished just the way it should be.

Two weeks after leaving Wales, we were standing once more at the top of the blossoming mountain garden and looking at the bare, pine strewn peaks of Snowdonia.

And I was in heaven again. I was high up on Kaspinsky Pass, among the cedar and pines and rosemary, where I once stood with my son and old friend, who was lost at some point in my wanderings and was now found again. And the rainy, translucent clouds, moving above the limitless Altai, touched with their foggy, scattered edges the nearby peaks, behind which still flowed the Katun, pouring its green-blue, frothing, rapid and vivifying waters around its rocky, coniferous islands.

And the Altai air, impregnated with the drizzle of the cloud drops and the clear, inimitable, resuscitating freshness of the primordial wet wind embraced us – giving us the feeling that the world is a single homeland, giving us that longed-for feeling that I seek daily in love, in work and in melancholy moments...

But isn't that same feeling, whether I am coming back or going away, given to me in the silences of the Unity?

On the top of yet another hill, from which the whole of London flickering in the twilight is visible, I close my eyes, and the life-giving wind of Kaspinsky ridge, unspeakably rustling in the foreign trees, touches my forehead, joining with the beating of my heart in its ever-living movement in the clear flow of universal existence, in which before God there's nothing small or large – there is the unity of a hope...

...a hope that you will finally be understood, especially by those who prefer silence to conversation and are not afraid to interrupt the ineffable speech halfway through a sentence...

March-August 2001